A Guide to Bearded Irises

A Guide to Bearded Irises

CULTIVATING THE RAINBOW FOR BEGINNERS AND ENTHUSIASTS

For Roger –
Enjoy the book
and the rainbow flower!

3/5/15

Kelly D. Norris

Timber Press ✻ Portland | London

Contents

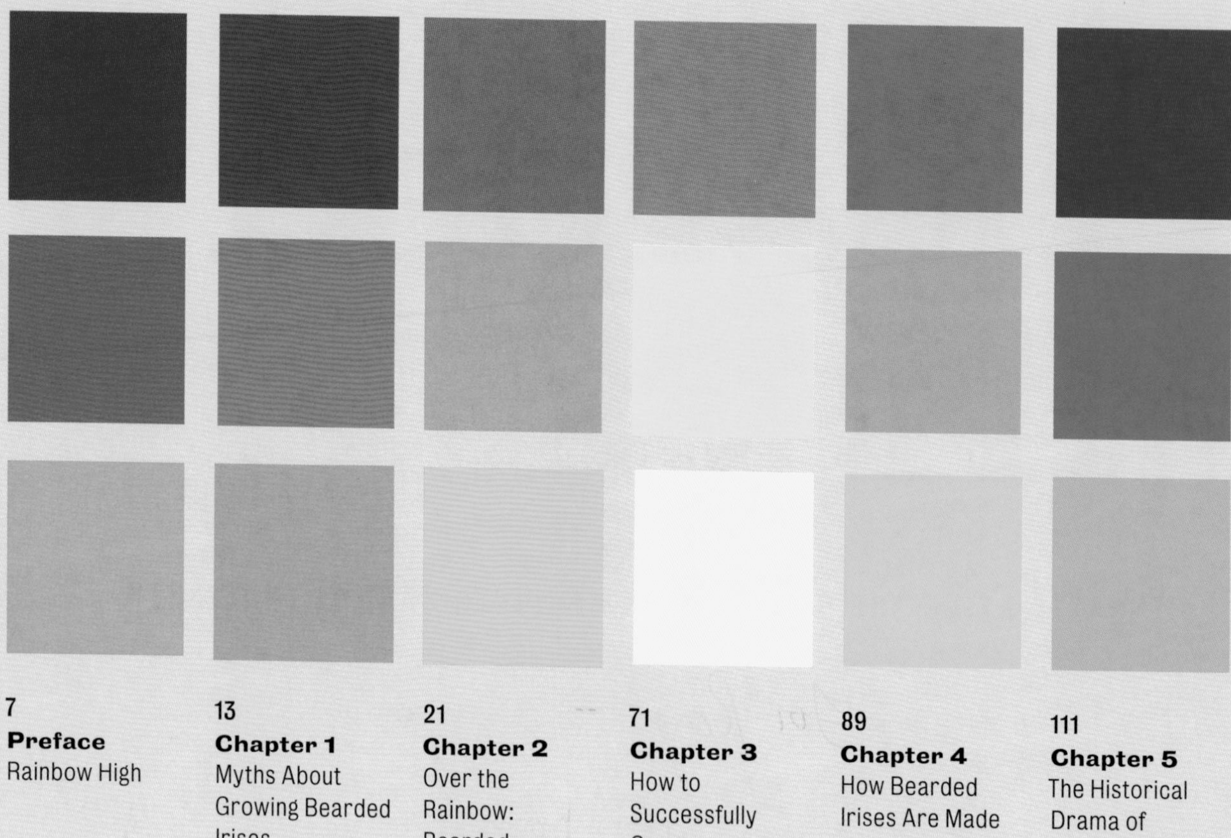

Preface Rainbow High

"To make me fantastic, I have to be Rainbow High/ In magical colors"

"Rainbow High," *Evita* (1976)

I love irises — all kinds, really. But I'm head-over-heels crazy for bearded irises. I guess it all started in 1999 at the kitchen table of Cal Reuter, a well-known irisarian from Wisner, Nebraska. Irisarian — that's the proper terminology for someone crazier about irises than a normal person would think healthy. I'm one, and I'd venture a guess that if you aren't one already, you will be, by book's end. I was all of 12 the summer I sat at Cal's kitchen table, poring through his small-type catalog in search of what I didn't know would become an all-consuming passion. I walked away with ten cultivars that day, vowing to keep track of their names as a promise to Cal. He dug them from his expansive front-yard "field," marked them, and sent them home with me in a box that got stuffed under the backseat of my grandma's van. I remember feeling giddy about the whole excursion, and as we ambled down the dusty road, away from Cal's Spruce Gardens, I checked over the seat to see that my box of plants was riding snugly, as the trees at the edge of Cal's property faded in the distance.

Fast forward three years. In that short span of time, those ten irises cultivated something deeper in me than I did in them. My collection had grown to almost 350 varieties by the summer of 2002, when I sent an email

OPPOSITE: 'Rainbow High' (Keppel 2009)

to a man named Cliff Snyder, who at the time owned Rainbow Iris Farm in Bartlett, Texas. Though I had no idea then, my life changed on 30 July 2002.

To make a long story short, I (a mere 15-year-old) talked my parents into flying to Texas, buying, and subsequently relocating Rainbow Iris Farm to our farm in rural Bedford, Iowa. We tilled up seven acres, spent 320-plus man-hours planting 40,000 rhizomes, and watched a former cattle pasture grow into a field of dreams. We opened for business on 18 May 2003 and haven't looked back, except to chuckle at our craziness, since.

With this book, I feel like I'm telling an epic story about how to grow and love magically colored bearded irises, complete with a dashing cast of characters, a rich historical backdrop, and an optimistic and enterprising protagonist — you. This is a book for iris lovers — plant lovers of a special kind who seek out rhizome sales like garage sales, track the comings and goings of bearded irises with unabashed addiction, and approach color-laden standards, falls, and beards without fear. If you're holding this book, you're an iris lover already, or one in eager training. I hope reading it will be like having a dirt-inspired conversation over a cuppa or a flute of bubbling Moscato. And here's full disclosure: I hope to cultivate nothing less than an all-out obsession in you by the time you close its cover.

More than ever in the 21st century, gardeners demand that their gardens look and feel like them, with plants that express their character and sense of style. Gardens should teem with our favorite plants. Mine teems with bearded irises, and with any luck yours does (or will) too. Bearded irises are a part of our horticultural heritage, grown throughout the world for a millennium and revered for their inarguable place of honor at the colorful table that is spring. From humble beginnings in the wilds of the Caucasus and central Europe, these "flags" evolved into banners of that season, thanks to the efforts of hybridizers from the 1840s to the present. They're timeless, classic perennials. Grandparents, aunts and uncles, and next-door neighbors brought bearded irises into the lives of a new generation, decade on decade, sharing their passion for the rainbow with every twinkly-eyed neophyte that strolled past on a mid-May afternoon. In that way bearded irises are beatnik passalongs, entering gardens more often through the back gate in a paper grocery bag than through the front in a black plastic pot.

The diversity of bearded irises rivals that of any herbaceous perennial we can grow in temperate climates, sporting nearly all colors of the rainbow and innumerable permutations and variations thereof. With such a banquet of cultivars and types to relish,

we're going to have a merry time. Amplify that with the tending-toward-hyperbolic way I talk about plants, and this conversation is going to get thick in no time. I have so many cultivars to share but limited pages in which to share them! I've consulted with my fellow "lovers" in the iris world to help me winnow the thousands of worth-growing varieties into a dashing selection of must-haves and can't-live-withouts in the six classes (taken on one at a time in chapters 6 through 11). After well over a decade of growing and loving bearded irises, I hardly lack for an opinion!

Sitting in front of my bookshelves, looking at my nearly complete collection of the *Bulletin of the American Iris Society* from 1920 through the present, I'm daunted by the legions of passionate iris soldiers that have gone before me — breeding, writing, lecturing, judging, and exhibiting for decades before I was even born. Though a little overwhelmed by the magnitude and depth of inquiry possessed in these tomes, I've found relief in one unifying idea — their body of work exists because of an undying love for the genus *Iris*. I've taken it as a rallying cry to translate that love into words and images in this volume, which I hope will keep a special place on shelves next to works probably wiser than mine.

Much of the bearded iris story has to do with passionate gardeners who swapped pollen through the mail, gathered in the lobbies of malls to exhibit flowers, and drove to little country churches to talk to garden clubs. Many works on the genus *Iris* have focused on these characters. With all respect, I choose instead to write more about their plants, which brings to mind one of my favorite quotes from J. Marion Shull's excellent *Rainbow Fragments* (1931):

> But all of these workers, mostly still in the prime of life and many of them with splendid new varieties to their credit, to single out any one for special mention would be invidious, and so their work must be left to speak for them, with the next generation of garden lovers, of *Iris* enthusiasts, to sit in judgment on their comparative merits.

Bearded irises are staple perennials, sure. But generations of gardeners in search of springtime doers planted undownable bearded irises, sometimes along the back fence and nearly forgotten, or in the dooryard and kindly treasured, in a simple quest for May beauty. Thankfully for us, those dooryard and back fence irises evolved into a deeper obsession for many — a horticultural quest for more of that satisfying color that only irises do so well. Playing as kids in these dooryards, some of us touched an iris for the first time, pulled gently at its silky petals for a closer sniff, and then giggled with

ABOVE:
'Jesse's Song'
(Williamson 1983) at
Rainbow Iris Farm

delight. Why are bearded irises so special? I'm eager to share everything I know in answer to that question. We'll tour and I'll teach, and after it's all through, you might say that we've been on a rainbow high.

Acknowledgments

Trying to put together a list of people I'd like to thank was harder than writing the entire book. I've decided to list only those who've closely assisted me in its production, whose contributions far outsize the few words given in acknowledgment here.

Lindsey Smith-McCartney, my best friend, editor, confidante, and sister-in-life — who routinely reminds me of my overuse of the em dash and at times uncomfortable relationship with apostrophes and commas.

Rita Gormley — who listened to me muse and moan from time to time on sundry subjects, most often iris-related, including this book during its early evolution. She is missed, but she'll always be celebrated.

Tom Fischer — the single most patient editor I've ever known.

Judy Keisling — for taking the time during the busiest month of an irisarian's year to review the first manuscript of the book. She was gracious as always, and her comments greatly clarified portions of this book.

Robert Pries — for providing valuable feedback on the miniature dwarf chapter during its genesis.

Terry Aitken, Lowell Baumunk, Paul Black, Barry Blyth, Roger Duncan and Rick Tasco, Tom Gormley, Thomas Johnson, Doug Kanarowski, Keith Keppel, Fred Kerr, Becky and Elizabeth Rankin, Schreiner's Iris Gardens, Janet Smith, Marky Smith, Hugh Stout, Mike Sutton, and Mike Unser — for patiently and happily responding to last-minute requests for photography and assistance, even to sharing glimpses of the bearded irises of our future gardens. Your passionate work is inspiring.

A whole slew of friends, family, ardent supporters, and colleagues go unmentioned in name but not forgotten in thought. You know who you are. I'm truly blessed.

1 Myths About Growing Bearded Irises

"Growers cannot… take one garden for an exact guide. They must learn to know and love their plants. Then it becomes literally true that they can… 'ask the plants,' and get from them as definite an answer as if these plants had the power of speech."

John C. Wister, *The Iris* (1927)

Myths and rumors — the stuff that tabloids, reality TV shows, and gardening have in common. I suppose every plant group has their own suite of them — the misconceptions that get passed on from one generation of gardeners to the next as well-intended but sorely misguided advice. Mention roses to the self-described black thumb gardener, and instantly you'll hear a bunch of excuses and insecurities like "oh they get diseases" or "I can't ever get mine to bloom well" or "those hybrid teas just won't grow for me." Better yet, say bearded irises to the doubting skeptic and you'll hear things like "they get so many diseases" or "all mine changed colors" or "the weeds just love them." I think I've heard it all when it comes to myths and excuses about why someone can't grow bearded irises. Too often those of us in the profession take a little too much pride in making the horticulture behind the gardening seem complicated. You don't need a degree to grow a beautiful garden, or to grow beautiful bearded irises. Instead, let's put aside the myths and misconceptions in favor of good, smart gardening practices, cold hard facts, and a little dirty know-how.

Myth: Bearded irises change colors.

Well not exactly. Over the years I've found this to be a pretty contentious subject with some people, most of whom adamantly report that after several years bearded irises en masse seem to spontaneously change colors, often drastically too, from white to purple or vice versa. The science isn't here on this one. Bearded irises reproduce asexually via rhizomes, which is why when we dig and share a rhizome we can be assured that the rhizome we plant will bloom and perform similarly in flower to the original clump. It's sort of like plant-based cloning. While it is possible for a mutation to occur, it is exceedingly rare (in ten years of commercial iris production and almost three million plants later, I've seen it once in our fields). The likelier answer takes one of two forms. First, ever notice those pickle-shaped pods at the end of the bloom season? Those are seedpods — the result of a little busy bee action in the garden. If not picked, it's plausible that the products of those labors might germinate in your iris patch, grow, and eventually bloom, resulting in a surprise color or two. Second, if you trade irises with fellow iris lovers or buy irises from commercial gardens, mix-ups happen. In nearly all those adamant reports of color shifting, the unknown color can be traced back to a bag or box of irises of suspect identity and origins ("I dug them up alongside of the road" or "Maybelle dug some up out of her back garden for me"). No bones to pick with the roadside or Maybelle here — just realize that the chances of something getting mixed up along the way are pretty high. After digging from the roadside and trading with Maybelle, I'm here to say it's happened in my own garden more than once. It's also possible that the suspect newcomer might really be a lingering former resident, a leftover of a tiny piece of rhizome that's sprouted, persisted, and finally bloomed. Take heed, and if you're dividing or transplanting, beware those little pieces left behind.

Myth: Bearded irises attract grass.

Attract probably isn't the right word. It's true that grass and nutsedges often commingle with bearded irises. But that's not to say bearded irises attract these weedy pests. Think about it from an iris's perspective. Bearded irises don't really form a canopy over the ground like a shrub might, for instance. Instead, their foliage jumps upward in a linear fashion, not covering much ground, and leaving it open, often with free space in between individual plants. Weeds are adventitious organisms. The little crack between the bricks of your sidewalk or the fingerling of space between two bearded iris rhizomes amounts to home-sweet-home for virulent weeds like yellow nutsedge (*Cyperus esculentus*), annual bluegrass (*Poa annua*), or the like. What to do? First, keep the grass clippings out of the bed, unless of course you have a perfect, manicured lawn free of every possible weed. When you prevent weed seeds from making contact with the soil around your bearded irises, you make long strides toward preventing serious weed problems in your garden beds.

Second, edge your beds, or avoid planting irises right at the margins of your planting spaces. If lawn surrounds your beds or abuts your borders, it's easy enough for grasses to spread via stolons or runners right into the iris clump. Edging in early spring often does the trick. If you've "double dug" your beds, the "lip" between the soil level and the grass often is enough to keep wandering grass stolons at bay.

Third, enjoy companion plants with your irises. Gardens with rich plantings often have fewer weeds, and why not enjoy the seasonal diversity of annuals, perennials, and shrubs long after your irises have left the stage?

Myth: Bearded irises have a lot of problems.

I disagree. In fact at some point in our gardening lives, we're bound to encounter problems with some plants we grow. Let's face it — all plants aren't created equal. Don't let one or two bad experiences with a plant taint you for good, particularly with bearded irises. With so many thousands of cultivars on the market, you're bound to find a dud. Believe me, they're out there, as with any plant or product, for that matter.

Bearded irises aren't stalwarts of the gardening tradition for nothing. Hike on over to your local cemetery, and you'll probably find a clump of bearded irises, purple or yellow, maybe white, growing effortlessly along the fence or atop a gravesite. They probably get mowed off in June each year, and yet for decades they've persisted. Sure, they don't make them all this tough anymore, and like everything, irises do best with some care and attention. For bearded irises, this basically means keeping them groomed and divided, in a sunny, well-drained spot.

Myth: Bearded irises are bulbs.

Even though garden centers and nurseries often sell bareroot bearded iris rhizomes alongside bulbs in the late summer and fall, the two are not the same. While some irises are true bulbs, like the familiar, early spring flowering *Iris reticulata* and *I. danfordiae*, bearded irises grow from rhizomes. Technically speaking both rhizomes and bulbs perform similar functions in plant biology, serving to store starches for biosynthetic processes. But a rhizome is actually a modified, horizontal stem found just at or below the surface of the soil. A rhizome produces roots and shoots at nodes along its length, and in the case of bearded irises culminates in a terminal fan of leaves. Bulbs are underground, vertical shoots that store food in modified leaves or thickened leaf bases (think of peeling an onion — those flaky, papery layers are actually modified leaves and leaf bases surrounding a central bud). Perhaps the most important distinction to make between rhizomes and bulbs — they aren't planted the same way. You can translate a rhizome's affinity for the surface as the reason you should plant bearded irises shallowly, instead of at depths where tulips and daffodils belong. I'll never forget the woman who approached me after a mid-winter lecture and told me of planting over 100 bearded irises at depths of 6 to 8 inches because she was told that they were bulbs. A painful lesson in the importance of terminology.

Myth: Bearded irises don't play well with others and need to be kept separate from companion plants.

Baloney. Somehow, somewhere, the rumor got started that bearded irises need to be quarantined. The critics (haters) of bearded irises justify their exile with words like leaf spot, rot, and brown foliage, at which point I usually stop listening. They must have "Red Cross" gardens — essentially sterile environments in which to cultivate Miltonian paradise. Please.

Of course, I'm not blind. I've seen gardens where clumps of bearded irises, planted in the spotlight, sulk in midsummer. Their foliage dies back and turns brown, and the memory of spring's flourish is forgotten in the face of the now-deserted stage. It happens and what's a gardener to do? But I've also been to some fabulous gardens where bearded irises pair wonderfully with an assortment of perennials and shrubs, look good throughout the season, and add contrast to the garden scene long after they've bloomed.

First off, don't rush to judgment after one or two poor experiences. There are an unfortunate number of cultivars on the market, too many in fact! And some of them are awful. They grow horribly, succumb easily to disease, and look bad when not in flower. I wish I could out them from the catalogs and nurseries on your behalf.

Second, consider how you're growing your irises. True, they are tough plants. But just because they can thrive under a range of circumstances doesn't mean we should always pit them against the worst or offer them neglect. Use bearded irises to punch up your gardens with color and springtime life. They're bold plants with rich histories and unprecedented colors. Surrender the stage!

Myth: Bearded irises have no place in small gardens. They get too big!

Fortunately for all gardens, whether patio-scaled or measured in acres, bearded irises come in a wide variety of sizes from the tiniest miniature dwarfs that bloom at only a few inches in height to the skyscrapers of the tall bearded class at a rarefied 60 inches tall (see "Horticultural Classification of Bearded Irises," at the back of the book, for the complete rundown). If you have a smaller garden, you may not have room for dozens and dozens, but surely a nook alongside a pathway or beyond the backdoor begs for just a little iris or two. The dwarfs and medians, diminutive but hardly lowly members of the bearded iris tribe, grow and reward in these small-scale scenarios. Truly versatile in every respect, bearded irises as a whole offer any gardener and garden, big or small, the chance to savor the rainbow.

Myth: Bearded irises are so much work. You have to trim the foliage back every summer!

Give yourself a rest from this unnecessary chore. It's a bit of gardening folklore that at the slightest sign of browning leaves, gardeners should rush out with sharpened implements and pare their bearded irises back into tidy little pitched fans. Sure, if the foliage for some reason has completely died back or become severely dry, it isn't harming anything to cut it back. It keeps things looking tidy and less unsightly. But you only really need to cut back the foliage during transplanting or dividing.

In fact, needlessly trimming the foliage back in the middle of the season actually breaks an iris's dormancy, kick-starting foliar production. This can take away from root mass accumulation and even from reserves meant to support flowering the next spring. I've traced consistently poor flowering in some gardens to regular foliar butchering the previous summer more than once on a help call at our nursery. On a natural cycle, new foliar growth often begins during periods of cooler temperatures in mid-autumn.

The easy truth about myths is that they're always untrue. Don't let these horticultural tall tales get in the way of growing and enjoying bearded irises. In the chapters ahead I'll cover the essentials for cultivating healthy, robust bearded irises. With myths dispelled and hope restored, why deny these famously familiar perennials a home in your garden

2 Over the Rainbow: Bearded Irises and Your Garden

"Here to our hand is a magic palette furnished with living colour with which to paint our canvas."

Gwendolyn Anley, *Irises: Their Culture and Selection* (1946)

Ask any irisarian to tell you how they got interested in irises, and you're liable to make a new friend. Iris lovers, indeed all plant lovers, always seem more than willing to divulge the details of the day their obsession began, in short story form. Mine began in Cal Reuter's Nebraska garden and continued when my new prized possessions bloomed the following spring. For many iris lovers, irises become the object of collecting and ordering into rows, beds, and plantings, with perhaps a few other companions thrown in for good measure. While that's all well and good, my passion demanded more. While I tended to start any new garden project with the acquisition of bearded irises, my plant obsessions didn't just stop for things with fuzzy beards and multicolored flowers.

Regardless of the vintage — 1920s and lingerie-esque in color, or the ruffles and flourishes of the 21st century — bearded irises own the scene in April and May, singularly or pluralistically, no matter where and with what they're planted. I think every garden should have at least one, but then I'm a teeny bit biased. In fact given the diversity of types, forms, and colors of bearded irises, I imagine I could come up with at least one cultivar for anyone who wanted to try. Every garden can grow at least one. What other group of hardy perennials offers that much possibility and excitement?

Irises in general have a historical record dating back thousands of years; they appear on the tombs and temples of Egypt, symbolize the Virgin Mary in Christianity, and were revered with near religious conviction in Greece. The fleur-de-lis, a stylized version of the beardless yellow flag (*Iris pseudacorus*), is associated with Florence, Italy, and French history, even to the Quebec flag and the New Orleans Saints. Van Gogh's famous *Irises* depicts sinewy waves of *I. germanica* (German flag). Colloquially, gardeners have known irises of all sorts as "flags," an apt description for their pennant-like flowers.

Humanity's obsession with bearded irises specifically, as symbols of regality, life, and color, is self-evident throughout western culture. The "poor man's orchid," as it was often called, crept into gardens of all shapes and sizes from continent to continent and coast to coast. Some still grow where gardens once were, making do amid tall grass and weeds — a testament to their durability. But I wonder if said durability has demoted bearded irises, in the minds of some, to a lowlier, commoner's rank?

Growing up as a bright-eyed iris lover, I got the feeling that some iris lovers hated the idea of mixing it up, planting their beloved treasures in the company of non-irises. How pitiful it was, I thought, to condemn bearded irises to a row just east of rhubarb or two rows down from sweet corn in the vegetable patch. Why relegate such stately blossoms to solitary lines of troops anywhere in the garden? But I know that many customers of our nursery — after walking through seven acres of iris production and two acres of gardens filled with irises and sundry plants — walk home, line out a soldierly row, and plant. So be it.

However, I'd like to imagine for you a garden filled with all your favorites alongside each other, bearded irises included. I'm convinced that somewhere in the annals of garden time some famous horticulturist decreed publicly that bearded irises shame their garden home, make poor neighbors to other spring-flowering perennials, and should therefore, if enjoyed or *tolerated* at all, be off somewhere by themselves. How mean. In all seriousness, I can appreciate how bearded irises have earned a reputation for being a little messy. But I tend to think that banishing them to a far corner

of nowhere doesn't really solve what are really cultural concerns and requirements. Just as with any of the plants we love, everything deserves a "just right" home in the garden.

Color

Imagine walking out into a garden absent bearded irises. After controlling your grief, where do you put a bearded iris? Let's talk shop about a key element of design — that practical artistry that results in beautiful garden spaces.

What makes a bearded iris look so fine? Answer: color, color, color, a key (if sometimes fleeting) aspect of garden artistry. Irises aren't for nothing called the rainbow flower. The genus is named for Iris, messenger to Mount Olympus and goddess of the rainbow in Greco-Roman mythology, who symbolized the connection between the heavens and humanity. She's represented in art and literature as a young maiden with wings on her shoulders or simply by the rainbow itself. Linnaeus couldn't have chosen a more perfect name, given the genus's profound range of colors.

As you'll discover in the pages ahead, my mind spins a constant reel of planting combinations with bearded irises — marriages, often based on color, that make or break the art of crafting an appealing garden space. But starting out in the world of bearded irises is like dropping a blind tourist into the middle of a crowded city without a map. Where do you begin, what with a monumental variety of colors, sizes, and types to enjoy? This overwhelming feeling, the kind that grips your stomach while your head spins with excitement, has no doubt intimidated many gardeners awestruck by the beauty of bearded irises.

But first, a prelude to my romping treatise on color. Dissect an iris flower into discernible parts, and know that *every* aspect of each discrete piece has its own complex, multivolumed history, with characters ranging from genes to hybridizers. Colors in standards, falls, and beards morphed, evolved, blended — and were lost. On that note, it's probably best to simply run through the main colors of the rainbow, adding in tones, shades, and hues along the

ABOVE: 'Code Red' (Aitken 2003)

2

way. Put on your sunglasses, color is about to hit the page.

Red

So-called spectrum red is the most elusive and sought-after color in the bearded iris firmament. To breeders caught up in a colorful crusade for floral epithets of fire engines and candied apples, red isn't just red — it's the pursuit of 43A on the RHS (Royal Horticultural Society) Colour Chart. A few cultivars push the envelope a little closer to the ideal each generation — 'Code Red' (Aitken 2003) and 'Red Hot Mamma' (Spoon, reg. 2010) in the tall bearded class — but alas, a true red bearded iris remains a dream. Why? The answer is convoluted but mainly attributable to the limited success breeders have had in moving lycopene (the red pigment) from beyond the beards. But if you lust for fuzzy red beards on your irises, you've got several nice cultivars to choose from.

In the genus *Iris*, red as a flower pigment shows up most notably in section *Hexagonae*, or Louisiana irises, as they are commonly known. The familiar *Iris fulva*, the copper iris of legend and lore across the U.S. Southeast, sports showy rust-colored flowers that smack of red, or at least what most people would think of as red. But apparently it hoards those genes, not letting them mix up with bearded irises, a lamentable state of affairs for sure. Some nice flirtations with red do crop up in the standard dwarf bearded irises, most admirably with 'Jeweler's Art'

ABOVE, LEFT TO RIGHT: 'Smooth' (Craig 2004)

'Play With Fire' (Schreiner 1987)

(Lankow/Aitken 1993), a sumptuous ruby red and amethyst bicolor selected by Terry Aitken from Carol Lankow's many red seedlings after she died; 'Red Rabbit' (Spoon 2002), a red with a bluish cast; and 'Smooth' (Craig 2004), a deep vivid red with a matte finish.

But there's more to red than fire engines and candied apples. What about bricks and adobe, cherries and salmon? In fact, the floral spectrum of red runs from the pale tints of crimson we know as pink to shades of maroon. The Schreiner family markets an ever-expanding collection of brawny reds worth growing, including 'Warrior King' (1984), 'Play With Fire' (1987), 'War Chief' (1992), and 'Dynamite' (1997). Others in the red-range family include the bronzey red 'Valentino' (Painter 2008), the violet-blue-blended red 'Candy Apple Classic' (Maryott 1999), the familiar garnet red 'Lady Friend' (Ghio 1981), the punch-colored 'Rip City' (Schreiner 1999), the bubbly copper-red 'Bev' (Richardson 2008), and as a token representative of reddish bicolors, the blazing 'Solar Fire' (Tasco 2003).

ABOVE, LEFT TO RIGHT: 'Solar Fire' (Tasco 2003) 'Crackling Caldera' (Aitken 2003)

2

Orange

The citrusy range of tones we call orange makes my mouth water. Orange bearded irises sparkle and gleam on warm spring days, the perfect show for a mid-afternoon stroll through the garden with a mimosa. An orange bearded iris of some kind is an essential plant to grow. Two tall bearded oranges from Terry Aitken of Vancouver, Washington, should top any list of must-haves: both 'Chariots of Fire' (2000) and 'Crackling Caldera' (2003) roil in ruffles lacquered with fluorescent blends of peach, pink, and juicy citrus. Barry Blyth's 'Mango Entrée' (1996–97), a ruffled concoction of honey apricot all the way from Down Under, grows into a grand clump. And two oranges from the Schreiner family grow well around the country — the timeless 'Avalon Sunset' (1994) and the newer 'Magical Glow' (2003).

The history of orange bearded irises, at least in the TB class, traces back to breeding efforts with yellows and pinks, work that was by no means easy. Some of the first orange-colored irises, blends of off-colors or faint allusions to orange by present definitions, lacked good floral substance and architecture. Some of the best examples of these new colors came from crosses involving median irises (standard dwarf bearded, intermediate bearded, miniature tall bearded, and border bearded) and early dwarfs like Schreiner's unregistered yellow 'Carpathia', coupled with further line breeding and use of apricot-colored irises that were the by-products of pink breeding. Many

ABOVE, LEFT TO RIGHT: 'Magical Glow' (Schreiner 2003)

'Clockwork' (Keppel 2003)

breeders have risen to the challenge of developing orange irises with distinctive colors, good form and substance, and sound growing habits.

In the medians, orange came about largely thanks to Bennett Jones, who spent much of his career in pursuit of carrot-shaded irises; he was successful with standard dwarfs like 'Orange Tiger' (1988), a deep orange self with darker orange beards, and 'Sedona' (2002), a pink and orange blend with red beards. Marky Smith used the Jones influence in her work to produce the sizzling hot SDB 'Marksman' (1999). Keith Keppel did the same with the SDB 'Clockwork' (2003) and the MDB 'Fission Chips' (2005). Blends and permutations in this color range can't be ignored either, though dream for a minute of the huge number of irises that have arisen when things like 'Orange Tiger' were crossed into other color groups — a rainbow of vividness abounds. One of my favorite yellow-orange blends to come from the founding germline of orange is 'Classic Sunrise' (Jones 2005), an SDB with yellow standards over orange falls with a rose ring tending close to an orange beard.

Yellow

I think we take yellow for granted in the iris world, despite the fact that clarifying it from sodden and sullied to lustrous and sparkling was one of the greatest challenges of iris breeding in the 20th century. Many have credited the venerable 'W. R. Dykes' (Dykes-Orpington 1926), the iris named for the godfather of the genus, with starting it all — stirring frenzy on both sides of the Atlantic for sun-kissed tints on iris flowers.

The range of yellow could cover continents in geographical terms. From the palest butter and white blend like that of 'Melted Butter' (Fan 1994) to the eye-searing, dark cadmium yellow blossoms of 'Throb' (Weiler 1991), yellow unspecifically describes many colors.

But for much of the iris's existence, yellow was a rare color, save the few golden or dirty yellow examples of *Iris variegata* or *I. pumila*. The earliest yellow, and at that a pale naphthalene yellow, was probably 'Flavescens' (De Candolle 1813), an old-fashioned diploid still found along highways and around old homesteads. It seems that generations of gardeners have passed this variety around, or it's seeded with vengeance beyond the confines of its planting space. Either way, it's still a simple charmer worth having in stock should an ugly fence or shed need some herbaceous company.

But early diploids like 'Flavescens' were limited in their ability to transcend their own murkiness and fulfill a breeder's quest for shiny, lustrous yellow. The conversion of diploids to tetraploids made this jump effortless. The originator of the most important yellow of the 20th century, W. R. Dykes, earned the honor of having a clear yellow tetraploid seedling of his named

CLOCKWISE FROM TOP: 'Melted Butter' (Fan 1994)

'Flavescens' (De Candolle 1813)

'Sunblaze' (Keppel 2004)

posthumously after him. Though the parentage remains unknown and subject to speculation, there's no arguing that almost every yellow tall bearded iris and many median irises trace back definitively to 'W. R. Dykes'. 'W. R. Dykes' had two horticultural drawbacks. One was its tendency toward flecking, perhaps due to the remnants of a virus that once infected the plant (the streaking reminds me of the so-called Rembrandt tulips that set off the Dutch Tulipomania of the 17th century); regardless of the cause it's unusually lovely. The second drawback was its unshakable reputation for being difficult to grow; though I've not found it all that persnickety in my own garden, it certainly qualifies as a slow increaser.

I could probably write an entire chapter on what happened to yellows after 'W. R. Dykes'. Numerous hybridizers picked up the reins and introduced many more great irises, ensuring yellow's popularity as a principle color of bearded irises. The 1940s were probably the peak years of the yellow boom — 22 new yellow irises received the American Iris Society's Award of Merit (not to be confused with the RHS's AGM, Award of Garden Merit) and three went on to win the Dykes Medal, the top award in irisdom. Of those, 'Ola Kala' (Sass 1942) probably earned the most immediate praise, holding the top spot on the AIS popularity poll for eight years and surviving as a memorable, historic favorite even now.

Contemporary yellow irises beam in all sorts of colors and forms. The dwarf and median realm boasts blue-bearded yellows like the SDB 'Experiment' (Black 2005) and the IB 'Blue Eyed Blonde' (Ensminger 1989). MTBs still carry the colors of their ancestor *Iris variegata*, but 'Yellow Flirt' (Fisher 1998) burnishes up that old-school look. It no doubt inherited some of that pizzazz from ever-so-happy-looking 'Chickee' (Dunderman 1980). My go-to yellow BB is the award-winning 'Little Mary

ABOVE: 'Lion's Share' (Jameson 1992)

Sunshine' (Roderick 1990), a ruffled daytime yellow with white on the falls. 'Debby Rairdon' (Kuntz 1965), the 1971 Dykes Medal winner, is a handsome, timeless yellow TB with bluish beards. Modern TBs like 'Sun Power' (Johnson 2004) and 'Sunblaze' (Keppel 2004) seemingly harness solar energy into a colorful glare that brightens any garden setting in late spring.

If you have a taste for softer yellows — buttery, creamy, and the like — there are plenty of choices. The tall bearded 'Lion's Share' (Jameson 1992) is one of the finest in this category, though unfortunately not as widely grown as it should be. 'Italian Ice' (Cadd 2001), a recent Wister Medal winner, also deserves mention in this category for its floral reconstitution of a tasty dessert. Space prohibits me from splicing yellow further into its many shades and tints, but rest assured that variations on the yellow theme abound in all six classes — enough for more gardens than any of us, no matter how cheery and happy, would care to plant.

Green

Green flowers baffle many gardeners. They wonder why on earth you would want a flower colored just the same as the foliage. It's a fair point, but why not? Green flowers, like brown flowers, have a mystical quality to them, almost as if they exist to be strange. For some reason, at the thought of green my mind immediately jumps to green chrysanthemums, an increasingly common symbol of modishness along with jade stones and clear, streamlined vases. Green irises aren't quite as ubiquitous. Some verge on olive, a moniker some would translate as muddy meets meh. Others sparkle in chartreuse. All six classes sport some example of green, but whether they all amount to your definition of green is up to you.

ABOVE, LEFT TO RIGHT: 'Jubal' (Innerst 1993)

'County Cork' (Schreiner 2007)

Breeding for green isn't really something most breeders have worked for, given the inevitably poor sales forecast for any thus-colored variety once released. A few have striven for a "Christmas" iris — an imagined flower cast in green with red beards, but few introductions have come close to that image. Breeding for green is also difficult by design — essentially a breeder is trying to develop a flower that sports chlorophyll in its cells or other co-dominant pigments that don't individually override one another to yield a single, definable color.

The medians trump the rest of the bearded iris gang by boasting more green irises than all the rest. Sure there were so-called green tall beardeds like 'Pride of Ireland' (Noyd 1971), which made me feel robbed when it bloomed for the first time, revealing a mostly yellow flower with some underlying hints of green. Some white TBs like 'Christmas' (Gatty 1991) have a heavy flush of green on the undersides of their falls with plenty of white on top. For green iris lovers, this is mostly what we settle for in the TBs. In 2007, Schreiner's introduced the peculiarly but fascinatingly colored 'County Cork', best described as very pale yellow with shadows of willow green. A 2011 Award of Merit winner, it's easily one of the most unusually colored TBs I've ever seen, flirting with the green realm most stylishly.

But back to the medians. The SDB 'Limesicle' (Chapman 2000) is probably the closest to a true green of any bearded iris, a cool blend of lime and cream. In fact the Median Iris Society — in establishing the modern horticultural system of classifying median irises — based the SDB class on 'Green Spot' (Cook 1951), named for its true green fall spot. In the olive shades, 'Jubal' (Innerst 1993) and 'Jade Maid' (Aitken 1996) have grown in my garden for many years as personal favorites, admittedly a partiality most of my gardening friends do not share. Many other greens defy even simple description. The popular 'Lumalite' (Aitken 1995) is an IB best categorized as a white and green-yellow bicolor with attractively loud red beards. 'Dew Buzz Bye' (Adams/Coleman 2006) glows from across the garden in blends of light yellow, olive, brown, and lime. Several years ago I discovered a green-washed IB in my seedling patch. Unfortunately color was its strongest suit — it was a miserable grower and quickly got to know the compost pile in an intimate way.

Blue

Iris lovers heart blue. Actually, I think people heart blue. We've been long lost on a quest for true blue in nature, and when we do encounter it, it holds us in deep rapture. Fortunately for iris lovers that rapturous experience storms the garden each spring, laden with ruffles and sassy, audacious flowers.

ABOVE: 'Dew Buzz Bye' (Adams/Coleman 2006)

Like yellow, blue covers a lot of ground, describing the world from the ocean to the sky. Color experts would distinguish true spectrum blue (105C on the RHS Colour Chart) from the violet-blue group of colors we register as wisteria blue, cornflower, bluebird, medium blue, and so on. Looking over the cumulative list of Dykes Medal winners, you can easily pick up on the judging electorate's bias toward blue bearded irises. Starting with 'Sierra Blue' (Essig 1932) in 1935, more than 18 irises of bluish colors (approximately 25 percent) have won the American Iris Society's top honor, including some of the world's most familiar and most often grown bearded irises: the light blue 'Babbling Brook' (Keppel 1969),

ABOVE, LEFT TO RIGHT: 'Babbling Brook' (Keppel 1969) 'Blue Rhythm' (Whiting 1945)

the cold ocean water 'Shipshape' (Babson 1969), the waterfall-esque 'Victoria Falls' (Schreiner 1977), the bay-reflecting 'Yaquina Blue' (Schreiner 1992), and the tempestuous medium blue 'Sea Power' (Keppel 1999).

The bearded iris world sports thousands of blue irises throughout the range just described, but spectrum blue bearded irises are inexplicably rare, with only one confirmed report in the *Bulletin of the American Iris Society*, from Virginia hybridizer Don Spoon, of its turning up in a seedling patch. Almost as rare are the blends with green — mainly turquoise. The SDB 'Tu Tu Turquoise' (Black 1989), the most famous turquoise iris, has given risen to other popular dwarfs of similar color, including 'Miss Meredith' (Spoon 2002) and 'Bombay Sapphire' (Black 2007).

In bearded irises, the quest for the true blue iris has had many fortunate detours. The flood of blue tall bearded irises from the 1930s through the 1950s stems from 'Great Lakes' (Cousins 1938), 'Blue Rhythm' (Whiting 1945), and 'Cahokia' (Faught

ABOVE: 'Bombay Sapphire' (Black 2007)

1948), which when crossed with other blues of the day and whites like 'Snow Flurry' (Rees 1939) and 'Purissima' (Mohr-Mitchell 1927) gave rise to a tide of new introductions from breeders across the country, including the Schreiners of Oregon, who still lead the crowd of blue breeders. The same quest led hybridizer Paul Cook to discover the amoena pattern, incorporate new species (namely *Iris reichenbachii* and *I. imbricata*) into the genealogy of modern irises, and create a whole new class of irises — the standard dwarf beardeds. His Dykes Medal–winning 'Whole Cloth' (1958) and 'Emma Cook' (1957), an iris named for his wife, were the grand culminations of his work. But Cook discovered these pearls en route to a dark blue bearded iris free of influence from violet. The best representative of his work in this line was 'Allegiance' (1958), "universally recognized as one of the finest iris Mr. Cook has introduced" (*Schreiner's Iris Lovers Catalogue*, 1958).

Purple

Purple, almost to annoyance, is the quintessential iris color. Though a rather vernacular word for any number of specific colors between red and blue, including in this case indigo and violet, it permeates the rainbow in gardeners' minds when someone utters the word "iris." Like blue does for delphiniums or gentians, and yellow for sunflowers or daffodils, purple in many ways defines the genus *Iris*.

ABOVE: 'Allegiance' (Cook 1958)

I've often heard veteran iris lovers blithely, dryly, and/or analytically remark that purple irises grow, smell, and bloom better than all the others. In many ways it would appear so. A careful reading of the great works on the rainbow flower reveals an almost uncountable tally of the word; it shows up in descriptions of all sorts of irises in the wild — the apparent default of evolution for flower color. But to go so far as to suggest that that color directly correlates with the vigor and floriferousness of a plant — well, my scientific intuitions balk at the notion. I may not rank it a myth, but I cannot give it a ringing endorsement of my own.

Given its default status in the iris realm, many breeders have avoided working with this color class specifically, unless on the way to goals involving blacks or maybe even complex bicolors. Purple bearded irises otherwise just happen. With so many thousands in existence, I always shake my head when I see another "new" one pop up on the market, with some minor distinction like ruffling or bud count accompanying its introduction as justification. Really, what could be further improved upon? I'll always grow purple bearded irises, even if I secretly plot their exit in favor of something a little less typical and a lot more outlandish.

White

Even though for a gardener's purposes white is really just an absence of color, we cannot forget the many

ABOVE: 'Purissima' (Mohr-Mitchell 1927)

different "ways" absence is marked by this spectral shade. White irises remind many gardeners of weddings, their pristine, crystalline petals whispering the strains of Pachelbel's Canon and conjuring up visions of bridal tulle. Whether planted next to a swarm of black irises or intermittently between lupines, white bearded irises occupy hallowed places in many gardens. For my part, I've spent years putting down white flowers of any sort — particularly white irises, after watching so many wither into mucus-like blobs of wet tissue after a rain storm. In all fairness that isn't really the color's fault; it's more an issue of substance.

The first white bearded irises were diploids from *Iris pallida* and *I. variegata*, and lacked in the pretty department due to drabness or marked flowers. With the introduction of Sir Michael Foster's tetraploid 'Kashmir White' in 1912, a door opened for clearer, prettier whites as well as better, cleaner blues. Two generations of breeding

ABOVE: 'Pure Innocence' (Sutton 2006)

later and we greeted 'Purissima' (Mohr-Mitchell 1927), hailed at the time as the finest, most robust white ever. Following this line of notable irises, 'Purissima' gave rise to 'Snow Flurry' (Rees 1939), now considered one of the most important bearded irises of all time. Bred by Clara Rees of California, 'Snow Flurry' was the result of a cross between 'Purissima' and the orchid-pink 'Thais' (Cayeux 1926) that produced a miserly two seeds, one of which was so shriveled it was thrown straight away. From the one remaining seed — also nearly tossed out by Clara and her sister, Ruth, who weren't sure it was worth wasting time with just one seed — grew an iris of phenomenal importance, just the kind of underdog, up-to-divinity story that every good tale of horticulture needs.

Whites today have come a long way since the days of their famous ancestor. Ruffles, lace, and a sun-catching characteristic of the flower's cells, colloquially called diamond dusting, top the list of adjectives used to

ABOVE, LEFT TO RIGHT: 'Ghost Train' (Schreiner 2001)

'Sable' (Cook 1938)

2

describe white irises. Mike Sutton's 'Pure Innocence' (2006) typifies the modern white iris, all ruffles and poise. Whites haven't stayed pure either. Breeders over time have added a mixed lot of beard colors to their virgin surfaces — yellow, red, blue, and near black.

Black

The mainstream gardening public is smitten with blue, but the horticultural deviants of the world lust for black. Black flowers are seductive, luring gardeners in with a color it seems we're just not supposed to have. Black irises rev it up a notch with large, ruffled flowers and silken petals that drip with color; their novelty and rarity entice the senses and the checkbook. Fortunately for iris lovers, black flowers run the gamut of the bearded iris continuum — from the petite MDB 'Bete Noire' (Smith 2009) to the Dykes Medal–winning 'Before the Storm' (Innerst 1989). Always about packing plants together into whatever space I have, I love black irises for all the things you can do with them in the garden. Black and yellow, black and white, black and red, black and orange, black and pink all sound colorfully exciting because of the drama and contrast they bring to the garden setting. What plant can really bring as much drama to the herbaceous border in May as a black bearded iris? (Yes, there are even nearly black-bearded bearded irises, too!)

The road for black begins all the way back in the 1920s and '30s, in Lincoln, Nebraska, with the Sass brothers. The first "black" iris was introduced from their gardens in 1934 as 'The Black Douglas', though to be fair it was just a purple bitone with really dark purple falls. The real deal came along in the form of Paul Cook's 'Sable' in 1938, an astounding almost black shade of blue-violet with a lustrous sheen; the iris world went crazy, and for years this breakthrough iris was commonly known as "the black iris." *Iris aphylla* is credited with intensifying pigmentation of black irises, its contribution said to be anthocyanic vacuolar inclusions (protein matrices that bind and trap anthocyanin pigments), which yield a deeper, saturated coloring at the surface. Most black irises have arisen from crosses between darker purples and blues.

Blacks hit their high point in the 1990s with TB introductions like 'Hello Darkness' (Schreiner 1992), the ever-sootier 'Midnight Oil' (Keppel 1998), and 'Anvil of Darkness' (Innerst 1998). More modern award winners and head-turners include Marky Smith's 'Obsidian' (2002), Roger Duncan's 'All Night Long' (2005), and three Schreiner introductions, 'Ghost Train' (2001), 'Fade to Black' (2002), and 'Badlands' (2003).

Pink

Pink was second only to yellow as a color sought by 20th-century iris breeders; it long eluded them and richly rewarded those who finally attained it. The long

TOP TO BOTTOM: 'Dozen Roses' (Meininger 2009) 'Fashionably Late' (Keppel 1998)

road to pink irises began with what were called "pallida pinks," orchid-pink blends that owed their ancestry to *Iris pallida*. These lines continue to this day, though a more chic moniker would be rosy pinks. Modern showgirls like 'Fashionably Late' (Keppel 1998) and 'Dozen Roses' (Meininger 2009) best define the present color category; however, in the 1940s these pinkish orchid irises took second chair to the tangerine pinks, an astounding and unparalleled color classification, and the predecessors of our modern pink bearded irises.

The discovery of "tangerine factor," as the gene was called, gave rise to a frenzy of hybridizing activity that attempted to exploit new tangerine-colored beards and pinker and pinker flowers. Surprisingly, the origins of the trait are a little murky, maybe because everyone was all caught up with breeding yellow irises at the time. P. A. Loomis, a Colorado iris breeder, even exhibited some of his best pink seedlings at the 1933–34 Chicago World's Fair, to criticism that he had dyed the soil with something to turn the flowers pink. Irisarians rigidly believed at the time that pink was an impossible color in the bearded iris realm.

The major progenitor of pinks was the Illinois-based breeder David Hall, father of the "flamingo pink" irises popularly introduced in the late 1940s and early 1950s. His first eight introductions were the results of 17 years of effort and over 12,000 seedlings, a daunting dose of realism even for a plant breeder. He ultimately earned a Dykes Medal for 'Cherie' (1948) in 1951. His pink irises, distributed by Cooley's Gardens, earned international acclaim and fame.

As with the stories of any of these color groups, development of pinks barreled on through the generosity of breeders with each other. Kindly letters accompanied by packets of pollen, seeds, and even boxes of rhizomes advanced the iris flower as much as the most innovative ideas. Few stories in the iris world begin and end with just one or two major players — by close of tale, they often encompass scores of people from all over the world.

ABOVE, LEFT TO RIGHT: 'Happenstance' (Keppel 2000)

'Just A Kiss Away' (Baumunk 2009)

2

Pinks today easily outshine any of the brightest hopes of gentlemen like David Hall. Some — such as the TBs 'Happenstance' (Keppel 2000) and 'In Love Again' (Keppel 2004), and the BB 'Eye Candy' (Keppel 2004) — gloss over pink with an almost silken texture. French-born 'Buisson de Roses' (Cayeux 1998) approaches true hot pink, particularly in cooler climates. Steve Poole's inbred pinks like 'Georgia's Dream' (2010) and 'Kaelin's Lipstick' (2011) max out the color intensity of blush pink with superb stalks and near-plastic floral substance. In addition to apricots, another by-product of pinks was more yellows, a trait combination still being explored by breeders and fueled by a market ever interested in the exotic and bizarre. Though bred from pink and white parents, Lowell Baumunk's 'Just A Kiss Away' (2009) epitomizes my definition of yellow-pink blends, complete with more lace than you can imagine.

Brown

Brown, like black, has an allure for color-crazed folks keen on one-upping the gardening neighborhood. Sure, everyone has some bronze-colored mums in September, but who has cinnamon and chocolate and copper in May other than an iris lover?

Most brown irises trace back to antecedents like *Iris variegata* and a Havana-brown tall bearded from

ABOVE, LEFT TO RIGHT: 'Daybreak' (Kleinsorge 1941)

'Single Malt' (Baumunk 2010)

France called 'Jean Cayeux' (Cayeux 1931). But it was an Oregon doctor, Rudolph Kleinsorge, who really transformed the iris world, with irises like 'Aztec Copper' (1939), 'Daybreak' (1941), and 'Goldbeater' (1944). These new color breaks took the iris world by storm. Kleinsorge's crowning achievement, 'Tobacco Road' (1942), was a selection from a three-way cross between his own 'Far West' (1936), 'Jean Cayeux', and 'Aztec Copper'. Despite winning one of only three-ever-awarded AIS Board of Director's Medals and being one of the most important tall bearded irises of the 20th century, 'Tobacco Road' is impossibly rare in cultivation and perhaps even extinct.

Though I'd love to find and grow 'Tobacco Road', I'm just as happy to enjoy other fine examples of Kleinsorge's work with 'Daybreak' and 'Bryce Canyon' (1944) topping my list of favorites every year. New age examples worth growing and swooning over for their coppery sheens include the burnished 'Corona Gold' (Maryott 1997), the Dykes Medal–winning 'Golden Panther' (Tasco 2000), the ever-popular 'Copper Bubble Bath' (Cadds 2002), and newly brewed 'Single Malt' (Baumunk 2010).

ABOVE: 'Corona Gold' (Maryott 1997)

Patterns and Color Combinations

Now let's jump into a brief overview of patterns and color combinations that every iris lover should know.

Amoena

An iris with white standards and colored falls. The bearded iris realm owes the existence of this pattern to the little species *Iris reichenbachii*, from which iris hybridizer extraordinaire Paul Cook teased the genes into the IB 'Progenitor' (Cook 1951). The glamour of this pattern and its perfection of contrast are obvious in person — stark white standards grant artistic license to whatever falls below. A reverse amoena (or darktop) is just what you'd expect: pigmented standards and white (or lighter) falls.

Bicolor

An iris with standards and falls of contrasting colors. Bicolors make the world go round. Sure, I love elegant all-one-colored irises too, but spice it up with bi-, tri-, and quadricolored flowers, and now you're talking. The term is a little misleading in a way. Amoenas, after all, are bicolors, but a specific one ("white and . . ."). Bitones are also bicolors, just variations in shade. For simplicity's sake, let's just say

ABOVE: Amoena, 'Last Laugh' (Shoop/Keppel 2000)

that broadly speaking if two or more colors show up on the tepals of an iris flower, it's a bicolor, regardless of the nuances. Bicolors provide remarkable contrast with other companion flowers, creating possibilities for animated conversations in the garden. They can also stir up chatter that leads to full-on gossip — too much yakety yak, amounting to visual noise instead of pleasant harmony. It's a matter of taste and style: the eccentric gardener will love them, the understated gardener will respectfully decline.

Bitone

An iris with standards and falls in different shades of the same color. Bitone irises add drama, while offering an olive branch to those otherwise turned off by color-busy bicolors. The subtle variation of shade and hue can add just a little more visual interest than selfs. They're great for monochromatic gardens, harmonizing the extremes of spectrum into one pleasing yet subdued combination. Typically the falls are the darker of the two.

Blend

A combination of two or more colors mixed, overlaid, or swirled into each other. A succinct way of describing an otherwise indescribable iris, one that is, ideally, a tantalizing visual feast. Flamboyant, dramatic, and over-the-top, these irises definitely inspire opinions! I love

ABOVE, LEFT TO RIGHT: Bitone, 'Leading Light' (Shoop/Keppel 1999)

Bicolor, 'Finalist' (Gatty/Keppel 1994)

the broken-colored look of creatures like 'Anaconda Love' (Kasperek 1999) and 'Flamingo Gringo' (Kasperek 2009), but I'm not always sure what to plant them with. Others like 'Silicon Prairie' (Stanek 1991) baffle the mind — what color is it, exactly? Blends can work well with full-color palettes, gardens awash with a chromatic medley. They shine like divas in the spotlight in gardens where just a few colors mingle — potentially a pro or con, depending on your intention. In essence they need a moment of garden space to shine in their time. For fearless color gardeners, there could never be a more perfect iris.

Luminata

An iris with white or yellow hafts, with the remainder of the flower washed with white veins. Genetic relatives of the plicata, luminatas have a characteristic washed or veined appearance, with color excluded from the veins and immaculate white or yellow hafts. The prototype for this fancy pattern was 'Moonlit Sea' (Sass 1942), eventually succeeded by Keith Keppel's 'Mind Reader' (1994) and 'Spirit World' (1994), both variations of purple veined with white or cream, and by Lowell Baumunk's 'Elizabethan Age' (2005) and 'Queen Eleanor of Aquitaine' (2007). Luminatas come in a range of colors, more often tending toward purples and variations thereof (i.e., mostly anthocyanin pigments). Like blends, their presence in garden vignettes never goes unnoticed, and with so many colors contributing to their composition they converse well with other plants, aesthetically speaking.

TOP TO BOTTOM: Blend, 'Silicon Prairie' (Stanek 1991) Blend, 'Flamingo Gringo' (Kasperek 2009)

Neglecta

A bitone iris in blue or purple shades. Neglectas conjure up images of stormy seas or thunderclouds, varying from shades approaching black to tints glimmering azure. Richly colored blossoms of 'Best Bet' (Schreiner 1988) and 'Proud Tradition' (Schreiner 1990) create perfect moments of drama in the springtime garden. In a season when pastels and white abound, adding the saturated colors of ocean and sky is an entirely understandable act of defiance.

Plicata

A color pattern featuring stippled, dotted, or stitched falls and/or fall margins over a lighter ground color. The plicata pattern is the "it" pattern of the iris world — at some point everyone's taken a fancy to it, genetically or otherwise. Captivating and eye-popping, plicatas boast bands of darker colors, often purple or browns, overlaying a "ground" color such as white, yellow, or cream. At the technical level, the difference is in the pigments — the band color is comprised of water-soluble anthocyanins (purple-based pigments) found in the vacuole, the storage container, of the plant cell. Biologists surmise that elaborate patterning in flowers like the iris probably results in response to pollinators. It's hard to imagine what iris patterns look like to bees or other insects, but it may be telling that the plicata pattern is genetically recessive to self flowers. The next time you're in the garden, just imagine what a bee thinks.

Self

An iris with standards and falls of the same color. This "pattern" is fairly self-explanatory and despite being common by default, it's still a valuable addition to the garden. In fact, visitors to my nursery often ask for them by name, preferring solid colors to bicolors and wild patterns. To each his own — the iris world can satisfy! Though I tend to prefer unusual colors and patterns in my own garden, I'm still a sucker for a clump of a dark black iris or competing clumps of cardinal and gold, the colors of my alma mater. Nothing beats the audacity of unblemished color in full force in late spring.

Variegata

An iris with yellow or near-yellow standards and darker falls of brown, red, or purple. Named for *Iris variegata*, this distinctive bicolor pattern is well represented in all six classes. In tall beardeds, cultivars include 'Jurassic Park' (Lauer 1995), 'Mine' (Headrick 2004), 'Kathy Chilton' (Kerr 2006), and 'Born to Please' (Rogers 2006). The original pattern of yellow and brown still colors many irises in the MTB class but has probably tired just as many gardeners because of its limitations. I mean really, how many ways can you do yellow-brown-red in

CLOCKWISE FROM TOP LEFT: Luminata, 'Moonlit Sea' (Sass 1942)

Neglecta, 'Best Bet' (Schreiner 1988)

Self, 'Black Is Black' (Schreiner 2010)

Plicata, 'Aunt Mary' (Stanek 2000)

variation before it becomes a little trite? But jaded eyes aside, the variegata pattern makes great art in the landscape. The pattern plays off the familiar colors of yellow and purple in other plants, while jazzing up the color display more than something white or pink might.

Zonal

An iris with a white or lightened area around the beard. Zonals look like lights — a little bulb beaming from the center of the flower. They look smashing in combination with white or cream flowers that play off the glow emanating from within. Plant a clump of a zonal and watch it flower into a fantastic focal point.

ABOVE, LEFT TO RIGHT: Variegata, 'Born to Please' (Rogers 2006)

Zonal, 'Flash of Light' (Johnson 2008)

Planting Combinations: Divas and Dancers

Bearded irises are uncannily versatile in garden spaces. To think that bearded irises look just as at home in a New Mexican xeriscape as in a cottage border on Nantucket baffles me. But it's true. Whether due to their rock star status as the diva of spring, or their simple familiarity to gardeners of all stripes, bearded irises grow and show well in just about any garden setting that meets their basic biological requirements, in concert with a medley of similarly cultured plants.

If there's one thing I love doing, it's assembling thriving plants together in combinations. But planting something in my garden can turn into an agonizing creative process if I haven't given it a little thought. I march around from bed to bed, pots and plants in hand, sorting through the rush of ideas in my head. Should I put this here or here? What plant needs to go there? It can paralyze a gardener's workday, particularly if you're prone to overthinking decisions as simple as what to order at your favorite restaurant. So why not spend a little time dreaming and scheming beforehand about which plants go with each other? After all, it's really, really, fun.

Texture

Aside from coming in virtually all colors of the rainbow except a true red, bearded irises can spike the texture in your garden scene. When I think about texture, I really just think about contrast. So imagine a clump of bearded irises with their blue-green foliage paired with a soft ornamental grass like a muhly (*Muhlenbergia*) or fountaingrass (*Pennisetum*). Picture the difference? Less metaphorically, how could you use that pointy, bluish green foliage to hide something that's not quite ready for showtime, or what bold, thickset leaf will offset that spiky iris look? A contrast of textures creates impact that's hard to beat. Don't forget to dream ahead to late summer and consider how those iris leaves hold up — maybe something, like asters, anemones, or goldenrods (*Solidago*), should give them a little privacy while they hover in semi-dormancy until cooler weather arrives.

ABOVE: 'Lullaby of Spring' (Schreiner 1987) with columbines

Without diving into a long philosophical treatise on how I marry plants into vignettes and then vignettes into a larger garden, I'll pose one metaphor with two characters — the diva and the dancer. As a devout iris lover, I firmly believe that every garden needs a diva — an iris, if you will. But if you know anything about theater, you know that few shows go on without a supporting cast, a chorus line of dutiful players that meld together the larger elements of a production into an enjoyable whole. A garden isn't any different. While I love bearded irises to obsession, a garden of them without a supporting cast would be just a little too much for me. Besides, I have too many other plants to love, just as you probably do. With this cast of characters in mind, let's explore some possible dancers to keep those divas looking their best in spring and beyond.

Herbaceous perennials

The array of plants that could be paired with bearded irises is vast. If we started making lists, we'd never finish; they would easily go on for pages. If there are any rules when it comes to choosing perennials, beyond grouping those with similar cultivation requirements, it's that bearded irises often need space — they are the diva, after all. Many dwarfs and medians will easily succumb to competition from taller, more robust plants that shade them

ABOVE: 'Sherwin-Wright' (Kohankie 1915) with *Baptisia australis*

out in the months following flowering. Tall bearded irises pack a little more staying power, but no clump will look its dandiest shoved in the shadows of shrubs. Beyond giving them a little breathing room in the garden, the possibilities for pairing bearded irises with herbaceous perennials are limitless. That said, let me suggest a few ways — grounded in the gardens of iris lovers the world over — to go about staging the production.

First, think florally. Though I'm not much of a floral arranger, this is when I dream about "in-garden nosegays," dynamo combinations of twos and threes that look as if they reversed fortunes and leapt from the vase to the garden. They accent each other in color and shape and end up together, often flower against flower. Picture dangling black columbines popping up between the stems of ruby-colored IBs like 'Ruby Slippers' (Keppel 2002) or 'Garnet Slippers' (Keppel 2005), or sprays of false indigo (*Baptisia*) alighting alongside just about any white or yellow iris.

Now give some thought to size. The shortest miniature dwarfs could easily get lost in the rambunctious herbaceous border if they're not grown at the margins. They would appreciate the sunny exposure of the rock garden, hunkered down between stones somewhere, or even mounded up in the center of a hypertufa trough. The miniatures sing in concert with many familiar rockery plants including rockcress (*Arabis*), creeping phlox (*P. subulata*), the tidy tussocks of emerging succulents, *Alyssum saxatile*, thymes, and even other early spring irises like the Juno iris (*I. bucharica*).

The SDBs work just as well in the rock garden, keeping in mind their slightly larger size. A vigorous swath of dwarf species like *Iris subbiflora* and *I. aphylla* is always easy on the eyes surrounded by saxifrages, androsaces, or geums. Standard dwarfs work into the open border with ease too, showing off neat

ABOVE: 'Flaming Embers' (Willott 2003) on the edge

and tidy mounds of foliage at the feet of taller neighbors like speedwells (*Veronica*) and salvias, silken clusters of pasqueflower (*Pulsatilla*), and even coral bells (*Heuchera*) and foamflowers (*Tiarella*) at the margins of shady areas. Their show often begins just as deciduous trees and shrubs leaf out, so don't be shy about putting them in what you think of as a shady spot in high summer — because when they bloom, it isn't really all that shady. A whole host of "edge" plants that thrive at the margins of sun and shade look endearingly aesthetic with SDBs — woodland phlox (*P. divaricata*), *Lamium maculatum* (so long as it's kept in check and not allowed to overrun the irises), *Ranunculus repens* 'Buttered Popcorn', smaller trilliums, *Polygonatum humile*, shooting stars (*Primula*), golden ragwort (*Packera aurea*), and of course violets. Though not a bearded iris, *I. cristata* is also suited to shady spots and makes an equally lovely companion of SDBs.

Intermediates, miniature talls, and border beardeds all deserve homes mid-border or even at the edges, where their delicate airs will capture attention. I've done this on many occasions with miniature talls like 'Bumblebee Deelite' (Norrick 1986), which always draw me and visitors to the garden with clouds of buzzing flowers on waspy stems. The airiness of MTBs suits them for mingling; whether rising from behind pinks (*Dianthus*), a rocketing clump of trollius, or a windy mass of *Linum perenne*. In my back perennial border, I once had a low, pink stream of *Primula sieboldii* 'Pink Snowflake' running underneath a clump of 'Joseph's Coat Katkamier' (Katkamier / Tankesley-Clarke 1930 / 1989), a delightful broken-colored MTB, and a stand of variegated loosestrife (*Lysimachia punctata* 'Alexander'); the wild and free colors were repeated by other iris-plus-perennial combinations throughout the border.

The intermediates and border beardeds, while standing at the same height as the MTBs roughly speaking, look a little more like their tall bearded cousins in flower. That proportion lends them to pairing with shorter herbaceous peonies, the early flowering eastern beebalm (*Monarda bradburiana*), spiderworts (*Tradescantia*), mountain bluet (*Centaurea montana*), and spring sweet pea (*Lathyrus vernus*).

Traditionally, tall bearded irises appear in the back, buffered, accented, and supported with the remaining structure of the garden — shrubs or still taller perennials like spring favorites Oriental poppies (*Papaver orientale*), delphiniums (opt for the species instead of the hybrids), or lupines. I'm a huge fan of *Thalictrum* 'Black Stockings', and early meadow rues in general. Another to use for late tall bearded accompaniment is *T. flavum* subsp. *glaucum*, the irresistible yellow meadow rue that begins flowering in early summer, just as the tall bearded irises wane.

Don't forget other irises for the well-companioned border: the chief complaint of irises is the brevity of their bloom season, so why not just keep the irises coming, to extend the season? The miniature dwarfs begin in early spring, and then give way to the medians of mid-spring, which let the tall beardeds take over in late spring and early summer, passing the baton from there onto late-flowering Siberians and spurias, and from there, Japanese irises. A calendar garden full of irises is entirely plausible and wholly necessary.

Don't forget to dream beyond spring. What perennials help show off your bearded irises, and how do they go together in the garden? Do late summer doers billow over clumps of irises or simply, gently disguise their margins? The list again could be long, but I'd be remiss for failing to voice positive endorsements of daylilies (*Hemerocallis*), lilies (*Lilium*), coneflowers (*Echinacea* and *Rudbeckia*), and beebalms (*Monarda*). The fall is a time for asters, goldenrods (*Solidago*), and the pendulous stems of lespedeza. If you happen to garden with rebloomers, hope for the chance to really throw off your gardening friends with an in-garden nosegay of autumn flowers spiked with bearded iris.

ABOVE: 'Hello Darkness' (Schreiner 1992) with *Thalictrum* 'Black Stockings'

Variegated irises, discussed later in this chapter, provide a double shot of artful value in garden planning — foliage that looks good through spring and summer and the bonus of flowers, though unfortunately not as showy. A few modern cultivars exist, but the best-growing, best-thriving variegated varieties are older things like 'Argentea' (Goos and Koenemann 1906) and 'Zebra' (syn. 'Pallida Variegata'). They show up in public gardens with regularity, but home gardeners are a little shy about using them. If you appreciate strong, colorful foliage that holds forth with conviction and eye-thrashing color, you'll want to grow them.

As a final thought — I'm not wedded to the idea of layering herbaceous borders like people in a stadium, though when it works, it works famously. If you'd rather have a border full of really tall plants and tall bearded irises gracing the boundary between bed and lawn, do it. Don't forget that if something doesn't work, just trash it for a new idea. Bearded irises are relatively forgiving in the grand scheme of plant tolerances — fear not. Replant them in the fall when you overhaul your design, and they'll reward you from their new spot the following spring, just as before.

Bulbs

A garden without bulbs is like a life without music, and fortunately bulbs make excellent companions for bearded irises of all sizes.

Daffodil lovers have it swell — just about any of the 13 divisions look even better with dwarf bearded irises in tow. I'm particularly fond of *Narcissus bulbocodium* running around with MDBs and a groundcover like bugleweed (*Ajuga reptans*) — a gang of three that will bring you only joy. The little triandrus daffodils with small, nodding flowers look dandy alongside SDBs, and both keep similar schedules! Daffodils plus dwarf irises plus groundcovers equals the easiest way to welcome spring into the garden with three fail-proof plants that just can't help but look good.

On the tulip front, I'm bewitched by species tulips, the preternatural charms of which combine naturally with smaller bearded irises. In the dream garden in my head, I conjure up a meadow of soft grasses, outcroppings of bearded irises, and highlighting drifts of red and yellow species tulips. I've enjoyed great vignettes with *Tulipa vvedenskyi*, *T. batalinii*, and various *T. kaufmanniana* hybrids in my own garden and elsewhere. Smart planning makes the tedious effort of planting drifts of bulbs worth it. And when you go to stick those tulip bulbs in the ground come fall, you have the benefit of actually seeing where the irises are, whereas other dormant bulbs or perennials, which have already gone hiding for the season, leave you wondering where exactly they grow.

Jumping outside the mainstream bulb offerings, you'll find the possibilities are tremendous, everything from camassias to fritillaries. I can't help but swoon when I see *Fritillaria pallidiflora* ring out sulfur-yellow bells over brown or red SDBs or IBs, but I get just as giddy when ominous rods of *F. imperialis* backdrop tall bearded irises. I love a mass of camassias standing up next to any iris taller than 16 inches, or spring-flowering onions like *Allium karataviense* rolling around in thick, succulent leaves at the base of any median iris. In the arena of delightful minor bulbs, I'm somewhat embarrassed to endorse the often weedy star of Bethlehem (*Ornithogalum umbellatum*), but must do so, simply because it can carpet the ground below armfuls of tall bearded irises — the simplest way to make a little heaven with just a few plants. I'll respect your right to cuss and disagree if you'd rather not permit such "stars" to enter your premises! Though I haven't grown them myself, I imagine other species like *O. pyrenaicum* and *O. fimbriatum* would look just as chic while showing at least a little more taste.

My bulb-iris pairings continue into July, with the thought of airy scapes of *Caloscordum neriniflorum* poking up between dwarf irises in the rock garden, the by-products of an always fruitful reseeding the season before. Speaking of midsummer, *Canna*, *Caladium*, *Colocasia*, and *Gladiolus* species go great with flowerless clumps of tall bearded irises, borrowing the stage while our divas take a rest.

Grasses

I'm really surprised at how few gardeners grow bearded irises with grasses. Maybe at first the idea seems a stretch, the thinking being that the textural differences between the two aren't sufficient to make a pairing pop. I'm not sure that's true at all. An ongoing project in my own garden is to convert a tough spot rife with veins of sticky clay into a prairie-style garden highlighted by tall bearded irises in spring. Beyond the obvious challenge of building up the soil structure and finding an ample palette of thriving plants for the job, I'm having a giddy time interspersing bearded and beardless irises with smaller, lower growing native grasses like prairie dropseed (*Sporobolus heterolepis*), sideoats grama (*Bouteloua curtipendula*), and little bluestem (*Schizachyrium scoparium*). The concept doesn't stretch far enough to include fall-fabulous maidenhair grasses (*Miscanthus*), at least in direct combination with irises, but that's okay. Other grasses that have proven soldierly handsome between strapping clumps of tall beardeds include the rigid, tall wheatgrass (*Thinopyrum ponticum* 'Jose Select'), the just plain big, big bluestem (*Andropogon gerardii*), and the vase-form indiangrass (*Sorghastrum nutans*). Taller, potentially rangier grasses like these work well behind the irises or interspersed as specimen plants that contrast in shape and architecture.

Though not true grasses, sedges and grass-like plants like liriopes grow superbly with bearded irises. Sedges dial the contrast meter in the opposite direction, taking the eye to a finer scale. Mondo grass (*Ophiopogon*) does the same, though stops short of the soft look of sedge in favor of a little more leaf surface area for color exposition. I could go on for pages about the thousands of combos I've dreamt up using the ultra Gothic black mondo grass (*O. planiscapus* 'Nigrescens'), but the bottom line is the same — it looks great alongside just about anything, especially if you need to feed that black plant addiction.

I'm fond of Appalachian sedge (*Carex appalachica*), mainly because it knows how to reseed politely and always in the most serendipitous spots. Despite its diminutive proportions, it looks grand with bearded irises of all sizes, keeping the company of shorter bearded irises along rocks or forming a meadow beneath towering tall beardeds. This same idea applies to sedges like *C. morrowii*, *C. eburnea*, *C. flacca*, *C. retroflexa*, and *C. elata*. Sedges and shorter bearded irises go together like cheese and wine — the perfect combination makes your mouth water.

Groundcovers

Though this really isn't any more than a horticultural designation for something moderately rampant at ground level, I love groundcovers for two reasons — they're quick and simple, the cleverest way to tie a few bearded irises and other perennials into a pleasing in-the-ground bouquet made for primetime. Afflicted by an addiction to succulents, I'll first praise groundcover sedums. My garden would be seriously incomplete without *Sedum spurium* 'John Creech' and *S. apoleipon* crawling underneath little clumps of standard dwarf bearded irises. But there are so many more! The gold-splashed *S. sieboldii* 'Mediovariegatum' politely mingles with any SDB, offering excellent contrast of leaf shape, size, and color. A combination I'm very fond of in friends' gardens is dwarf and intermediate bearded irises underplanted with a dense layer of *S. acre* and *S. album*. Despite my intuition that this mat might run over the irises in time, they've thrived beautifully, kept in check no doubt by a tighter planting scheme initially. If

ABOVE: 'Maui Moonlight' (Aitken 1987) with *Carex elata* 'Aurea'

you want to give your irises a fighting chance, plant them closer to start with and then let the groundcovers fill in. One last sedum endorsement — I'm head-over-heels for *S. album* 'Murale' for its dark chocolate color in the earliest days of spring. Toss in some grape hyacinths (*Muscari armeniacum*) and some little yellow irises, and you'll have the plant world's equivalent of dancin' in the streets.

The rock garden is full of ground-hugging possibilities beyond the sedum realm. Scotch moss (*Sagina subulata*) forms a neon mat between dwarf irises and hens and chicks (*Sempervivum*). Later in the summer, little tussocks of gentians like *Gentiana septemfida* or *G. acaulis* color in the void left by dormant dwarf and median irises. Other rock garden staples like skullcaps (*Scutellaria*), woolly yarrow (*Achillea tomentosa*), creeping baby's breath (*Gypsophila repens*), and even hardy ice plants (*Delosperma*) make smart companion choices throughout the season with color and textures that offset the green architecture of iris clumps.

If you enjoy shorter irises along stone or pebble paths, you'll probably want a variety of steppable plants in their midst. Imagine thymes (*Thymus*), clovers (*Trifolium*), and cotula (*Leptinella*) running between. Not only do these fast-growing groundcovers look good, but they serve a practical purpose of keeping pesky weeds out from between clumps of small irises, which can be a little difficult to weed among anyway. With so many choice selections of bugleweed (*Ajuga reptans*) available these days, ranging from the ultra modern 'Black Scallop' to the geeky 'Planet Zork', you'll probably want to experiment with those, too. Have a wall's edge to plant an iris or two? Why not go for a taller median like an intermediate or miniature tall bearded behind a spilling mass of ornamental oregano (*Origanum rotundifolium* 'Kent Beauty') or creeping phlox (*P. subulata*)?

ABOVE: Irises arising from a mat of sedums

Shrubs and small trees

The great revival of interest in shrubs couldn't be more welcome by iris lovers, particularly if you're fond of tall bearded irises. If you've got an iris-brimmed garden, put shrubs to use as backdrops for color echoing and contrasting and as intimate companions during flowering season and beyond.

A staple combination for many years in my garden, drawing upon winsome, old-fashioned charm, was a clump of navy blue 'Stellar Lights' (Aitken 1986) and a pink weigela. But with so many *Weigela* cultivars from which to choose, you shouldn't feel constrained by old fashions. Graceful boughs of sooty-foliaged cultivars like Wine and Roses™ and 'Elvera' (Midnight Wine®) provide a dramatic backdrop to any bearded iris taller than 16 inches. If you really like dramatic, why not assemble a few of the blackest irises around like 'Before the Storm' (Innerst 1989) or 'Anvil of Darkness' (Innerst 1998) in the company of a white-flowered weigela like 'White Knight'? One last weigela combination I've just pieced together in my own garden — one of the yellow-flowered weigelas (like *W. middendorffiana* or *W. subsessilis* 'Canary') with dark purple or black irises. Dreamy!

Not a weigela fan? What about Dream Catcher™ beautybush (*Kolkwitzia amabilis* 'Maradco')? Its foliage, dripping with gold and flushed with bronze, could simmer in the background behind any number of intermediate or border bearded irises. Keeping with the chartreuse theme, why not spot a few clumps of something silky, dusky, or brunette alongside *Spiraea thunbergii* 'Ogon'? It would be a great opportunity to pull in 'Dynamite' (Schreiner 1997), 'Warrior King' (Schreiner 1985), and other brick reds, or even some dark blue-purples like 'Dusky Challenger' (Schreiner 1986) and 'Polished Manners' (Keppel 2000).

Ninebarks (*Physocarpus opulifolius*) make great backdrops too, particularly the satiny purple leaves of 'Diablo'. Against such a dramatic foil, anything pops! For greatest contrast and effect, try lighter blues and whites. In one garden I saw a 'Diablo' planted in the center of a large mass of an old clone of *Iris pallida* — a vignette for the senses. Not only was the blue against burgundy color combination striking, but enjoying the fragrance while taking in the view was a real treat. No iris gardener in zone 6 and above should be without a large specimen Japanese maple (or two, or five); they are exceptionally vibrant as backdrops. West Coast gardeners no doubt feel the same way about ceanothus, and I'd love to find an iris lover using the rad and slightly avant garde *Ceanothus* 'Tuxedo', with its lacquered black foliage, as an all-season backdrop.

Another popular shrub or small tree in many iris gardens is fringetree (*Chionanthus virginicus*). Filling out into a pendent, arching shrub or a statuesque small tree, fringetree looks handsome lording it over comely clumps of bearded irises. Given

2

fringetree's delicate appearance, white or pale pink irises always seem to look most chic with it, maintaining a monochromatic theme. If you're unable to find fringetree, you could just as easily substitute a silverbell (*Halesia*) or snowbell (*Styrax*), which have equally seductive, pendulous white flowers.

On the theme of small trees, the very popular dappled willow (*Salix integra* 'Hakuro Nishiki') trained into a formal standard can look especially posh accompanying bearded irises. Variegation poses a classic challenge; it is too often too busy, leaving gardeners acting as plant neighborhood planners struggling to know what exactly to put "next door." Bearded irises to the rescue! I've seen the combination many times, and I've never once thought, "Oh darn, that variegated willow just does too much for me." (Honestly? My thought is always, "Who the hell has to prune that willow into a ball on a stick?") In fact, big, bold, colorful bearded irises always steal the show, backlit by these manicured willows, a great opportunity to use either a happening bicolor or a strong self.

ABOVE: 'Footloose' (Schreiner 1993) with *Physocarpus opulifolius* 'Diablo'

Let's think beyond putting flowers alongside flowers. What about midsummer, when the irises are done and the show must go on? Roses, hydrangeas, and butterfly bushes (*Buddleia*) might come, sure. All these and any other bold diva shrubs you can think of have enough jam to divert attention away from what are now simply clusters of green blades. Butterfly bushes look especially great, rising from behind irises with rocketing, richly fragrant clusters that draw the eye from ground level to the tips of their flowers.

Personally I've never much liked clumps of bearded irises planted at the foot of large shrubs like viburnums. At some point in the summer the whole scene looks a little blah, something I'm always trying to fight in my garden. I'm not blah, you're not blah, and our gardens should never be blah. That's not to say they have to be a circus, but really, if a garden doesn't entice the senses, what good is it? But back to that viburnum (though I really don't mean to pick on them). While beautiful in every respect, a clump of tall bearded irises really can't go toe to toe with a doublefile viburnum (*V. plicatum* f. *tomentosum*) in terms of sheer "wow" power. They need a second act, something like a meadow rue (*Thalictrum rochebrunianum*), a phlox (*P. paniculata*), or even a smaller shrub like summersweet (*Clethra alnifolia*) that blooms in another season and boasts foliage that covers the scenes while the divas take a break in the green room.

In a parting nod to shrubs, let's not forget about reblooming irises. Jumping back on the stage for a fall encore, rebloomers offer that rare moment to turn heads, defying seasonal expectations and adding just another few dozen options for dynamo combinations. Think about that stalwart white rebloomer 'Immortality' (Zurbrigg 1982) in concert with a bluebeard (*Caryopteris*) or a hardy fuchsia, or a fail-proof purple rebloomer like 'Eleanor Roosevelt' (Sass-McDade 1933) planted at the feet of yellow-burnished witchhazels (*Hamamelis*) or spicebush (*Lindera benzoin*). Talk about turning heads. Your neighbors just might ask what's wrong with that iris!

In the Cutting Garden

When it comes to cutting and arranging flowers, I'm generally clueless. I've mastered the scissoring part, but that's about it. Oh, and the bucket too. So basically I can get them cut and in a bucket of fresh water. Then I snap my fingers for the magic florist. But I do think that bearded irises have been ignored too long as cuts in the height of spring, likely because most people don't grow miniature tall beardeds — the best of the six classifications for cutting and arranging. At one point in the history of modern iris development, the MTBs were known as table irises, a far more descriptive name. The term fell by the wayside over the years and generally didn't conform to the naming standards that most of the other iris groups abided by. But that vocabulary does serve a very fundamental purpose in describing their worth, merits, and use as fresh cut flowers.

If you walk out into my garden in mid-May, just about the peak bloom time for MTBs, it's immediately apparent why they cut so well. First off, they're short, or at least shorter than their tall cousins. But shorter stems shouldn't imply stout or squatty. In fact, ranging in height from 16 to 27½ inches tall, their airy charm keeps them from succumbing to the weight of their own flowers (and they don't topple over after a rainstorm, like so many of their taller cousins do). Second, not only are their stems short, they're flexuous, easily stuck into arrangements and maneuvered without being fractured or broken. Many MTB cultivars retain tremendous vigor, putting up several stalks per clump, each loaded with buds, resulting in longer vase life.

Like most bearded irises, the MTBs have delicate flowers. Great care should be taken when handling them as they're easily smashed in a bucket. (This goes double for larger cuts of TB stems, whose flowers always wanted to flop into each other and lock petals as if determined not to leave the bucket.) Frequent flower show exhibitors (of which I'm not one) have elaborate contraptions for hauling their precious stalks to show. You may wish to adopt their techniques if you're keenly interested in keeping every flower intact and in proper form. I'm told a favorite system involves a deep box or basket with milk or wine bottles half-filled with water.

MTB stalks sequence well for floral arranging purposes, often with three buds open at once (one terminal bud and two branches). If cut just as the first terminal bud is opening, the rest of the stalk usually opens up within 24 hours, in warm water indoors. Given the number of requests I've had over the years for cut irises, I can't imagine why cut flower growers wouldn't grow these shorter varieties.

In Containers

If you love container gardening, or are restricted to it because you garden only on a patio or deck, you can still grow bearded irises. Trough gardens might be the most logical place to start. Any dwarf iris would fit perfectly into these faux stone homes, but keep in mind (as you should anyway, when building a trough) that drainage is paramount. Any other proportionally small container with good drainage would also fit the needs of most dwarf irises.

I know several patio gardeners who have successfully cultivated tall bearded irises in large containers. Size, scale, and drainage are the most important factors to consider. Even a small clump of tall bearded irises flowering at 30 inches tall in a container can get a little woozy in the wind, so the larger container the better, to support not only the weight of the plants in flower but their roots as well. Bearded irises are typically not thought of as deeply rooted plants, but if grown in a fertile substrate, their roots often extend several inches down from the rhizome. The largest container available to support robust plants, particularly those that have been lightly fertilized, will guarantee the best chances of success. Some gardeners over the years have shared anecdotes about slightly smaller flowers from irises grown in containers, though I'm not prepared to give a horticultural reason as to why they may have experienced that.

Iris Novelties

As with any hyperevolved group of plants, novelty forms of irises have arisen, to the delight and excitement of collectors and enthusiasts. Some iris lovers shrug these off as fringe ideas, content on enjoying the abounding diversity of the norm. Some, however, hanker for the rare, the obscure, and the unusual, ever in a quest to one-up the neighbors when it comes time for the annual spring garden tour.

Variegated foliage

A few dozen or more variegated bearded irises exist, or at least did at some point, according to the American Iris Society registry. But few populate nursery catalogs and benches, and even fewer end up in gardens, with the exception of the clones of *Iris pallida*, 'Argentea' (Goos and Koenemann 1906) and 'Zebra' (syn. 'Pallida Variegata'). I can often find at least one of the latter two at a big box store in the fall, if I arrive on the same day as the truck delivering them. They get snatched up fast, and rightly so. After all, what better wow factor to add to the garden than an unexpected variegated riff on a common theme? But it's almost certain you'll be disappointed by the flowers — I cut them off hastily with pruning shears once while giving a tour of my garden, to the horror of onlookers. Though blue and fragrant, their dowdy, droopy form is a stark contrast to their wider, ruffled neighbors. While I have nothing against an old-fashioned look, some modicum of taste is in order. And after all, the excitement is the foliage.

Irisarians have long pondered the reasons behind variegation in bearded iris foliage. Many have suggested it's a viral disease, though that's debatable. Variegation in plants can be grouped into different categories based on general appearance relative to its cause. Variegation caused by viruses generally looks washed or haphazardly smeared, almost as if mixing shades of green and white together into a

murky, but often dazzling swirl. While I haven't grown every single cultivar of variegated bearded irises, not by a long shot, I've yet to see a variegation pattern that makes me think "viral." I think the more likely answer is genetic — a random mutation, perhaps caused by a transposon (the so-called jumping genes famously associated with mottling in corn kernels), or a chimeral mutation that yields two distinct types of tissues, one with chloroplasts, one without.

Whatever variegation's exact origins, iris breeders know the only way to transmit variegation to seedlings is maternally (and those who have ventured to prove otherwise have been disappointed every time). Most variegated cultivars are tall bearded. There are a few variegated medians, but they just aren't that stable. Over the years, at least a half-dozen seedlings in my own median breeding lines sported lovely, splashy variegation, but they either flat out died or reverted slowly over the course of the next season. I've tried my hand at 'Pink Marble' (Austin 1955), an intermediate iris derived from embryo-cultured seed, and 'Striped Britches' (Short 1977), a border bearded, but killed them both before they flowered. The variegation didn't impress me all that much anyway.

Breeding for variegation isn't something that tops the list of goals for most hybridizers, but Brad and Kathie Kasperek of Zebra Gardens in Utah have given it some attention. Brad and Kathie have

ABOVE: Dwarf iris, happy in a faux stone home

focused their efforts on improving the flower form of variegated irises (which I so handily trashed earlier), bringing them up to modern standards. One of their best and best-growing variegated cultivars in my garden is 'Zebra Bluez' (2004), a modern-formed, ruffled blue tall bearded. The combination of cobalt blue flowers and consistent, smoothly blended green and cream foliage is outstanding. The foliage even looks good well into summer, providing a nice foreground to loosestrife (*Lysimachia punctata*) and beebalm (*Monarda didyma*) around the Fourth of July. Despite this appraisal, I should note that like many if not all variegated bearded irises, its growth rate tends to hover somewhere between "sulking" and "poky."

While never unhealthy, clumps of variegated cultivars just don't increase at the same rate as other varieties (remember the part about half as much chlorophyll?). From a practical standpoint, this works out well if you need a focal plant that won't run you out of house and garden. Then again, who likes to wait around for something to decide whether it's going to grow or not? Don't be afraid to give your variegated irises a little extra fertilizer in the spring and fall to keep them growing strong. You'll reap the rewards of lush variegated foliage for seasons to come.

Other tall bearded varieties worth trying for their special foliar flair include 'Canadian Streaker' (Chapman 1997), 'Fantastreaks' (Jedlicka

ABOVE: 'Zebra Bluez' (Kasperek 2004) with *Lysimachia punctata*

2007), 'Neglected Zebra' (Kasperek 2007), 'Quite the Same' (Ensminger 2002), and 'Verdict' (Johnson 2004).

Though technically not variegation in the scientific sense, you've no doubt noticed while puttering around the iris patch that some irises sport handsome flushes of purple pigments at the base of their fans. In iris lingo, they've got PBF (purple-based foliage). Many irises exhibit PBF to varying degrees; the Dykes Medal–winning 'Honky Tonk Blues' (Schreiner 1988) has an especially rich flush of purple-red. Notable among species is *Iris purpureobractea*, so named for its purple bracts; it's reportedly a diploid, and most closely resembles a miniature tall bearded iris, which class it'd be most likely to improve if hybridizers used it more frequently in crosses. A handful of enterprising geeks have taken on the challenge (including yours truly), dreaming about fans of almost entirely purple coloration, purple buds, and even purple stalks. Bearded irises with purple, ornamentally aesthetic foliage would be a major coup. Stay tuned!

Space-agers

When I utter the words "space-age iris" in conversation or a lecture, the look of bewilderment that follows on the faces of all present is priceless. What on earth could a space-age iris be? Space-age irises boast some kind of appendage at the terminus of the beard, on a scale from horn (the smallest protrusion) to flounce (the largest). In most cases, horns are simply beards that rise away from the plane of the fall into mid-air, poking upward. Some cultivars sport spoons, thin petal-like projections that rise or dangle off the end of the beard. Flounces are petaloids, literally small petal-like pieces lobbed onto the end of the beard like some ostentatious hairpiece. If you love bling, you'll love space-age irises. Fortunately the trait shows up in about every class of bearded irises — from the tiniest MDB 'Punk' (Ransom 1998) to TBs like Tom Burseen's extravagantly flounced 'I Wuv Woses' (2009).

Space-agers are with us thanks to the observant eyes of Lloyd Austin, a USDA pomologist and budding iris breeder, who in 1944 discovered a horn-like projection at the end of the beards on a plicata seedling

ABOVE: 'I Wuv Woses' (Burseen 2009)

(introduced as 'Advance Guard' in 1945) in Sydney Mitchell's garden. Professor Mitchell, a renowned iris breeder himself, apparently had no interest in the trait and offered to let Austin use it for some of his very first crosses. Austin made crosses and grew out hundreds of seedlings before introducing five "horned irises," as he called them. The first and perhaps most famous of these original space-agers was 'Unicorn' (1954). Austin introduced over 200 different irises, most of them space-agers and various novelty irises. I've enjoyed 'Horned Tangerine' (1960), a pink blend with orange beards lifting into small orange horns, for many years in my garden.

Iris breeders have continued to dabble in this fashionable novelty trait, even against the opinion of mainstream irisarians, who for many years looked down on space-agers as gaudy and tasteless. The most successful was Monty Byers, a young California hybridizer who in the 1980s and early 1990s introduced several space-agers that have redefined modern irisdom, including two back-to-back Dykes Medal winners — 'Thornbird' (1989) in 1997 and 'Conjuration' (1989) in 1998. Though many gardeners look right past their rising beards without ever noticing them, space-agers offer just another flavor of interest for those who've caught the iris bug.

Rebloomers

It seems that rebloomers are the most asked-about irises these cost-conscious days. Everyone wants an everblooming iris that begins in early May and continues, without pause for summer, until the early days of October (then that's enough). Sadly, Don Quixote, that iris doesn't exist. But that doesn't mean hybridizers aren't trying.

Reblooming, or remontant, irises essentially cruise through summer without going through dormancy, like their once-blooming cousins. Remontancy is fairly common in many herbaceous perennials and is practically expected from stalwarts

ABOVE: 'Thornbird' (Byers 1989)

Cyclic rebloomers (daylength dependent). These varieties complete two distinct cycles of growth—flowering and increasing—each growing season. The second cycle of growth does not require vernalization to produce flower stalks. Cyclic rebloomers typically rebloom in the fall, when shorter daylengths mirror those of spring.

Repeaters. These varieties produce additional stalks on old growth immediately following the first spring flowering cycle, typically within a few weeks to a month.

Continuous rebloomers (soil temperature dependent). Rebloom in these irises occurs whenever new rhizomes mature, throughout the growing season, often without pattern. Their remontancy correlates well with soil temperatures, not daylength.

like daylilies, geraniums, tick-seed (*Coreopsis*), and many salvias. But irises lag a little on this front. Blooming nonstop costs photo-synthesis and chlorophyll, in plant terms, and sometimes with an interest rate that makes bearded irises cringe. While there are many cultivars that do rejoin the garden in flower late in the summer and through the fall, a good many more don't. Will it be the norm some day? For the sake of customer service, I can only hope.

So what makes a bearded iris a rebloomer? Though we in the iris world lack specific data, it's reasonable to assume from general botanical research that the capacity to flower more than once in the growing season is a quantitative trait, meaning that (as with human eye color) a variety of genes and environmental factors influence the outcome. Rebloomers are loosely categorized by these factors and the timing of their rebloom.

Where you garden plays a role in how reliable rebloom will be in your garden; for example, it's fair to say that rebloom in zones 3 to 5 can be an iffy proposition. While I've certainly rebloomed many varieties in my iris life, and even experienced two years where I had some sort of iris in bloom at least one day out of every month from March through November in zone 5a, I don't get to enjoy them as often and in such numbers as my gardening friends in warmer zones. And as you well know, a Tennessee zone 7 isn't exactly the same as a Texas zone 7 — so both USDA hardiness zone and climate figure in. Warmer nighttime temperatures tend to induce dormancy in bearded irises, which means if you live in the Deep South, rebloom might not show up until later in the fall. Short autumns, too, often prevent rebloom from happening in northern climates. Many reblooming varieties, particularly those bred and developed on the West Coast and in Australia, don't get a chance to flower in the fall once temperatures start falling near freezing, though it's not uncommon to see flower stalks tinged in hoarfrost emerging on chilly mornings in October. Weather often prohibits their complete development in the garden at these late dates, but you can cut them and bring them indoors. I remember cutting a stalk for the Thanksgiving table one protracted fall, drawing several weird looks and inspiring inquisitive conversation.

But all this honest truth about rebloomers shouldn't discourage you from trying the growing crowd of them on the market. To keep the fun going, you basically want your reblooming varieties in "constant growth mode," meaning that instead of letting them sink into the doldrums of dormancy you might consider ways to coax them through the hotness of July and August to an encore performance. Rebloomers don't mind a low-nitrogen fertilizer or a little extra water, especially if a drought sets in. A little extra water might mean a once- or twice-weekly splash from the sprinkler hose (if you've got such a thing running around the yard), an occasional dousing with the water bucket as you check on your newly planted shrubs, or an inch of precipitation every ten to 14 days — if the rain gods are benevolent. Take care that the soil still drains well; a steady accumulation of water in the muggy, humid days of summer is not a recipe for success.

Broken colors

Pileated, variegated, and broken-colored are all adjectives used to describe the splashed and streaked flowers of bearded irises under the likely influence of a transposon (a jumping gene). Though the genetic history remains a little foggy, what matters most is that this phenomenally novel genre has rightly taken the bearded iris world by storm.

Scandalous-looking, no doubt, these irises have graced the gardens

2

ABOVE, LEFT TO RIGHT: 'Orangutan Orange' (Kasperek 2009)

'Joseph's Coat Katkamier' (Katkamier/Tankesley-Clarke 1930/1989)

of avant-garde iris lovers since the 1970s. But like many new trends seized upon by stylish people, broken-colored irises have been around longer than most realize. A 'Zebra', in commerce in the 1890s, reportedly had white flowers with blue stripes throughout the standards and falls, but that name is now reserved for the familiar cultivar of *Iris pallida* and its variegated foliage. The earliest extant broken-colored cultivars date back to sports (chance mutants) from 'Honorabile' (Lémon 1840). Two of these, 'Kaleidoscope' (Katkamier 1929) and 'Joseph's Coat Katkamier' (Katkamier/Tankesley-Clarke 1930/1989), look like confused variants of their wild ancestor *I. variegata*. There is some dispute about the identity of the true 'Honorabile' and whether it still exists; some have suggested that 'Sans Souci' (Van Houtte 1854) long ago replaced 'Honorabile' in commerce, but I'm not about to wade into those waters.

The Sass brothers of Nebraska probably were the first to dabble in breeding broken colors, likely as a by-product of their crosses for better plicatas. But it was in breeder Allan Ensminger, also of Nebraska, and later Brad and Kathie Kasperek, the Utah-based proprietors of Zebra Gardens, that these broken-colored irises found champions. The form of broken colors steadily improves, as does their stylishness. Whereas in their earlier days they were blatantly gaudy, they are now something closer to chicly frenetic.

*

I trust you'll only plant irises that appeal to your tastes. But don't overlook the properties of the flower itself after you've gone gaga over its color or pattern. Good form and substance go a long way toward enjoying coveted bearded iris blossoms. Though we iris lovers may value individual traits of bearded irises differently (I, for instance, nearly demand that modern bearded irises have round, fat form and wide hafts), the qualities that define a modern bearded iris of merit don't vary that much between us.

The real measure of any bearded iris is whether or not it lasts for several seasons in the garden. What impact does that plant have in its third or fourth year? Does it flower freely, hold up well in the wind and rain, increase abundantly, and contribute to the beauty of the garden? Or is it stingy with its blossoms, prone to withering in the slightest breeze, a wimpy increaser, and embarrassing to look at? If you happen to grow the latter already, find a sharp shovel and do what must be done.

If you have the privilege of visiting gardens in the spring or checking out iris specialty nurseries, give a watchful eye to those irises that grow into swoon-worthy clumps. Take note of American Iris Society (AIS) award winners, but recognize that the awards system isn't flawless. With so many plants coming onto the market each year, many get overlooked in the awards process.

You can grow bearded irises of all kinds, forms, and colors to flattering effect in your garden, large or small. The concepts I've introduced, the combinations I've proposed, the players I've sketched out in this chapter simply hit the highlights — a few major ideas worth sharing between one iris lover and another. No garden should be without these exceptional, versatile garden plants.

3 How to Successfully Grow Bearded Irises

3

"For decorative use in the home, then, it is quite appropriate to discuss ways and means of securing the most satisfying effects."

J. Marion Shull, *Rainbow Fragments* (1931)

If you asked me if bearded irises are easy to grow, and restricted my answer to one word, I'd shout, "Yes!" In the grand scheme of things, this is abundantly true. I can think of plenty of plants much harder to grower — Himalayan blue poppies (*Meconopsis*) and noble rhubarb (*Rheum nobile*) come to mind, both of which fall well outside the realm of even marginal plant snobbery. But bearded irises, difficult to grow? Rubbish. After covering the basics, the finer points deserve a closer look, just as with any other plant group. If gardening were as simple as soil, water, and light, humanity would have made paradise a long time ago.

Like any smart gardener, you know too that all plants are not created equal. Across this vast planet, plants have evolved and adapted to a range of conditions, from minute fissures in rock walls to unfathomably deep loam in mid-continental prairies. Fortunately for gardeners, bearded irises don't need elaborate cliff faces or endless feet of topsoil. In fact, given the hybrid nature of most modern cultivars, they're really highly adaptable in gardens. Anyone who's tossed a ragged clump or two of bearded irises over the back fence and watched them bloom blithely the next spring knows exactly what I'm talking about. Sure, not all cultivars are created equal either.

Some are duds. Some are rock stars (we'll get to those later). But for now, let's focus on getting a solid understanding of the cultural basics — how to grow the best-looking bearded irises.

When to plant

The best time to plant bearded irises is late summer through early fall. This magic window of time coincides with the ripening of the rhizome and a summer dormancy that irises go through on their way toward winter. During the spring months, just before and after flowering, bearded irises set down new roots that rapidly feed the plant through flowering. It's an auspiciously busy peak in a life cycle that largely takes place above ground, except for the aforementioned root development. The roots that you remember seeing as you planted your rhizomes last fall die away at this point — iris roots are deciduous in this way.

After flowering, a cascade of physiological changes takes place within the plant, essentially powering it toward flowering the next spring. Rhizome buds increase in size due to rapid nutrient uptake, growing from small spikelets at the heel of the rhizome into a colony of new rhizomes. Different cultivars increase at different rates, ranging from as few as one or two increases (considered poor, and often the one you're most anxious to have more of) to eight or more (considered robust, and too often the ugliest of varieties, which nobody wants more of). Flower buds also develop for next spring within these new increases. Most species and cultivars mentioned in this book typically undergo these changes within six to ten weeks after flowering and end up in pseudo-dormancy at some point in July or August, depending on your climate.

Naturally, it would make sense to divide and plant irises after their physiological maturity, when active growth has suspended for the season (ignoring, for the moment, rebloomers, of which more later). Upon division and subsequent replanting, active growth resumes, so long as the soil remains moist for a good ten to 14 days after planting. This encourages new root growth and foliar growth, and often results in a "greening up" of the plant overall.

Where to plant

For best performance, plant bearded irises where they'll receive six to eight hours of full sun during the growing season. That statement is as generic as it sounds, but it's true. While I've managed to grow bearded irises, when I had to, in the shade of oak trees, I wouldn't recommend it to someone out to create a beautiful garden that includes bearded irises. Bearded iris species grow natively in relatively treeless steppes and saxatile environments throughout central and eastern Europe and Asia. That's not to say that some bearded iris types won't grow in a little shade — in

3

fact, the miniature dwarfs do just fine because during their flowering season most trees aren't even leafed out! But please don't exile your irises to lonely rows. Let them marry with other plants in vignettes throughout your garden. Their charm and great beauty are wasted in straight and narrow lines.

Where to buy

Though bearded irises are sold in a variety of venues, you'll obtain the best selection of plants by ordering from an iris nursery. Likely, these passionate iris lovers are in the know about the latest, greatest varieties and can offer real-life experiences about all the varieties they raise. You'll come across carloads or UPS-boxes of different varieties, all of which will have to have a home in your garden.

While not a steadfast rule, if you can buy irises bred and developed or at the very least grown near your garden, you're more likely to have success. That's not to say that varieties developed on the West Coast won't do well in the Midwest or on the East Coast, but it's sort of unreasonable to expect by default that they

ABOVE: Bareroot rhizomes at Rainbow Iris Farm

should. Fortunately breeders have developed many hundreds of varieties over the years with broad tolerances to a wide swath of climates.

As a buyer's beware, don't let rhizome size influence you. Rhizomes vary by genetics and environment, and often rhizomes purchased from West Coast growers are phenomenally larger than those purchased from growers elsewhere due to a plusher, less stressful climate and thus a greater opportunity for tissue formation and swelling. While logically indicative of a good-quality product, the genetics of that plant will ultimately determine whether or not it's successful in your garden. You'll have the easiest time establishing bearded irises purchased bare-root as opposed to container-grown plants.

What's the soil like?

Bearded irises need soil underfoot that supplies them regular water but drains well. They were born to thrive in light soils with a coarse or gravelly texture. I've tried at all costs to avoid using the single most generic phrase in all horticulture — "moist but well drained." Let me explain. Good soil, by bearded

ABOVE: Rhizomes potted at a garden center

iris standards, should provide consistent water throughout the growing period, even if rain or irrigation isn't abundant (reflect on their native origins — mid-continental Eurasia can undergo lengthy periods of dryness). The chemical and structural composition of your garden's soil will ultimately determine how well and for how long it can fulfill this capacity.

If you have really sandy soil, you have a soil mixture that doesn't by nature hold water very well for very long. Bearded irises do just fine in sandy soils, partly because they're fairly drought resistant, like many plants with underground storage structures, and because the increased porosity of sandy soil affords their roots a greater opportunity to grow around. Sandy soils also keep moisture from hanging around too long, fostering the growth of microorganisms that could infect the roots or rhizome.

Bearded irises also do just fine in loamy to semi-clayey soils, mainly because they're fairly tolerant of water hanging around for just a while and because this range of soils is often nutrient-rich, accounting for its darker colors and crumblier texture.

Clays are a mixed lot as far as soil types go. It's possible to grow bearded irises in clay (I've even seen some tough bearded irises sticking it out in heavy clay), but I'd be foolish to say that a majority of cultivars or species would tolerate such abuse.

With a little amendment, even the most lackluster soil can support thriving clumps of bearded irises.

Sand
Improves drainage, increases tilth (avoid using with heavy clay)

Compost
Improves structure, enriches soil with organic matter and microorganisms

Peat
Improves aeration and structure, increases permeability

Pea gravel or grit
Improves drainage and structure

ABOVE: Planting demonstration

If you have a soil that's down on its chemistry, you can pep it up with a variety of additives to make it more amenable to cultivating bearded irises. See page 76 for a grid of four common amendments and their benefits.

How to plant

Plant bearded irises shallowly with anchorage. "How do I plant bearded irises?" is by far the most common question I get asked, usually from someone who's planted them too deeply at first. Mythbuster redux — *bearded irises are not bulbs*. Despite its bulb-like appearance, a rhizome is in fact a modified stem that grows at or just below the soil surface and serves as the main stem of the plant while also storing nutrients. Rhizomes should be exposed or only slightly covered after planting at ground level.

Many iris growers insist on leaving dangly strands of roots attached to the plants they ship out. I'm not here to tell anyone what they're doing is wrong, but if that bulky mass of roots gets in the way of planting, feel free to chop them back a bit. Initially, most of that root mass just provides anchorage for the plant and will quickly die off in the weeks after planting. Once the soil starts to form around the roots and the physics and chemistry kick into gear, those roots grow new root hairs and start supplying your newly planted irises with essential nutrients and water. Pruning off the lower third of that root mass stimulates callusing and additional root hair formation, thereby helping (not harming, as some believe) your bearded iris rhizomes.

In all good gardens, the magic starts below ground. Digging that first hole for a new bearded iris can be the simplest thing you'll do in the garden come late summer/early fall. Grab a trowel and make two parallel troughs about 4 to 6 inches long. Place the rhizome on the crest of soil that you've just left behind, taking care to splay the roots out into the troughs. Backfill around the rhizome, barely covering it, or with up to an inch of soil in areas with light, sandy soils or high summer heat and sun exposure. If you live in one of these areas, a little over-the-top protection will keep your rhizomes from scalding, drying out, and heaving.

If you have only one rhizome, you can stop reading here. But if you've gone overboard (something I totally condone) and have several rhizomes to plant, you may find yourself asking how close you can space them together. My naturally wry response is "plant them as close as you like, if you want to divide them every year." Truly, spacing is conditional. If you have a bed of just irises, you're likely to want to get as many in as possible. But the closer you plant each of them to one another (12 inches or less), the more likely you'll have to divide every two to three years instead of every three to five years. Give them a little room (12 to 18 inches) and you'll give them more time to fill in, and thus put off division. If installing your irises with other plants, spacing may be up to the design of

the border. You may craft vignettes to specially suit your irises, at which point you'll have to plan for them crowding themselves and other plants in the vicinity.

A trick of the iris trade — planting in triplets. Three rhizomes, all facing the same direction and planted a foot apart, at the points of an imaginary 12 × 12 × 12 inch triangle, will grow into an "instant clump" of sorts in just a few growing seasons. The earlier warning holds true — they'll need to be divided sooner on account of the initial closeness — but if you're impatient and would prefer a quick established look, you'll likely want to adopt this method.

Water around the rhizomes and keep the ground moist until new growth starts to appear, usually within a few weeks of planting. Watering every two days makes sense; more frequent applications are called for in extreme drought conditions.

Feed me or . . . ?

Fertilizing your bearded irises depends on your soil and your preferences as a gardener. The nurturing nature of gardeners leads many people to ask what they can do to make their gardens grow better — principally, what can they feed their plants? For a long time I avoided the question with campy, lighthearted answers, barely disguising the fact that I rarely considered this question in my own garden. I took a slightly militant view on the subject, likening nurturing to coddling, which can often lead to shortsightedness about the lackluster performance of certain plants in the garden. "I don't have time for weaklings," I mumbled, while lumbering toward the compost pile with a wagonful of misfits and rejects that for whatever reason failed to make the cut on that particular day in the garden.

But I've softened a little. In fact as the question relates to bearded irises, it's quite thoughtful. Like many perennials that can overexert themselves in an honorable attempt at glory once every season, bearded irises do benefit from a nutritious growing environment. Some gardeners like the idea of fertilizing, while others like the idea of just "doing it right the first time" — starting with a good garden soil to begin with. Regardless of your position or its ways and means, the outcome ultimately looks the same — a floriferous, hardworking clump

ABOVE: Overgrown clump of bearded irises

of bearded irises that'll make your friends envious.

If you're in the "feed me, feed me" camp, consider a fertilizer that's low in nitrogen, 6-10-10 or something thereabouts. Fertilizers of this blend can be difficult to find, so you may opt to make your own, or have it custom-mixed at a farmer's cooperative or other source of agricultural supplies. There's no need to starve the plants of nitrogen entirely. Just keep that first number low. Too much nitrogen for a bearded iris means fast, succulent leaf growth and very few flowers. Nitrogen-rich foliage also happens to top the delicacy menu of iris borers. What chomping, chewing insect wouldn't mind a fresh batch of greens for breakfast, lunch, and dinner? Keep the nitrogen low, and you get healthy, green foliage and lots of flowers.

The second and third numbers don't have to be equal, but they shouldn't greatly outdo each other. Plants mainly use phosphorus (the second number) for converting light energy to chemical energy during photosynthesis, totally justifying its position in the Triple Crown of macronutrients; it also contributes to flower formation (a good thing, obviously). The third number represents potassium, which plants use to regulate water storage and form flowers.

Bearded irises greatly benefit from fertilization at two points during the growing season. The first application should occur six to eight weeks prior to flowering, usually in the early spring. Most pelletized fertilizer takes several weeks to break down into forms readily used by plants, hence the length of the lead time. Ideally, a three-year-old clump of irises contains several flowering-size plants, which will benefit from one to two clumps of fertilizer spread around the ground in their immediate vicinity. Take a moment to work this in with a trowel or hand rake, and better results are guaranteed: you're putting the fertilizer in direct contact with chemically active soil, which will expedite its decomposition. The second application of fertilizer should be just after transplanting, or, for any existing clump, in midsummer — an essential, "hungry" period in the iris life cycle, when new increases are being formed.

If you'd rather go wholly organic, you can top-dress bearded irises with well-aged compost. Fresh, hot compost will cause you serious grief, likely in the form of luscious ultra-green growth (remember the part about too much nitrogen?) or, paradoxically, burnt-looking leaf tips and weak plants. The older the compost, the less likely it is to contain high levels of any one macro — or micronutrient that could counteract your good intent.

Certainly any new bed involving bearded irises would benefit from a starter shot of well-aged compost or manure. One of my favorite additives to a new perennial bed or iris trial garden is a hefty load of aged manure. Steamy, dark, and luscious, aged manure gets bearded irises off to a great start producing stout plants with deep root systems. While I use a combination of organic and inorganic fertilizers in my garden and nursery, I'd take a load of compost and manure any day over a bucket of pelletized fertilizer. But make sure it's well aged! Fresh manure is often too high in nitrogen and will overfeed your irises.

Keepin' it good

Bearded irises need division every three to five years to maintain their glam and charm. As a gardening mentor of mine used to say, if it's okay to remodel the house, it's okay to remodel the garden from time to time. I know many gardeners have a strong aversion to division — it disrupts the status quo. But honestly if you don't keep up with the pace of your bearded irises, they'll quickly bloom themselves into nothingness, which isn't exactly beautiful (unless you have a strong taste for just spiky green foliage). With so many plants and so little time, it's easy to let bearded irises slip into various states of discontent. Most gardeners start to cry foul when suddenly one spring, one or two stalks of flowers appear where dozens did previously. Remember that range of numbers about increase, under "When to Plant"? If a variety is increasing at any number larger than two or three, it doesn't take very long to run out of room.

In list form, here are the usual warning signs that division is overdue:

1. Poor or no flowering. Sort of a "and then there were none" situation. With relatively shallow root systems, crowded clumps of bearded irises can easily compete for nutrition. If you do see any bloom stalks, they'll likely be restricted to the outer perimeter of the clump — the easiest place to garner the appropriate nutrition to facilitate flowering. You may even notice a donut hole of sorts in the middle of the clump where old "mother" rhizomes have died out, leaving behind tight entanglements.

2. Small rhizomes or poor-performing plants. A robust clump of bearded irises can quickly give way to fingerling rhizomes and strappy-looking plants when not regularly divided. Growth may also slow throughout the season, leaving a sad, underperforming mess in place of former beauty.

3. Outbreaks of rhizome-based diseases. Soft rot is a "misery loves company" disease. The closer and tighter plants are to one another, the easier it is for bacterial soft rot to spread between multiple plants and consume an entire clump. It leaves behind mushy rhizomes and softening, collapsing foliage, much to the dismay of the gardener.

So what's a gardener to do with a clump of overcrowded bearded irises? Grab your favorite spade or digging fork and get going. Dividing irises couldn't be more fun. It's a great stress-relief activity, and it's pretty hard to screw up. Here's the scoop:

1. Lift the entire clump with a spade or fork. Take care to shake off as much dirt as possible. This makes it easier to work with and less heavy.

2. Scope out the situation. You likely have lots of green fans and rhizomes, which in all likelihood are growing very close together or directly on top of each other.

3. Take a sharp knife or your hands and begin to split apart the clump into smaller pieces, either as "mini" clumps with two to four increases each or into individual rhizomes. If the rhizomes seem smallish, you can leave them attached to larger, "mother" rhizomes (sort of like life support until they develop further).

4. Trim back the foliage by at least half. Doing so allows the plant to recover more quickly, creates less of a mess in the garden, and makes the plants easier to handle. Consider this: newly transplanted plants lack a fully functioning root system, which means they deliver nutrients to the leaves at a slower rate than they would normally. If a handicapped root system has to support the development of new growth, plus maintain all the growth the plant had before transplanting, it can really take some time for that new plant to establish. In a nutshell, cutting back the foliage reduces the photosynthesis load on the developing root system.

5. Feel free to trim back the roots a bit too.

6. Once you have a pile of freshly clipped rhizomes, you're ready to plant as you normally would (see "How to Plant," earlier in this chapter).

Site your bearded irises well, keep them tidy every spring, give them some room to grow in abundance, and the only thing you'll have to worry about is division every three to five years, depending on how fast they grow. Some cultivars will probably need division after only two years (the ones you already have too many of anyway, remember?), while others will patiently "focalize" well into their fifth season (the slow pokes).

LEFT TO RIGHT: Yes, these will appreciate division!

Splitting apart the clump

"Mini" clumps, ready for foliage and root trimming

Healthy iris clump

Pests and Diseases

If not for full disclosure, I might forget about this section altogether. I fully appreciate how important it is to be aware of potential pest and disease problems associated with the plants we grow and love, but sometimes I feel it's like a physician's desk reference or WebMD — it brings out the hypochondriac in us. I've chosen to cover the biggest potential problems here with the underlying sentiment being "bearded irises are relatively carefree." They aren't hybrid tea roses, after all (I know the rose people among us just cringed a little).

Iris borers

Of any pest or disease problems you might encounter, this takes the prize for being the most difficult to cure, the most frustrating, and, sadly, the most detrimental to the health of your irises.

Iris borers are the larva of the iris borer moth (*Macronoctua onusta*), a nonnative moth first introduced to the eastern United States. The moth itself is rather nondescript, a brownish sort of thing with sometimes darker spots on its wings. It's in the same family as corn earworm (*Helicoverpa zea*), a rare and uncommon pest of irises (in over a decade of growing bearded irises, I've only observed it once, eating through a row of intermediate beardeds, not too far over the fence from a cornfield).

If it weren't for the devastating damage of iris borers, we'd probably never even notice their existence. In the main, the pest limits its palate to irises — U.S. natives like Virginia iris (*Iris virginica*) and crested iris (*I. cristata*), and garden irises, including bearded, Japanese, Siberian, and even the blackberry and candy lilies, *I. domestica* and *I.* ×*norrisii* (no relation), respectively.

Managing, controlling, and eradicating iris borers depends on a sound knowledge of their life cycle. The adult female moth lays her eggs in late summer, usually amid garden debris like dead iris leaves, mulch, and even nearby plants. Troubling to say, a single female moth can lay up to 1,000 eggs, making it fairly obvious how a one-time problem can balloon into an infestation over the course of the fall and winter. Small, round, and pearl-like, these eggs overwinter and hatch in the waking days of spring. Brown larvae emerge and grow to 3 to 5 cm in length, largely thanks to the bountiful buffet of fresh, verdant iris growth in your garden. The larvae first chew through the leaf and then head by some evolutionary instinct for the rhizome below. Signs of their entry often show up as watery holes or wet stains along the margins of the fans. Tunneling through the leaves, they leave a trail of bacteria-laden frass behind, which often results in bacterial soft rot. Gardeners usually don't notice soft rot until it's too late —

most often the borer has moved on to another plant. A single iris borer can handily damage several plants, exiting through the rhizomes via a small hole. Most damage occurs between mid-April and mid-June, after which the larvae pupate and emerge as moths again in late summer, ready to deposit the eggs of the next generation.

The best iris borer control comes down to one simple rule — preventing their infestation in the first place. Keep your iris beds free of dead leaves and debris and minimize the use of heavy, hardwood mulch around the crowns of iris rhizomes. You can accomplish this during fall or early spring cleanup. By lessening suitable nesting sites for roving female moths, you'll limit or eliminate egg-laying entirely.

But let's face it — debris happens, right? So for the pyromaniacs in the crowd, the most active control method involves a propane or butane tank and a match. Please proceed with caution and check with local ordinances if you live within city limits as to the use of fire in your backyard. Early in the spring before much growth has taken place, gather the necessary tools for making and managing a fire, take a stiff shot of hard liquor, and tromp toward the most suspect clump of bearded irises. Carefully burn off any leaf debris remaining from the year before, and don't worry if you happen to lightly toast the surface of the rhizomes. After years of doing this I can tell you that despite its seemingly drastic nature, burning your iris clumps in the spring is the single best way to control borers without adversely harming your irises. The fire removes the eggs, effectively eliminating borers, and in my experience can hasten growth of the clump.

If using pesticides, keep in mind that iris borers are most vulnerable in their larval stage. Spraying a clump of irises in late August when the moths are hatching from their chrysalises or late in the fall won't do much good. Time spray applications during and immediately following bloom season, or whenever

ABOVE, LEFT TO RIGHT: Iris borer feeding on rhizome

Iris borer feeding on foliage

you directly observe foraging by living borers. Imidacloprid (Merit®), for example, is systemically applied early in the spring, while acephate (Orthene®) is locally applied once every two weeks. As with any pesticides, take great care in applying them, follow label instructions carefully, and avoid using near food crops.

If you notice iris borers during the growing season, take efforts to destroy them. Dig the entire clump, trim back the foliage, attempt to physically remove the borers, and then soak the remaining, undamaged rhizomes in a 1:1 water:chlorine bleach solution for up to an hour. Many gardeners choose to relocate their irises, which is a perfectly logical choice if you're confident you've removed all preying borers from the plants (if the borer is in the rhizome, it may not emerge during an "emergency procedure" as described here). If the damage is extensive, with significant marring of the rhizomes and complete decimation of the foliage, it may be best to dispose of the plants entirely—a disheartening choice no matter the circumstances.

Bacterial soft rot

This is often, though not always, an aftereffect of iris borers. Many thousands of bacteria species populate our garden soils, some beneficial and some not. In wet years, it's especially common to notice some rotting at the base of iris clumps and other perennials with fleshy crowns, most often caused by *Erwinia carotovora*, noted for producing a terribly foul odor. Incidents of rot in wet years likely have little to do with iris borers and more to do with persistently wet growing conditions. At any rate, rot is fairly manageable in the iris garden if caught early, so be observant. With spring outbreaks, the easiest control involves a bucket of bleach and a tenacious attitude. Just apply bleach directly, either straight from the jug or diluted by half with water (depending on your level of tenacity), to the base of the clump. As drastic as this may seem, your irises won't sweat it. You'll notice disappearance of the rot within a week or so after application.

If on the other hand you discover rot while dividing a clump late in the summer, the most logical method is to dunk the rhizomes in a bucket of the aforementioned bleach solution for up to an hour. As recommended for borer control, this treatment handily disinfects your rhizomes of bacteria. Replant as before and don't worry about needing to "treat the soil." The soil isn't to blame as much as the organisms in the soil, and they likely became a problem only because of weather or a pest like iris borer. Consider it one last thing to worry about. Replant and enjoy.

To avoid bacterial soft rot in the future (or in the first place), ensure your soil has good drainage. Second, avoid overfertilization: green, fleshy foliage is a banquet to bacteria craving nitrogen. If you use raw manure,

do so with care since soils with too much manure can lead to a similar overgrowth of foliage in the spring. Aged manure or compost works much better anyway.

Gray mold and crown rot

Bearded irises can fall prey to other rots, such as crown rot (caused by the mustard seed fungus, *Sclerotium rolfsii*) and botrytis (*B. convoluta*), aka gray mold. Botrytis seems to be more of an issue in climates like the Pacific Northwest, where prolonged periods of wetness contribute to the germination and colonization of a fuzzy gray covering of mold on the surfaces of the rhizomes. It has a way of desiccating rhizomes to an almost corky condition but will often not infect new developing increases. If a serious threat is posed, spraying triadimefon (Strike® 50 WDG) per label recommendations has been known to control further spread of the disease.

Crown rot, aka southern blight, is fairly ubiquitous and has a history of infecting a variety of horticultural and agronomic crops. It too occurs during wet periods, particularly in the Midwest and South during wet winters and in soils with poor drainage. It shows up as sclerotia, dormant fungal propagules that resemble small seeds, usually at ground level. It tends to be something of a silent killer, going unnoticed until fans start collapsing, revealing softened crowns and rhizomes and an abundance of tan or black sclerotia. If infestation warrants chemical treatment, and at that only in the severest of cases, fungicides containing PCNB can be used, if available. PCNB is heavily regulated, and many products have been cancelled for use in the United States. Though an unpleasant thought, destruction of plants and surrounding soil is another strategy for eradicating the disease.

Fungal leaf spot

A variety of soil-borne fungi can cause leaf spot on irises. Rarely do they prove fatal. If spraying is warranted, copper-based fungicides usually do the trick when regularly applied during the wettest parts of the spring. At the very most these yellow to brown circular dots are unsightly, and some cultivars of irises prove more resistant than others. Tough, tolerant cultivars will often display clear, waxy blue-green foliage when their less-resistant neighbors sport ill-looking, yellow-brown foliage. Regrettably, breeding for disease-resistance to foliar maladies like leaf spot just isn't on the radar for most iris breeders. Without launching into a litany of recommendations, I'll happily suggest 'I Repeat' (Roberts 1998), a ruffled blue rebloomer, as one of the most consistently leaf spot tolerant irises in my nursery for several years running now.

Iris scorch

Iris scorch is a bizarre malady of irises, and one poorly understood by science. Researchers have attempted to tackle the disease without arriving at much of an understanding of

TOP TO BOTTOM: Iris rhizome with bacterial soft rot

Iris rhizome with crown rot

what causes it, how and if it's preventable, and what it actually does to the plant. The symptoms are easy enough to spot — the fans start to assume a burnt look with red and bronze tips migrating down the blade until the whole clump looks "fried." In established clumps the affliction seems to start from the center and work its way outward concentrically. New growth often looks stunted or deformed, but strangely enough a clump affected in the fall of one season might be perfectly healthy and normal the next. Some experts have previously recommended digging up a plant at the onset of symptoms, though it's unclear whether this has any impact on the plant's survivability or not. If you do decide to dig up and isolate plants for replanting at a later date, you'll notice that while the rhizomes remain firm, the roots may have rotted and died. With little more than conjecture and observation to go on, it doesn't appear that the condition is infectious. I've observed scorched clumps in production fields of irises with no regular pattern of incidence or spread. A row of a thousand plants may have one scorched plant with others never showing any symptoms at all. In a word — bizarre.

❋

There is an element of experimentation in all gardening — don't be afraid to kill a few plants for the sake of knowing what thrives and what doesn't. The bottom line: don't fret about your bearded irises. It takes away from enjoying them. Listen to, learn from, and love them, and you'll be well on your way to keeping a healthy assembly of bearded irises alive and well in your garden.

ABOVE, LEFT TO RIGHT: Fungal leaf spot; Iris scorch

4

4 How Bearded Irises Are Made

"The whole aim in breeding irises is, of course, to raise varieties different from and better than all others."

Leslie Cave, *The Iris* (1959)

"There are plenty of things left to aim for…"

Wilma Vallette,
***Iris Culture and Hybridizing for Everyone* (1961)**

I was always that curious kiddo, poking around the kitchen as my grandmothers and mother whipped up magically palatable things. I was curious about how things were made, and that early fascination with process led me out of the kitchen and into the garden to make my first cross pollination between two petunias at the whopping age of 10. More than a decade later, I'm still fascinated by that process as a student of plant breeding, plant genetics, and horticultural product development. That curiosity is easily stirred with irises, whose fabulous, unfurling colors — blended, wrought, and gilded into the delicate structure of a flower — make for easy outbreaks of puppy love.

This chapter is thus dedicated to the subject of how, and really why, bearded irises are made. In the grand scheme of plant breeding, corn and wheat breeders can claim to feed more stomachs, sure. But few plant breeders can claim as much pride in beautifying the world as iris breeders. But don't let all that opulent ornamental beauty fool you: bearded irises are the products of tenacious breeding efforts — centuries of crossing, waiting, hoping, selecting, and discarding in search of the perfect flower. If I were in this game for ease alone, I'd much rather breed corn or wheat.

So You Want to Hybridize

For those with starry eyes and high hopes, like yours truly, the world of bearded irises offers many pearls and diamonds worth seeking. Resistance to the perilous soft rot, the miraculous key to rebloom, and other quests that sound vaguely Monty Python–ish pose great challenges to breeders who toil to keep alive the passion for the rainbow flower. More than ever, we demand that the plants grown in gardens thrive sustainably for many seasons. Anything less just doesn't cut it anymore. But not all plants are created equal — this is one of gardening's self-evident truths. Some plants shrink in the heat of summer, melt away by fall, and freeze into a crisp in the depths of winter. Others tough it out in the worst of weather, glimmering when the rest go dull, and laughing in the face of climate change. Bearded irises are no exception. After growing nearly 2,000 varieties in my life, I can roundly attest that some irises deserve to be grown and others don't deserve the time it takes to compost them, much less to plant them to begin with. With that tenacity for finding the best of the best, I want to share with you the things that I look for in good irises, the qualities that make one stand out from the others.

If you don't agree — great. In gardening, rules are meant to be broken anyway. But if you're looking to hybridize, take time to consider all the factors that add up to create a truly breathtaking plant.

Color

Color is on every iris lover's mind. The bearded iris flower runs on an engine of color and color pattern, and any up-to-snuff breeder knows it. While we all hammer underperforming plants for their lackluster growth habits, few gardeners buy ornamental plants for reasons beyond their aesthetics. Flowers rule. Each color class is a game with individual rules of its own; the broader stroke is to underscore why color is important and what breeders should be aware of when mulling over rows of gorgeous seedlings each spring.

Many iris books written over the last century make harsh judgments on the subject of color that don't always apply to modern gardening. New color breaks happen all the time, and with each new one, the ways in which we value color in flowers change as well. The final frontier for colors in bearded irises will probably never be reached — the genetics of our favorite flower are incredibly complex and still confusing to this day. In the broad sense, bearded irises are approximately 35 generations away from their wild ancestors, and as hybridizers continue to incorporate new genetic material from different wild species, the possibilities for out-of-this-world color are truly endless.

If there is one idea in the way of a rule though, it's that color should never disappoint the gardener. It's the whole reason any iris lover swoons, and it should be clear, not muddy or unattractively blurry. Blended colors send many iris lovers over the moon; I personally love blends, that swirled-together look I was after when mixing watercolors and oil paints as a kid. But I've also seen many flowers that resemble the less-successful concoctions on the palettes of my youth — muddy, drippy, and ugly. You'd think it'd be impossible for a bearded iris to approach ugly, but without an exciting application of color, it's surely less than beautiful. The infamous border bearded iris 'Jungle Shadows' (Sass-Graham 1960) comes to mind for its controversial medley of gray, black, and brown. What can I say? The perception of color is obviously subjective — in the eye of the beholder, as the cliché goes. Coloring of the hafts is another arena of controversy. Some iris lovers can't stand haft marks, insisting they look messy and detract from the effect. Others live for tiger-striping that adds character and attitude to an otherwise quiet flower. Colorful petals should always be sun-fast too — nothing is more disappointing than watching color bleach away hour by hour on a spring day. Bleached hair may happen, but bleached flowers don't have to. In short, color anywhere on the flower should always be an asset, not something that distracts or baffles.

Substance

I frequently kvetch on the topic of substance, probably because I've watched bearded irises blow into tissuey smithereens for so many years. Substance is what allows an iris flower to hold its body, shape, and form — the inner cellular structure that keeps it looking fresh. Some irisarians call this floral architecture, which I think clearly explains the idea. I write this as a warning to breeders pursuing the newest elaborations of the bearded iris flower — don't forget floral architecture. The nicest, sharpest, hottest iris won't win any popularity contests if gardeners have to pick pieces of it up off the ground after a spring deluge. I wish I were writing this for dramatic effect, but sadly there are cultivars floating around the market that have falls that break and tear in gusts of wind and standards that collapse for lack of anything better to do. If as artists we can't create flowers that stand up and hold out, we really aren't that good at what we do.

This whole gripe isn't just about flowers staying together. Good substance makes the color last longer and shine. Take for instance those old blue flags growing in the ditch (or by my backdoor). If you place your index finger on one side of the fall and your thumb on the other, you can feel just how thin it is, almost like crepe paper. But go up to some big, ruffled flower like that of 'Eye Candy' (Keppel 2004) and you'll find thick, nearly plastic petals. On average, flowers with better substance will have stronger colors, thanks in part to more layers of cells stacking up, like another coat of paint. The AIS Handbook for Judges and Show Officials states clearly that flowers of tall bearded irises (and in my opinion, all bearded irises) should hold their color, structure, and form for at least three days. Weather and genetics certainly play a role in this effect, and while we may not have much control over the wind, the rain, and the hail, we certainly can exercise some management of DNA.

That said, we know precious little about the genetics of substance, and why the flowers of some bearded iris cultivars hold up better than others. Yet breeders over the years have managed to turn out many excellent flowers that don't fall apart, tear, or tatter. The flowers of bearded irises should withstand all the usual rounds of weather, excepting of course extreme incidents, which nothing would survive. Amazingly, many tall and median bearded irises hold forth remarkably well against hail while still in bud. Though it may pierce or slightly tatter the blossoms, in many cases these flowers continue to open with few problems.

Form

The benchmarks for form vary widely across the six classifications of bearded irises. Regardless of the class, form is indisputably one of the most tremendous advancements in bearded iris breeding in the last century. The move from flaccid, low-profile flowers to flaring, high-profile concoctions of petals marks one

of the most vivid floral transformations in the horticultural world. The flower should always be well balanced and proportioned, regardless of the vintage of the iris. Some iris lovers are more particular about form than others, and others just enjoy good-growing, easy-flowering plants as staple garden perennials. Whatever the preference, gardeners should always have the best irises available to them, and the best irises should have flowers that support themselves, hold up under a variety of weather conditions, and display their color without your having to contort your body into strange positions to see it.

Fragrance

Given that it is a trait so longed for by society, it is strange that plant breeders have seemed intent on exterminating fragrance, or just plain ignoring it, even when they begin with the most aromatic flowers. Bearded irises were grown and appreciated for their scents long before their psychedelic flowers; it's pitiful that breeders haven't paid fragrance more attention when selecting cultivars. I doubt any rainbow-loving iris breeder did so with malice aforethought, but lack of premeditation is nonetheless a terrible excuse. Bearded iris flowers range in fragrance from spicy to sweet to tangy to pungent to none at all. Some emit a scent that fill rooms when iris lovers cut stems and bring them indoors.

ABOVE: Poor substance and form

CLOCKWISE FROM TOP LEFT: 'Fascination' (Cayeux 1927), historic form

'Citoyen' (Anfosso 1989), classic form

'Dream Team' (Johnson 2007), modern form

Fragrance is an asset, but don't look down upon bearded irises that lack it. The eyes can still enjoy them.

Lace and ruffling

Lacy, ruffled flowers drive me mad. I can't get enough of all that frilly stuff along the petal edges — feminine elegance in the state of a flower. That frilly stuff is, in fact, bunched-up cells, and it is those microscopic bumps that give flowers a jagged, frayed, or pinked appearance. It's a fussy ornament, but one that appeals to the taste of many iris lovers. Some classes of bearded irises (e.g., like miniature tall and miniature dwarf bearded irises) lack lacy flowers, probably due to their size and in the case of the former, their diploid nature. If you're looking to start breeding for lace, start your collection of parent stock with the hot orange 'Fringe Benefits' (Hager 1988) or Tom Johnson's orchid-lavender self 'Super Model' (2007). Ruffling, a wavy quality of some flowers, adds to the fascinating, three-dimensional architecture of the bearded iris flower. Most modern irises exhibit some degree of ruffling, even if only slight, as in the case of the diploid miniature tall bearded irises.

Branching

What's all the fuss about branching? Iris lovers would like to enjoy their prized flowers without their being buried in the foliage (in the case of the dwarfs and medians) or obscured by half-spent flowers on overly budded stalks (tall and border beardeds). Good branching displays the flowers without conflict, so that each one in succession can be appreciated. Many breeders brag about triple or even quadruple terminals — three

ABOVE: 'Super Model' (Johnson 2007)

OPPOSITE: Good branching

or four buds in the terminal position of the stalk — which is all well and good until the first two buds are spent, still hanging on and keeping the last from opening correctly. Mangled-looking stalks of bearded iris flowers don't sound like something most gardeners want to enjoy, least of which me. There are many different types of branching in the non-dwarf bearded irises, ranging from stalks with "wide candelabra" branching (imagine the arms holding five beautifully spaced candles) to "two branches and a spur" (which is fairly self-explanatory). Though the category of branching isn't all that important, ultimately the appreciation of each flower is. If you're going to spend years developing a super-awesome bearded iris flower, it really deserves to be appreciated to the fullest, and for that to happen, good branching is essential.

Bud count

The chief complaint about many bearded irises is the fleetingness of their bloom season. The higher the bud count on a stalk, the better — at least that's the way it's supposed to work. Each classification has its own ideal limit, and the particulars distill to practical sentiments. For example, if an established three-year-old clump of bearded irises has less than 25 percent of its fans producing flowers, you can understand how some gardeners might get a little crabby. Bearded irises should bloom abundantly and sustainably, which means that while the idea of pushing more and more buds onto a stalk sounds like a great idea, breeders sometimes ignore the consequential tax of those flowers on the plant. Botanically speaking, flowers of any kind consume a lot of resources, as well they should; the continued existence of the plant, through offspring, depends on them. But when too many flowers draw too many resources from the plant, the list of consequences looks like this: short-lived, poor-growing, and unsustainable after a few seasons. Hybridizers should find ways to maximize the bud count while maintaining health and vigor of the plants. New bearded irises that can't do both shouldn't bother to get out of the breeding bed.

Hardiness and vigor

A chief complaint of most new plants, whether rightly leveled or not, is that they lack hardiness and perennial vigor. My skeptical stance tends to think part of that is just seeing the past with rose-colored glasses — after all, genuinely terrible plants always have and ever will be with us, if for no other reason than to provide a little contrast to what's truly exceptional. That said, I'm not easily duped by claims of "new and improved" without trying it first myself, particularly as a northern gardener who shivers when he says the word "hardiness."

Hardiness and vigor are complex horticultural subjects; we have a poor understanding of the genetics behind them, which makes it very hard for breeders to select for them. Hardiness is also hard to define since gardeners in different growing environments tend to think about the topic very differently. To a Coastal Maine gardener, hardiness no doubt means surviving brutal midwinter Nor'easters and salt spray. To a Southern California gardener, hardiness means a plant is frost-hardy, thriving with minimal or no damage during irregular frost spells in early and mid-winter. Where do bearded irises fall in that spectrum?

With so many cultivars now on the market, and more waiting in the wings, it would seem prudent for hybridizers to focus on improving the performance of bearded irises regionally while maintaining their attractiveness to a gardening public that's very inclined to purchase plants from a national market. Some would argue that this is easier said than done. Probably so. But there are bearded irises that could just as easily thrive through a Maine Nor'easter as an Orange County frost, though cultivars with such broad-based adaptability are not the norm. A large majority of bearded iris breeding and development happens on the West Coast of the United States; you can imagine the complaints some gardeners in Maine and other northern places have on the subject of hardiness.

Some authors have speculated on the origins of hardiness and vigor, keeping in mind that most modern bearded irises trace back to a mere baker's dozen of founding species. To winnow it further, some of the progenitor irises used in early crosses by Sir Michael Foster and other hybridizing wizards were based on only a few collections from a few provenances. To illustrate my point, consider *Iris variegata*, a diploid widely used in crosses that yielded miniature tall bearded and tall bearded irises and which species is widespread throughout Europe's mid-continent, from Germany to Romania and north to Ukraine; given its range, it certainly encounters cold winters and wet-humid summers. In contrast, consider the more Mediterranean *I. pallida*, which in parts of its range grows evergreen without experiencing severe winters.

You could imagine that crossing the two species would lead to progeny with intermediate traits, even most likely for hardiness. Extrapolate this example a little bit more, and it's easy to conceive how after dozens of generations of intercrossing with other species and cultivars, the genetic arrangements for hardiness might end up a little mish-mashed. In one arrangement you might have an array of top-notch genes that yield very hardy plants, while in another you have an array of low-browed genes that yield very tender wimps.

The bottom line — trialing plants is of paramount importance. The logistics of it all get complicated quickly, but if breeders can get feedback from growers and gardeners in a variety of environments, it will ultimately improve the gardening public's perception of bearded irises. Thriving, star-studded cultivars that flower just as happily in Boston as in Los Angeles make everybody happy.

Rebloom

Most iris lovers would kill for repeat performances of bearded irises throughout the season. But for whatever reason — poor understanding of the genetics or just bad luck — the fabled everblooming or even reliably reblooming iris (at least in a northern temperate climate) remains a fixture of our iris dreams. Hope is not lost, though. As more and more wild germplasm enters the gardens of enterprising breeders, it's possible that a lucky iris lover will one day find a plant with formidable reblooming tendencies. A more rational hypothesis, however, is that through careful observation and planned crosses between the distinct types of rebloomers, an ingenious hybridizer will combine the right types of genes into an attractive plant and end up with a market-worthy reblooming iris that all iris lovers will want to grow. I remain optimistic that better reblooming bearded irises lie ahead.

Novelty flowers

Novelty flowers of all sorts have increased in attractiveness and desirability in the last 20 years. The genetics behind them are unclear, but with so many excellent modern cultivars in commerce, anyone looking to daub a little pollen toward this goal has plenty of options at their disposal. Space-agers I've loved from the start; those nifty little appendages, whether pointy little horns or extravagant flounces, add a lot of character to iris flowers. Broken-colored irises have come a long way but still could benefit from better form so that those splattered patterns show off to their fullest potential. The so-called flatties (bearded irises with a Japanese iris look, thanks to standards that become falls) have long been known as recessives, but not all hybridizers have had this experience; while I eschewed them as freaks of nature for many years, I've slowly come to adore these enormous flat-topped flowers.

Hybridizing and Growing Bearded Irises from Seed

Many feel hybridizing is only for the experts, but this simply isn't true. The mechanics of cross pollinating bearded irises are incredibly easy, but you must be patient: it takes two to three years, and occasionally longer, to see the results of your creation.

Inside each flower are both male and female sex organs. If you follow the beard into the throat of the flower, you will see the male stamen, an arrow-shaped wedge with fluffy yellow pollen on it (if you don't see pollen, the anther may be deformed or dysfunctional). Directly above the stamen is the style crest. After the flower opens, and on a dry, windless day, take tweezers and remove the stamen. Try to keep the pollen on the stamen intact. In Midwestern climates with fitful spring weather, the windows for hybridizing can be limited in some seasons.

Next, rub the stamen on the stigmatic lip of the style crest of another iris — this lip should almost glisten and appear sticky. Hybridizing with wet flowers is usually a wasted effort, and windy days often dry out the stigmas. Apply pollen to all three stigmatic lips of the receiving flower to increase the chances of successful pollination. If conditions are right (stigmatic receptiveness, fertility, weather), fertilization will occur; the pollen grain will germinate and grow down the style crest into the ovary, where the ovules (unfertilized seeds) await. This pollen tube will fertilize the ovules, which will then begin to develop into seeds. To keep your crosses organized, tag the stalk with the names of the parents used in the cross or a number recorded in a studbook that gives the same information — for example, 'Decadence' × 'Sea Power'. List the pod parent first, the pollen parent second.

After pollination, you must leave the flower on the stalk to form a seedpod. After a week or so you will see some swelling beginning just below the fading bloom that you pollinated. This swelling will continue until the spent flower has withered and dropped off, leaving a thumb-sized seedpod that will continue to swell throughout the next six to eight weeks. Once the pod turns brown or begins to split down its sides, harvest it and shell out the seeds. Let the seeds dry for one to several weeks, and plant in seed trays or in a garden bed in organized rows.

Over the winter the seeds will stratify, a process that as a result of cold and wet conditions will

physiologically ready the seeds for germination. In the spring the iris seeds will germinate. When seedlings, looking much like thick blades of grass, are 3 to 4 inches in height, transplant them to a suitable place where they can grow into mature plants, usually a row or bed in your garden. These seedlings can take another year or two before they grow into blooming-sized plants. Expect blooms of many different colors — bearded irises are highly heterozygous and heterogeneous, so the results of genetic recombination will inevitably surprise you.

CLOCKWISE FROM TOP: Iris seeds

Iris seedpod

Iris seedlings

From One Plant Breeder to Another

Over the years I've kept track of various pieces of advice from plant breeders, either conferred to me as nuggets of wisdom or absorbed through lectures and conversation. All are relevant to all plants, but they hold especially true for bearded iris breeders.

Search for opportunities. With bearded irises, the search won't be long. There are all sorts of challenges (many aforementioned) awaiting the fertile minds of newcomers and advanced breeders alike. These opportunities ensure you a ticket to the party and the chance to contribute a novel new plant to the gardening world while satisfying the wishes, hopes, and desires of a lot of iris lovers!

Have a goal. Inevitably you'll get drawn into side-adventures, pursuing new ideas and opportunities as they arise; the quest for better reblooming irises, for instance, may turn up all kinds of exciting irises along the way. Having a goal, a reminder about where you're headed, will keep the passion and excitement in check.

Use good parents. Any good breeding program, just like any good attempt in the kitchen, starts with the best of ingredients. Though advanced breeders go to special lengths to incorporate desired traits of interests, beginning breeders shouldn't cut themselves short. Always start with the best, even if the best isn't the newest iris on the market. What makes the best parent? That's probably more appropriate for a philosophical conversation, but consider all the traits of a good bearded iris just discussed. Is its color beautifully clear? Is its fragrance, or ruffling or substance striking? Are its branching and bud count what they ought to be? While it's easy to buy into the advice that the newest releases offer the most hybridizing potential, many introductions of the last 20 years are still waiting for their pollen to be applied to another plant. Get out the tweezers.

Plan crosses but follow your instincts. Make good use of long winters by dreaming and scheming. Planning crosses is a tremendously valuable exercise in learning about iris genetics, parentages, and the history of how unassuming iris species were fused together over generations to make the modern bearded iris flower. But never discount your gut instinct. Inevitably on a spring day, in a moment of spontaneity, you'll decide to cross two irises for no better reason than intuition. Do it. Just remember that if the cross takes and sets seed, that's more planting on top of what you already had planned.

Keep good records. Throughout the history of plant breeding, some of the greatest feats have been sullied by a poor record to support their achievement. Wouldn't it be awful for you to develop the first bearded iris resistant to soft rot and forget to record the cross? Not only are records important to documenting your work, they also help keep track of the progress you've made or have yet to make. I can't stress enough the importance of detailed, easily located, user-friendly record systems.

Train your eye to be critical. Remember the disappointment you felt the first time a plant you'd purchased turned out to be a dud? It didn't live up to the hype. It died. Whatever the outcome, that plant was a disappointment, and gardening isn't something anyone pursues in order to experience disappointment. Iris lovers want to be successful with their favorite plants, savoring the experience of the spring flowering season like the annual holiday it is. Train your eye to be critical and never introduce a dud. Be shrewd, ruthless, and remember that the more you toss, the more compost you'll have.

Evaluate your seedlings objectively and over time. The horticultural market of the 21st century is an exciting place, but it pursues plant development at a frenzied pace, releasing products to keep up with an ever-constant demand, often without the most thorough evaluation. Rushing a product to market can easily lead to disappointment — quit disappointing gardeners! Seedlings should ideally be evaluated in a variety of climates, but even then plants shouldn't be expected to thrive equally well in all places. If a seedling does, you definitely have something worth crowing about. But poor performance in one region or another shouldn't immediately disqualify an iris from introduction — ultimately it goes back to the goal of the hybridizer. If the hybridizer is trying to develop a plant with a certain color pattern to thrive in a particular climate, it's reasonable that that cultivar might only perform most admirably in one or a few regional markets.

Is it distinctive? While the AIS *Handbook for Judges and Show Officials* accords point values for distinctiveness to all classes, many judges and breeders overlook its importance. With thousands and thousands of irises to choose from, the general public needs garden plants that stand out. Distinctiveness is otherwise hard to define, but if it looks and grows like more than a couple of other varieties, what is the point of introducing a copycat? If it's a better white self for a particular climate, then that might be a worthy reason to introduce an iris. If it's a better rebloomer, then by all means the world needs to grow it. But if it's another well-formed, heavily budded, candelabra-branched purple and white plicata, I've got a giant list of available cultivars that I'll happily share with anyone. Distinctiveness is paramount to successful product innovation in any industry, and especially so in bearded irises.

Failure is inevitable. Every plant breeder is bound to encounter failure somewhere along their journey.

Must-have crosses won't ever set seed. Seeds won't germinate or will do so very poorly. Seedlings will get trampled, plagued by disease, or die off for mysterious reasons. But failures don't always mean dead ends. Another breeder's failure may just be another's success. Knowledge expands, new tools crop up, and the mechanics of approaching horticultural problems evolve so that the next generation of plant breeders can tackle age-old questions with renewed fervor and zeal. Take heed of past work, but don't get discouraged if a colleague in a bygone era failed to realize a goal you intently covet.

Join in the fellowship of kindred iris lovers. Join your local iris club and the American Iris Society (irises.org). The exchange of information and plants, and the camaraderie between similarly passion-crazed plant lovers will benefit your garden and your work immeasurably.

Beyond the Rainbow

Out and about, I'm often asked the loaded question "What's next for bearded irises?" With nearly 60,000 cultivars registered with the American Iris Society since 1929, and the expectation that we'll exceed that number before 2020, the possibilities for actual improvements might seem dim. Yet, I think that nothing could be further from the truth. In fact, despite so many varieties and after so many years of hybridizing, breeders have just begun to unearth the real rainbow behind our favorite flower. Here's a gallery of some of the newest, as-of-yet unintroduced flowers coming along from hybridizers all across the world.

OPPOSITE, CLOCKWISE FROM TOP: Kerr 05-057A TB

Schreiner PP1719-1 TB

Kerr 04-037A TB

Gallery

TOP TO BOTTOM:
Bunnell G30-5 MTB

Johnson TA18A TB

ABOVE: Johnson
TB124KK TB

ABOVE: Kanarowski
0406-1 TB

ABOVE: Keppel 07-176B TB

CLOCKWISE FROM TOP LEFT: Sutton TB seedling

Blyth Q24-B TB

Black P83B TB

Black Q95B SDB

5 The Historical Drama of Bearded Irises

"Anyone interested in irises should know something of when, where, and by whom irises were first brought into gardens to be enjoyed, watched over, and selected for their particular beauty."

John C. Wister,
***The World of Irises* (1978)**

The development of bearded irises is a long-running historical drama, a major production with countless acts. The stories behind the plants, the legends lurking in the garden, imbue the rainbow flower with far more than just cultural planthropology. From pastoral scenes in Europe dotted with clumps of wild irises to the suburban streets of America lined with clumps of prize-winning hybrids, the glamorous rise of the bearded iris is a feel-good tale of starry ambition. Classically beautiful stems waved tailored forms of simple colors — purples and lavenders — for millennia. But the introduction of the human eye, ever in search of beauty, set in motion a 300-year adventure that would turn Italian and Caucasian meadow wildflowers into one of the western world's most familiar herbaceous perennials.

The next time you stare at a bearded iris, know that it didn't just get there by happenstance; its arrival in your garden involved a cast of characters with as much or more personality than the flower you behold. Our favorite plants likely entered European horticultural commerce in the 17th century; in 1601, Flemish doctor and botanist Carolus Clusius described 28 varieties of tall bearded irises and famously wrote, "A long experience has taught me that iris grown from seed vary in a wonderful way." From chaos came order — irises, all of them, were first classified by Linnaeus in the 18th century and then given a modern taxonomic treatment by W. R. Dykes in his monumental *The Genus Iris* (1913); other authors have since attempted to modify Dykes' breakdown of the genus, the most lasting of these being Brian Mathew's 1989 revision.

Our horticultural whodunit begins with the 13 *Iris* species from which arose the most colorful collection of hardy herbaceous perennials the human race has had the privilege to cultivate.

The Founders

Some of the earliest accounts of irises in cultivation come from the shores of the Mediterranean, where species like *Iris pallida* and *I. florentina* were cultivated not only for their ornament but their fragrances, too. Fields of these, draped across sunny Italian hillsides at the outskirts of villages, were the sources for orris root, a fixative in perfumes and a common ingredient in many types of gin. Sun-dried rhizomes of these and many bearded irises in fact, emit a clean, violet-like fragrance. Aside from these few economically important species, the genus *Iris* is one of purely horticultural interest and intrigue.

As a group, bearded irises belong to the subgenus *Iris*, section *Iris* — known in botanical circles as pogon irises (in other words, they have beards). Beards are a funny subject: every gardener knows how to spot the trio of fuzzy appendages adorning the tops of falls but never really knows what to say about them or how to describe them. Ask a botanist, and he'll tell you that they're simply a collection of multicellular hairs, likely with some impact on reproductive biology — colloquially, a landing strip for pollinators, bumblebees in the genus *Bombus*. The other signature element that distinguishes bearded irises are non-arillate seeds, a trait of little interest or consequence to gardeners. An aril is a specialized outgrowth that covers or looks attached to the seed; they often serve to attract birds or insects, which carry off or ingest the seeds, ultimately aiding in dispersal. Bearded irises differ from other members of the subgenus, the so-called aril irises from the Middle East, in that they lack a protruding white aril on the surface of their seeds. The leaves of bearded irises are equitant, sword-shaped, and glaucous. In the wild, their flowers are often of a single color or have darker falls than standards. The shortest species are characteristically unbranched, while the taller species can have one to a few branches.

Approximately 45 species occupy the bearded camp of the iris world; the total remains in flux due to disagreements about taxonomy and the occasional new discovery of species from herbarium records or the wild. The group is broadly distributed across the Mediterranean, southern and eastern Europe, and eastward into central Asia and Russia — a vast geographic range taken as a whole, but many of the species occur in highly localized settings, often preferring dryer, open country and occasionally the endemic retreats of mountain ranges or foothills. Given the degree of variability encountered over wide but discontinuous populations, it's no wonder these magical flowers have come to dazzle and intrigue humans with a rainbow of floral possibility. Genetic variation abounds! From a horticultural perspective, wild bearded irises prefer summer dryness and overall good drainage but can tolerate higher amounts of water during the flowering season. Breeding has expanded, contracted, and melded these tolerances so that as a group, horticulturally, bearded irises make excellent garden plants with broad adaptations across a range of climates and zones.

Of these 45 or so species, only 13 species have greatly contributed to the highly budded, multi-branched stalks of luscious flowers we know and love in our gardens. Not merely progenitors of celebrated perennials, these wildlings merit a garden spot in their own right, and we shouldn't be afraid of incorporating them into sunny borders with good drainage. Though perhaps unrefined in comparison to their descendants, their simple charm is unrivalled, especially when cultivated in settings reminiscent of their homelands.

Iris aphylla Linnaeus 1753

When I first started breeding irises, the buzzword species was *Iris aphylla*, and so it remains. Noted for its superb branching, hardiness, and tetraploidy, this dark violet–flowered iris grows natively across much of central Europe, from Germany eastward to Russia. It's quite variable in size; some forms resemble modern-day MDBs in stature, others are more like MTBs. On average, the species is regarded as SDB-sized, but it has contributed to virtually all classes of bearded irises at this point. In the garden, selections of the species enjoy appreciation from rock gardeners in early spring and fall, as some clones notably rebloom. The foliage is completely deciduous.

Hybridizers didn't begin to incorporate *Iris aphylla* into the rainbow mixing game until the mid 20th century, and at that only a few people did so seriously. Much credit is due Jim and Vicki Craig, a breeding duo that set out to miniaturize tall bearded irises while maintaining their tetraploidy using *I. aphylla*.

Decades later, we are enjoying their successes in spades. Given its propensity for impressive, almost show-worthy stalks with surprising garden adaptability, the future of *I. aphylla* as an iris of promise in hybridization remains bright.

Iris cypriana Baker & Foster 1888

The giant, blowsy flowers of *Iris cypriana* no doubt called out to plant collectors when they first encountered it, though its continued existence in the wild is doubtful, alas. Reddish lilac flowers with white haft markings open on 3-foot-tall stems. A tetraploid originally discovered on Cyprus, *I. cypriana* proved a finicky grower for iris lovers in the United Kingdom and the eastern United States, though that didn't limit efforts to utilize it in hybridizing. Many notable irises stem from the various combinations of *I. cypriana* with diploid species like *I. pallida*, including the lovely blue 'Caterina' (Foster 1909), a personal favorite of mine because Caterina is a family name generations ago.

Iris germanica Linnaeus 1753

You might find it odd to learn that despite lending a common name to all bearded irises (known to many as German flags), *Iris germanica* played only a small role in the development of modern bearded irises (unless, as some do, you consider *I. cypriana*, *I. mesopotamica*, and *I. trojana* synonymous with it, in which case we

TOP TO BOTTOM: *Iris aphylla* 'Minnow'

Iris germanica, wild-collected in northwestern Greece

5

haven't space to sort out the taxonomic imbroglio on the naming of names). 'Amas' (Foster, coll. 1885), a wild-collected tetraploid hybrid, gave rise to founder cultivars like 'Lent A. Williamson' (Williamson 1918), 'Prospero' (Yeld 1920), and 'Dominion' (Bliss 1917). Otherwise, *I. germanica* has never been used abundantly in crosses, mostly because the forms in horticulture are sterile 44-chromosome plants. 'Amas' was collected in modern-day Turkey in an area historically called Amasia. Sir Michael Foster named this, and many other wild-collected clones sent to him, for its homeland. As such its history is a little hazy, and several other nearly identical clones might have been given different names — I'm sure you can see the haze thickening up into an intriguing horticultural whodunit fog from here. Whatever its origins, *I. germanica* has a firmly rooted place in iris history due to its vernacular association with bearded irises and its relative ease of culture, even when nobody in particular intends to grow it! Some might even slander this beauty as a weed.

ABOVE, LEFT TO RIGHT: *Iris imbricata*

Iris purpureobractea

Iris imbricata Lindley 1845

Though at face value this species doesn't seem to harbor much genetic potential, many authors have awarded it status as a founder species. It's not much of a show-off, donning yellowish to greenish flowers with reflexed form subtended by curiously inflated bracts on 12- to 20-inch-tall stalks — an oddity and novelty worth growing just because. Its exact influence in the early years of bearded iris development remains a little cloudy due to poor historical documentation; nevertheless, it was in cultivation around the turn of the century, and most certainly so in the gardens of Foster and others, who probably had exhausted its use in crosses with other diploids. In later years, Paul Cook used it in a line to develop reverse blue bitones. Experimental crosses by Frederic and Mary Megson in the 1960s and '70s demonstrated that *I. imbricata* inhibited anthocyanin pigments, a useful bit of information for iris breeders looking to breed better non-purple bearded irises. All told, breeders probably haven't utilized its genes enough in the development of bearded irises, and it most certainly has potential as a parent of MTBs, most of which are diploids, and BBs.

Iris junonia Schott & Kotschy 1854

As you've perhaps already learned to expect, the taxonomy of the bearded iris section is about as messy as a four-year-old at the dinner table. Some taxonomists point the finger at W. R. Dykes, whose formal circumscription of the genus was at times rather vague. Plus, given their promiscuous tendencies, wild populations of bearded irises continue to confuse botanists to this day — are these wild populations truly natural, reproductively isolated species or the products of bygone gardening left to persist in the absence of humans? Mysteries aside, the iris presently considered *Iris junonia* is an 8- to 12-inch-tall plant with bluish to yellowish flowers with white beards sometimes tipped orange; however, earlier descriptions of the species capture a taller plant, in the border bearded height range, with similarly colored flowers. Which one is the real *I. junonia*? Botanists agree that the species is an endemic of the Sicilian Taurus (a hill for which the city Taormina was named), but that's about it. Yellower forms resemble the purportedly close relative *I. purpureobractea* — another species I'd posit was at the proverbial "party" around the turn of the 20th century but isn't telling what it did.

Iris kashmiriana Baker 1877

An endemic of the remote Kashmir region in Afghanistan and Pakistan, *Iris kashmiriana* nevertheless played a critical role in the advancement of bearded irises. Trunked home by missionaries to the garden

5

ABOVE: *Iris lutescens*

of Sir Michael Foster, *I. kashmiriana* is one of the quartet of tetraploid easterners (the others are *I. cypriana*, *I. mesopotamica*, and *I. trojana*) that met their diploid western cousins for a little horticultural hanky-panky in the gardens of British hybridizers in the early 20th century. The iris world benefited from *I. kashmiriana* by way of two paramount cultivars, 'Miss Willmott' (Foster 1910) and 'Kashmir White' (Foster 1912), both of unsurprisingly suspect but well-guessed parentages involving this species. Foster is said to have grown three different forms of the species, varying in color from white to purple. These plants flowered on one- or two-branched, stout stems at 30 inches tall. Some irisarians blame *I. kashmiriana* for introducing a lack of hardiness into bearded irises, since its more easterly, mild disposition didn't always fare well in the gardens of western Europe or the United States. Whether true or not, such romantic conjecture is overshadowed by the historical significance of this species as an ancestor to thousands and thousands of bearded irises.

Iris lutescens Lambert 1789

Iris lutescens is sort of the dead-end species of the iris world, remembered more for what it wasn't able to produce than what it did. Formerly known as *I. chamaeiris*, its early involvement in MDB and SDB breeding proved useless as the hybrids were frequently sterile, though at times respectable as garden plants. Native throughout the Mediterranean, the species itself is a handsome plant, appealing to rock gardeners or anyone with a passion for growing and appreciating the diversity of plants from seed. It varies considerably across its range, and botanists have described a number of different varieties and subspecies. Trying to describe the color range would be an exercise in adjectives — patterns, combinations, and hues abound, and no doubt caught the eye

of early horticulturists, who anticipated more breeding value from the species than was actually there. William J. Caparne of the United Kingdom and the German breeding team of Goos and Koenemann were early explorers of the species' potential for developing colorful dwarf bearded irises. American dwarf iris breeder Samuel Burchfield raised several choice cultivars, including 'Burchfield' (1952), which was named and introduced posthumously.

Iris mesopotamica Dykes 1913

Curiously, this species isn't known from the wild proper. Some authors recognize it as an autonomous taxon; others regard it as merely a form of *Iris germanica*. Occurring in cultivation throughout the Middle East, this member of the eastern tetraploid quartet flowers in shades of purple with bronzy haft marks, on stalks upwards of 48 inches tall. *Iris mesopotamica* was used extensively by California breeders William Mohr and Sydney B. Mitchell, who produced and/or introduced some of the best tall bearded varieties of their early-20th-century day.

Iris pallida Lambert 1789

Though *Iris germanica* tends to steal the stage, it was really *I. pallida* that formed the foundation for modern bearded irises. Iris lovers owe much to this weedy wildling. Its widespread occurrence across Europe as a wildflower and perfume commodity coupled with its ease of cultivation (it's pitifully easy to grow) no doubt inspired interest in the genus. Despite being pigeonholed as a blue iris, other colors are represented in the wild, from deep violet to pink and mauve to white. In its native France, *I. pallida* was used by early French breeders to create a range of sweetly fragrant, diploid cultivars in blue and lavender tones. Wild-collected or man-made hybrids with *I. variegata* awakened an even greater medley of colors. The two

ABOVE: *Iris pallida*

5

CLOCKWISE FROM TOP LEFT: *Iris reichenbachii*

Iris ×barthii

Iris variegata

'Whole Cloth' (Cook 1958)

variegated forms, 'Zebra' (syn. 'Pallida Variegata') and 'Argentea' (Goos and Koenemann 1906), are undoubtedly of garden origin.

Iris pumila Linnaeus 1753

Easily ranked in the top five most important bearded iris species in horticulture, the allotetraploid (for those tracking the lingo) *Iris pumila* hauled the dwarf bearded irises back from the brink of boredom. Native from Austria east to the Ural Mountains, the species reveals flowers across the rainbow spectrum in the wild and is an enticing plant to grow in the rock garden from seed. It was used extensively in crosses with tall bearded irises to develop the standard dwarf bearded iris class and further enhance the offerings of miniature dwarf bearded irises. *Iris pumila* notably sports one flower per stem but compensates with an abundance of stems per plant, a trait that is quite noticeable in MDBs.

Iris pumila has hybridized with *I. aphylla* in the wild where their ranges overlap to produce *I.* ×*barthii*, a usually blue-bearded dwarf with exceptionally tasteful flowers of swirled and blended colorations, usually in the chocolate brown range. In a word — delicious, at least to the eyes, and a glimmering insight into the potential the two species have in hybridization.

Iris reichenbachii Heuffel 1858

Compared to other, older ancestors of modern bearded irises like *Iris pallida* and *I. variegata*, *I. reichenbachii* entered onto the scene rather late, thanks to Paul Cook, who used it to create 'Progenitor' (1951), which in turn gave rise to 'Whole Cloth' (1956), the first clean, modern amoena. *Iris reichenbachii* grows wild throughout the Balkans east to northeastern Greece. Flowers are typically yellow or violet (expect some lovely variation when growing wild-collected seed), carried on stalks no taller than 12 inches. The plants are compact and low-growing, with a tidy habit and dainty appearance — superb rock garden specimens indeed, thanks to the wonders of genetics. Both diploids and tetraploids occur in the wild, the latter no doubt facilitating the species' use with tall bearded irises in hybridizing. With some potential to throw a branch from its flower stalks, *I. reichenbachii* is worth further consideration from hybridizers of median irises.

Iris trojana Kerner 1887

Hailing from western Asia Minor, *Iris trojana* is the last of the eastern tetraploid quartet that helped to modernize bearded iris development. In the wild, 3-foot stems sport attractive purple flowers with varying degrees of yellow veining in the hafts. Foster was the first to utilize *I. trojana* in breeding, crossing it to *I. pallida* to achieve such notable cultivars as the blue bitone 'Lady Foster' (1913). The French firm Vilmorin-Andrieux et Cie released 'Alcazar' (1910) from a cross of a diploid seedling by *I. trojana*. J. Marion Shull earned national fame and recognition for his 'Morning

Splendor' (1923), a cross of *I. trojana* and 'Lent A. Williamson' (Williamson 1918), which married two major progenitors of bearded irises into one cultivar.

Iris variegata Linnaeus 1753

Iris variegata is another key bearded iris progenitor. Widespread across eastern Europe, this exceptionally hardy and vigorous species looks the part of predecessor to the diploid MTBs; however, its use in breeding tall beardeds, where it likely introduced genes for yellow and yellow-derived pigments, is what assures its seat at the head table. Pronounced veining or hafting gives *I. variegata* a more-than-distinctive look; in the wild, flowers vary in color from yellow to white for the ground color and yellow to blue to brown for the vein colors. Flowers tend to flare outward, too, in stark contrast to other species in the section, which droop or, worse, recurve. *Iris ×lurida* is just one of many examples of a hybrid between this species and *I. pallida*; the clone in my garden is reddish in color, has a tendency to rebloom or just bloom in the fall (a truly silly but amusing quirk), and grows quite well. *Iris ×sambucina*, another group of naturalized hybrids between *I. variegata* and *I. pallida*, often features characteristically splashed and blended falls of rose or brown-red colors.

ABOVE: *Iris ×lurida*

The Minor Players

A handful of other species have had a minor role in the development of modern bearded irises, in some cases so minor as to barely warrant mention. They're cultivated in the main (not to say, "if at all") by collectors, or utilized in hybridizing experiments, with few of their genetics ultimately reaching the broader gene pool (though some perhaps should and will get there in future, as enterprising breeders ferret out new challenges). Still, some are quite attractive in their own right and make excellent candidates for the rock garden. I mention four that intrigue me.

Iris albertii Regel 1877

Native to the Tien Shan and Fergana ranges in Kyrgyzstan, this unusual BB-sized species sports tailored flowers in lavender and violet with reddish brown splashes emanating from the hafts and terminating abruptly at the end of the beards; rarely, yellow flowers with similar patterns occur. Though the flowers are incredibly narrow in comparison to modern bearded iris hybrids, their novel provenance, inherent hardiness, and diploidy could add to the genetics of MTBs and even, through chromosome doubling, to the BBs and TBs. For anyone tempted by splashy flowers and outlandish coloration, this species whets the appetite for ever-gaudier bearded irises — my favorite.

Iris attica Boissier & Heldreich 1859

Considered one of the ancestral species of *Iris pumila*, *I. attica* looks and grows much like its progeny — a bearded iris of miniature dwarf size that thrives and flowers freely in soils with good drainage and aeration. Rock gardeners have long enjoyed the species' early spring flowers in crevices and troughs, or in between small stones. I've grown a red form for a few seasons now; with dainty, dapper white beards sparkling against a merlot seemingly meant for a glass, I'm a happier rock gardener every April for its presence. In the wild, *I. attica* varies widely in its native range in Turkey and Greece, coming in such an array of colors and flower forms as to make the fashionistas among us envious. Given the genetic contributions of *I. pumila* to modern dwarfs, it might make sense for breeders to dig a little deeper and go back to this primary source for improved miniature dwarfs.

Iris subbiflora Brotero 1834

Native to southern Portugal and Spain, this Mediterranean dwarf might bring more heat hardiness to dwarfs and medians that have a tendency to falter in the summers of the South and Southwest. Some authors (most gardening in areas with wet springs) have reported difficulty growing this evergreen species; still others have praised its carefree flowering habits. This species is another excellent plant for rock gardeners less interested in derived things and

more intrigued by native beauty. A very limited assortment of colors (basically variations on the theme of purple), but they can be quite intense, saturated, and pronounced.

Iris timofejewii Woronow 1924

Iris timofejewii is associated with several different species, everything from *I. pumila* (with which it shares seed capsule characteristics) to aril irises, whose flowers it sometimes resemble. In the wild it grows to 8 inches tall, bordering the horticultural definitions of MDBs and SDBs. Specialist growers report that seed-grown plants invariably vary. Its use in breeding has been very limited; being a diploid, it offers the most to MTBs and perhaps other classes through chromosome doubling and wide crossing. Earl Roberts introduced two cultivars from a primary cross between *I. pallida* and *I. timofejewii* in 1973, 'Paltime' and 'Timpala', both of which won AIS Honorable Mentions in 1974 and 1975, respectively. In 2008 John J. Taylor introduced four seedlings with a complex and unusual ancestry: 'Triplicity', 'Foursome', 'Sherman', and 'Hutch' all involve a seedling P-17: (*I. imbricata* × M-3: (*I. timofejewii* × *I. reichenbachii* 'Van Nes')) with approximately 25 percent of its genes from *I. timofejewii*. These four diploids are handsome garden specimens in their own right and could prove highly instrumental in breeding.

ABOVE, LEFT TO RIGHT: *Iris subbiflora* *Iris attica*

CLOCKWISE FROM TOP LEFT: 'Sherman' (Taylor 2008) 'Triplicity' (Taylor 2008) 'Hutch' (Taylor 2008) 'Foursome' (Taylor 2008)

Bearded Irises, Act I

Theophrastus once remarked upon "the miraculous way in which the torch of life passes from one plant to another through the medium of small cuttings" — an eloquent statement that might also be applied to the torches of horticultural careers. Seriously, you have to wonder if humans are as much a part of the evolutionary scheme of bearded irises as bumblebees. Through rhizomes, handshakes, and letters, bearded irises moved from their earliest center of appreciation in the horticultural markets of the Netherlands and France, to Germany, the United Kingdom, and eventually to the United States.

The earliest varieties of irises grown and appreciated by gardeners in the 16th and 17th centuries were likely wild hybrids between *Iris pallida*, the source of lavender pigments, and *I. variegata*, the source of yellow pigments. Early collectors gave them various names, some pawned off onto botanists as species names like *I. amoena*, *I. squalens*, and *I. neglecta*. Each represented a relatively distinct color group, but the variation seen between clones was highly suggestive of their hybrid constitution. These seed-grown bearded irises were variously distributed across European gardens from the mid-17th century on. It wasn't until the 1820s, when Parisian nurseryman Paul de Bure raised and named hundreds of seedlings, that the movement to popularize bearded irises gained a footing; 'Buriensis' (c. 1822) was his first introduction.

De Bure's work stirred the interest of another Frenchman, Henri Antoine Jacques, who earned his place in iris history with 'Aurea' (1830), steadfastly popular and highly praised as one of the best yellow selfs for nearly a century. He in turn influenced fellow Frenchman and nurseryman Jean-Nicolas Lémon, the son of Nicolas Lémon, an early breeder of herbaceous peonies. In 1840, the younger Lémon published a catalog offering 100 varieties of his own bearded irises; one was 'Jacquesiana', a velvety copper-crimson bitone, named to honor his inspirer. Lémon followed that success with 'Mme. Chereau' (1844), a plicata distributed worldwide and renowned as one of the best bearded irises well into the 20th century. Both are still grown, lasting reminders of the heritage of bearded irises.

By the 1870s the bearded iris fascination had crossed the English Channel, and early enthusiasts like Peter Barr were leading the production of new varieties in the British Isles. It was in the 1890s that many breeders, churning out dozens of new varieties each year, began to wonder if they'd reached the limit of the bearded iris's potential. One of these was Sir Michael Foster, a professor of physiology at Cambridge and by all accounts among the most esteemed iris connoisseurs of his day. Foster grew and experimented with all irises, including oncocyclus irises from the Mideast and spurias. Not long after the introduction of two popular whites named for neighbors — 'Mrs. George Darwin' (1895) and 'Mrs. Horace Darwin' (1888) — he speculated that the potential of diploids had indeed been realized in the prodigious outputs of the last half century. He worried that improvement of bearded irises would cease if new germplasm didn't enter the breeder's garden. Calling on missionaries he knew in Asia Minor, Foster successfully imported collections of bearded irises from new provenances. The origins of these gifted acquisitions, which I'll cautiously call species, weren't terribly mysterious; Foster gave them names that were often indicative of their nativity ('Amas' from Amasia, for example), but the status of those populations in the wild were iffy or unknown at best. In any case, thus it was that Foster became one of the first westerners to cultivate the quartet of plants later recognized by W. R. Dykes as *I. cypriana*, *I. kashmiriana*, *I. mesopotamica*, and *I. trojana*. These first tetraploid bearded irises to enter the European iris scene would dramatically hasten the progress of bearded iris development in the decades ahead.

Foster's death in 1907 preceded the introduction of some his finest plants and may have contributed to the loss of information about their exact parentages, such as it was, though they certainly involved his beloved tetraploids. Nurseryman Robert Wallace, Foster's neighbor, introduced the best of his friend's work posthumously as 'Caterina' (1909), 'Crusader' (1913), 'Kashmir White' (1912), and 'Miss Willmott' (1912), among others.

The equally impressive introductions from the French firm Vilmorin-Andrieux et Cie would have their own legacy abroad; among these were the first tetraploid tall bearded irises released to commerce — the lilac and rose bicolor 'Isoline' (1904), the blue-violet blended 'Oriflamme' (1904), and the pansy-violet blended 'Alcazar' (1910). These tetraploids boasted taller stems, better branching, and larger flowers, but some were notoriously difficult to grow, suffering through the wet winters of the East Coast with only marginal success. In spite of their at times persnickety reputation, American enthusiasts acquired these new plants from their European counterparts in droves and bred them to their own diploids in earnest.

The American interest in bearded irises originated with diploids. Bertrand Farr, a music shop owner from Pennsylvania, imported Peter Barr's entire collection (over 100 cultivars) and established a nursery near Wyomissing in the early 1900s. But Farr drew ideas and genetics from more than just Barr's extensive nursery catalog; he also imported collections of irises from Cayeux and Vilmorin in France, Goos and Koenemann in Germany, and William J. Caparne (known for his dwarfs) in Guernsey

— and marketed them with uncanny sensibility. His numerous additions to the bearded iris palette offset a century's worth of foolproof but somewhat dowdy varieties that had grown in American gardens and dooryards since the Colonial period — clones of *I. germanica*, *I. pallida*, and named hybrids or selections like 'Flavescens', 'Odoratissima', and 'Sambucina'.

Farr's 1,500-plant exhibit at the 1915 Panama-Pacific International Exposition, held in San Francisco that year, really put him and the rainbow flower on the American horticultural map. Farr sent to competition the best collection of British and Wyomissing cultivars, ultimately awakening a dormant lust of the gardening public for bearded irises. Considering that Farr began breeding irises in a time when so little about their refinement was known in this country, it's an amazing accomplishment that so many of them were superb varieties. A trio of his first introductions in 1909 — 'Quaker Lady', 'Juniata', and 'Wyomissing' — are popular even now among collectors of historic irises. Interestingly, Farr never took much of an interest in the French and British tetraploids and continued breeding with his own and foreign diploids for the rest of his career. At the time of his death he likely held the largest collection of bearded irises in existence, numbering over 1,200 varieties.

As America was catching the initial round of bearded iris fever, a schoolmaster from Godalming, U.K., was feverishly making crosses of his own. William Rickatson Dykes is the undisputed godfather of the genus, a position he earned partly through his association with Sir Michael Foster, a friendship begun at Cambridge while Dykes was a student there. Upon Foster's death, Dykes inherited, by way of a mutual friend, copies of his predecessor's notes and garden records, and like Foster, he bravely ventured into all sorts of deep and muddy waters with his experimental crosses between diploids and tetraploids

ABOVE: 'W. R. Dykes' (Dykes-Orpington 1926)

and dwarf and tall species. Dykes traveled extensively to document species in the wild and collect them for horticultural evaluation; in his short breeding career, he introduced 34 cultivars, most in the early 1920s. Dykes died following a car accident in 1925. Two fitting tributes marked the next year: his wife, Katherine, introduced the yellow iris that bears his name, and in June 1926 the British Iris Society created the Dykes Medal honoring the most outstanding variety of the year — an award still coveted by breeders worldwide.

A. J. Bliss, a British contemporary of Dykes, earned a reputation for 'Dominion' (1918), partly for its unspeakably lofty price of five guineas (equivalent to $275 today!) and ultimately for its poor growth habits. Nevertheless, 'Dominion' was used extensively by breeders and gave rise to other progenitor varieties like 'Cardinal' (Bliss 1919), 'Bruno' (Bliss 1922), and 'Grace Sturtevant' (Bliss 1926) — collectively known as the Dominion Race.

Back in America, Grace Sturtevant — an irisarian in search of a thriving yellow tall bearded iris for Southern

ABOVE: 'Dominion' (Bliss 1918)

California that didn't owe its ancestry to *Iris variegata* — realized her goal in 1917, when, as a seedling, 'Shekinah' (1918), along with two others that would become 'B. Y. Morrison' (1918) and 'Afterglow' (1918), earned her a silver medal from the Massachusetts Horticultural Society. Her contemporary Bruce Williamson gifted American irisdom with 'Lent A. Williamson' (1918), considered one of the greatest cultivars of its day. William Mohr of California is best known for 'Alta California' (Mohr-Mitchell 1931), a fine-growing yellow (involving no known yellow genes to date) that seemed to grow happily wherever planted.

From the 1930s on, the pace quickened. As often happens with genera marked by vast genetic diversity, the pursuit of sundry forms invites participation from more and more people at an almost exponential rate. In short, our stage production morphed into a television soap opera, with each new idea or discovery, however slight, bringing a twist to the plot.

ABOVE:
'Lent A. Williamson'
(Williamson 1918)

Diploids to Tetraploids: The Back Story

The so-called conversion of garden hybrids from diploids to tetraploids was the most significant event in bearded iris history. But first, what's a diploid? Diploid organisms have two homologous copies of each chromosome, represented by notation 2n=2x, followed by another equal sign and the chromosome number of the organism. Since humans and many other organisms are diploid, the "2x" is often dropped, leaving (to use the example of *Iris pallida* and its chromosome number) 2n=24.

Plants, and many organisms for that matter, don't just come in duple form, though. Ploidy levels can vary as a result of environmental adaptation and abnormalities that occur during cell division, natural hybridization, and evolutionary divergence. Tetraploids by definition have twice the amount of genetic material as diploids. To continue with the example just given, the notation for a tetraploid plant with 24 chromosomes and four sets of homologous chromosomes would be 2n=4x=24. Doubling the amount of genetic information contained within the cell of a plant can increase plant size, flower size, floral substance, fragrance, vigor, and many other horticultural traits — all exciting features that gardeners ultimately swoon over.

Crosses between diploids and tetraploids, faced with uneven pairings of the homologous chromosomes during meiosis, typically produce triploids (plants with three sets of chromosomes). However, on rare occasions, such a cross results in an unreduced set of chromosomes (from the diploid parent) that can pair evenly with its tetraploid mate. The resulting cell is then also a tetraploid. The failure rates vary in nature, and while some plant species tolerate ploidy mismatches better than others, there's no great hope that it will happen often or at all. It's a game of chance.

And remember: none of the major hybridizers of the late 19th and early 20th centuries knew any of this. Their forays into hybridization between diploids and tetraploids were purely intuitive. They made crosses, harvested inevitably little seed, raised seedlings, and made selections, without any awareness of the cellular biology of the plants they raised — all of which speaks to the nearly fantastical nature of their passion, a pursuit of beauty so authentic that even ignorance didn't foil their ultimate success.

Indeed, those swoon-worthy traits were motivation enough, and the formerly limited palette of the diploid bearded irises was transformed into a colorful cast of characters made for the world's garden stage. What had previously seemed like a group of prismatically flowered plants with limited breeding potential now looked capable of developing into popular herbaceous perennials. Iris godfathers like Foster, Dykes, Bliss, and others followed their intuition, took stock of the newfound tetraploids, and began making crosses — the fortuitous founding of the rainbow flower.

The Drama Continues

The founding of both the American Iris Society and the British Iris Society in 1920 and 1922, respectively, helped to solidify camaraderie among iris lovers worldwide. Offering an exchange of information and plants, a recognition of efforts, and a mechanism through which to promote irises, these societies flourished as the craze for all irises, not just bearded, swept the horticultural landscape. It's hard to imagine a garden absent hyper-blooming clumps of bearded irises, but without either of these organizations coalescing at the right time in iris development, the sweetly fragrant reality we enjoy today may never have been.

Contemporarily speaking, the majority of bearded iris breeding in the world takes place on U.S. soil, though many important players contribute from Australia, the U.K., and central Europe. Unfortunately the number of people breeding irises, as with so many groups of horticultural plants, is declining, and after more than a century of vigorous hybridizing, the horizon might seem less bright. Nothing could be further from the truth. The drama of bearded iris development continues to unfold with new quests and challenges — a spectrum, true-red iris; better rebloomers (better yet, an everblooming iris); improved vigor in modern TBs; tetraploid MTBs. Many of these tales lie ahead, in the chapters devoted to the six classifications of bearded irises.

So, let's raise the curtain on our current production, and see how everyday people with camel hair brushes and twinkling eyes took humble wild irises and gave them style.

6 Miniature Dwarf Bearded Irises

“I believe that the preoccupation of most gardeners and nearly all breeders with the tall bearded irises has reached its peak and that a return to much greater use of low-growing irises...will be seen.”

Sydney B. Mitchell,
***Iris for Every Garden* (1949)**

On blustery slopes in the Caucasus grow tiny tussocks of spiky green leaves which, in spite of snowcover, often bloom in the earliest days of spring — the “openers” for the colorful riot of montane meadows. These little sprites are *Iris pumila*, the wild dwarf irises whose genes hide in the background of thousands of bearded irises, particularly those of the miniature dwarf bearded class.

I’ve loved miniature dwarf irises for as long as I can remember. My great-grandmother loved them too and grew a huge colony of ‘Atroviolacea’ (Todaro 1856) in her dooryard garden under the dry shade of an eastern redcedar (*Juniperus virginiana*); commonly known as purple flags (or just flags), these familiar dark purple miniatures grows hardily along roadsides, at the base of cemetery monuments, and at abandoned farmsteads throughout the country, blooming at only a few inches tall. The cultivar's origins are a little unclear, but it's definitely a sterile hybrid discovered in the wild in Europe in the middle 19th century. Some botanists argue that it's a pure form of *Iris pumila*, the primary progenitor of our modern dwarfs, but nobody knows for sure, and few care. To paraphrase Shakespeare, an iris by any other name . . .

Officially, miniature dwarf bearded irises (MDBs for short) flower at less than 8 inches in height — the proverbial hobbits of the bearded iris realm — just as the perennial stalwarts of the spring garden begin to rustle from their winter rest. Pair them smartly, and you'll have miniature dwarfs in bloom with crocus and dwarf daffodils. As Gertrude Wister, wife of 20th-century horticulturist and irisarian John Wister, so eloquently wrote, "The flowers of late winter and early spring occupy places in our hearts well out of proportion to their size." That's a gentle way of sticking it to the man: my own dad, a lumbering six-foot-four-inch Iowa farmer, doesn't see what all the fuss is about so close to the ground. But let me tell you — if you haven't lain on your stomach peering past the beard into the center of an MDB flower, you really haven't seen one of the coolest perspectives on the planet. These little plants have drawn me down from my own six-foot-one-inch height into a bijou fairyland brimming with the rainbow spectrum.

Indeed the colors of MDBs sing as loudly as their taller cousins, and most certainly do so en masse. While nature has afforded tall bearded irises nearly 3 feet of stem for ample branching and buds, the MDBs function with a mere fraction. Thus, practically and biologically speaking, it would come at a great cost to the plant to attempt to send up more than one bud per stalk, but MDBs compensate for this by sending up multiple stems per plant. Floriferous is an understatement, at least when speaking of the best cultivars. A well-grown and established clump of miniatures will carpet the garden floor for weeks, inevitably drawing attention and envy from your neighbors as they stroll by.

Origins: From Romania (and Russia) with Love

The story of miniature dwarf irises in gardens begins in the same place we started this chapter — in the Caucasus, the alpine meadows of eastern Europe and Russia — but with a consort of species that excludes *Iris pumila*, at least for the moment. The earliest miniatures cultivated in gardens had as ancestors the species known collectively as the chamaeiris complex, most belonging to the present-day circumscription of *I. lutescens* (though in the early 1900s, these irises ran around with a host of names, including *I. italica*, *I. olbiensis*, and *I. chamaeiris*). These cultivars, of which there were many at the time, failed to persist in gardens and in the specialist iris firmament for a couple of reasons. First, breeders encountered sterility issues, mainly due to a lack of proper chromosome complements, which from a biological standpoint makes hybridization a challenge. Meiosis, the process of cellular division that occurs in germ cell lines and ultimately renders an organism capable of proceeding through the processes of sexual reproduction, operates best on an "even to even" policy. Mismatches, odd numbers, and mispairings tended to complicate the results or render them useless or impossible altogether. Thus these cultivars were often dead ends, unable to advance the ambitions of the breeder to widen the color palette, improve disease resistance (some species had a nasty habit of acquiring viral infections that mottled and streaked their flowers and foliage . . . the nerve!), or enhance the flower's form. They also lacked glam and sparkle, coming in few colors and combinations that would make them anything more than a collector's commodity.

Other species on the scene at the time included the arenaria complex, which to this day is a source of controversy among botanists; depending on your geographical position or which botanical team you root for, you may know them as *Iris arenaria*, *I. flavissima*, or *I. humilis*. Clones of each are still commercially available and most often encountered in rock gardens. I've grown *I. flavissima* for several years and marvel at its vigor, robust flowering habits, and alarmingly neon yellow color. Each flower lasts for one day, and a small pot that I purchased at a specialty nursery exploded into a dense clump of tiny green fans in just a few seasons. Amid creeping phlox (*P. subulata*) and shooting stars (*Primula*), you can't miss this dynamo rock garden iris.

Still another taxon, *Iris suaveolens* var. *mellita*, found its use in select crosses by enterprising breeders hoping to make hay from a species sadly known for slender, downward-looking flowers in drab colors. Ick. Though charming to the collector, most breeders couldn't make sense of it. Its most famous contribution was as the pollen parent of 'Buddha Song' (Dunbar 1970), a highly unusual miniature with purple colors like its pod parent, 'Rhages' (Mead-Riedel 1934), a tall bearded, but with the dainty habit of *I. suaveolens*. Seeing the two parents side by side makes you wonder what crazy idea grabbed hold of Bonnie Dunbar when she made that cross in 1963, and frankly, why nobody else had done it sooner.

Modern miniature dwarf irises may never have existed were it not for the introduction of *Iris pumila* into mainstream breeding circles in the 1930s, '40s, and '50s. Present-day cultivars owe much of their glamour and charm to this diminutive iris — a naturally occurring hybrid between *I. attica* and *I. pseudopumila* probably first originating somewhere along the mountains of the Adriatic coast. From there this versatile, adaptable, and environmentally adept hybrid migrated across much of the Balkans into present-day Austria and the Czech Republic and as far east as the Ural Mountains in Russia. This widespread range accounts for a sweeping array of flower colors and chromosome arrangements, both traits that breeders exploited in the decades after its introduction to western horticulture. In the late 1930s, Bob Schreiner of Schreiner's Iris Gardens imported seed from three sources — Romania, Crimea (Ukraine), and Austria — and introduced three notable (if unregistered) cultivars, progenitors of many more to come. 'Nana' (Latin for "dwarf") came from the Crimean seed and was notable for passing on lovely reddish hues to its progeny. 'Carpathia' and 'Sulina' came from the Romanian seed and likely were used the most by breeders in the early 1950s to widen the form of the rather strappy *I. pumila* to something fatter and fashionable for modern tastes (more surface area = more color). Nothing ever came of the Austrian seed directly, although Schreiner sent selections to his colleague Paul Cook in Indiana, who used them to create two of the bluest irises of the day, 'Remnant' (1955) and 'Sky Patch' (1955).

The road to the modern MDB essentially had two routes. The first cultivars tended to originate from crosses between different forms of *Iris pumila*. While these were often quite hardy and of the daintiest proportions, they weren't broadly adaptable to American gardens, suffering in the heat of the South and lasting only a few growing seasons, if that. The second and largely more successful cultivars originated when *I. pumila* was crossed with modern TBs (also tetraploids), followed by generations of selection for miniature proportions. The majority of modern MDBs derive themselves from these trailblazers and their advanced-generation hybrids. *Iris pumila*, in short, ranks as one of the most significant species where modern bearded irises are concerned: its genes contributed to the development of thousands of irises and paved the way for not only the miniature dwarf class but also the standard dwarf and intermediate bearded classes.

This species is easily the jester of spring in the wild. With flowers from purple to yellow to brown, and occasionally lighter colored versions with dark, saturated spots on the falls (called the "pumila spot"), this wild miniature also boasts some of the most memorable fragrances in all the iris realm. It varies for sure, depending on the nose, obviously, and the provenance of the plants in question. Some boast thick, heady smells reminiscent of heliotrope, others cleaner and classic, akin to vanilla or lemon. Most of all, it's the earliest bearded iris, the harbinger of spring, blooming from March through April in most areas of the United States. If you're looking for a dwarf bearded species iris for the rock garden, look no further.

Iris pumila typically goes summer dormant, a trait it passed on to many of its early hybrid MDB descendants. I know it's easy to get fussy about summer dormant plants. We complain because they leave bare spots, or because we forget where they're planted. True. But if you can enjoy this sprite-like iris in surroundings akin to its homeland (like a rock, scree, or saxatile garden), it may not make much of a difference whether it takes a nap in the hottest months of the year or not. In fact, if given ample drainage during its dormancy and a good, cold winter, *I. pumila* really shapes up into an enjoyable garden plant, which might even reseed politely once it settles in. Plants are readily available from rock garden suppliers, and seed from exchanges like that of the Species Iris Group of North American (signa.org) or the North American Rock Garden Society (nargs.org).

Worth Noting: A Storied Past

Now that your interest in the miniature realm is piqued — nearly 1,000 cultivars of MDBs are presently on the books with the American Iris Society, awaiting your gardener's ambition to grow them all, or at least as many as you can fit in your own garden, right? That's right: in the 1950s interest in the miniature dwarf bearded irises rocketed to fantastic heights and their heyday continued through the '80s. Walter Welch (the godfather of miniature dwarf irises and whose name, along with that of British iris enthusiast William J. Caparne, is associated with the medal that the American Iris Society awards the best MDB each year) stoked interest in this class for several decades from his well-known and oft-visited garden in Noblesville, Indiana, with the founding of the Dwarf Iris Society of America (zyworld.com/DISoA). His efforts to collect dwarf species besides *I. pumila* also resulted in new hybrids and a slew of popular cultivars for which he earned many awards.

The miniatures come from diverse backgrounds. The "old" pumila-derived MDBs are in the minority today compared to the "SDB-derived" MDBs, which are basically genetically stunted versions of their taller cousins (just imagine the figurative "short end of the stick" and you'll have a pretty clear idea of how chromosome architecture effectively makes these plants miniature dwarfs). The SDB-derived cultivars are equally showy and floriferous, but some purists balk that MDBs should come only from lines of exclusively miniature origins. For the iris lover, this is a moot point.

Expert Pointers: MDBs in the Garden

With so many cultivars from which to choose, the modern garden can surely sport a dozen or so whose flowers will span from the earliest stirring through the first few solidly good weeks of spring weather. Those flowers, though, aren't appreciated singularly. In fact, the real charm of this class stems from the clump, slight pun intended. The one-bud-per-stem of miniature dwarfs might at first read seem stingy, compared to their taller cousins. But, again, they gladly compensate with stem count, resulting in dense clumps of flowers that look like nosegays erupting from the ground. The best of them couldn't be more joyous in full bloom; check out my next-up list of top-notch garden performers: every one of them will reward you by thriving.

Such star performers needn't go solo in the garden. Miniature dwarfs are excellent accompaniments to many early spring flowering perennials like rock cress (*Arabis caucasica*) and alpine speedwells (*Veronica alpina*, *V. wormskjoldii*), and bulbs like daffodils, species tulips, and grape hyacinths. I could sit here and list favorite companion plants all day, as I'm sure you could too. Plant lovers often grow their treasures in overplanted company, something that might not bode well for success with miniature dwarfs. I'd hardly call them finicky, but they'll do best in full sun, not shaded by taller companions (though they will do fine at the edge of shady areas — because those areas aren't all that shaded when these early birds start to sing). I quickly learned the hard way, as a teenager rampantly collecting miniature dwarfs and stuffing them in left and right: beware the overcasting shade of taller plants. I had the (at the time) bright idea to plant a ring of MDBs at the periphery of a shady island bed, nearby newly planted swaths of spotted deadnettle (*Lamium maculatum*), bugleweed (*Ajuga reptans*), and assorted woodland sedges (*Carex*). Point for the sedges — these really do make fine companions in part-shade areas. A designer would give you an extra point for contrasting textures and foliar colors, and plus it just looks classically elegant. But the lamium and ajuga are cause for serious demerits. Their rampant vigor overwhelmed my MDBs in one growing season, and although the MDBs persisted and even bloomed the next spring, it was clear that it would be their last appearance if I didn't move them soon. The lesson here — it doesn't take much in the way of "tall" competition overhead to outcompete these diminutive irises. I think the mantra goes "right plant, right place."

Cultivating the miniatures is pretty straightforward. Plop them down in full sun, in soil that gets consistent moisture but drains quickly (the less mystical way of saying "well-drained soil"), and out of the shade of taller plants, and you're on your way. Keep in mind that these tiny little rhizomes are at the mercy of freeze-thaw cycles and do heave, at least in some years, due to their shallow root system. To keep them anchored, don't be afraid to put a small rock on top of the rhizomes in late fall — sounds drastic I know, but just think how cute a yard full of small rocks will look sitting on top of your irises. Or you can plant the MDBs in rock gardens, where pea gravel mulch is just the thing for keeping them nestled in the ground. Dooryard gardens, along walkways or the edges of borders, or troughs can work just as well. Always remember their origins — alpine meadows — when carving out a niche in your garden. While they're certainly adaptable plants, you can't easily escape their desire for wide-open sky above and dry feet below.

When it comes time to divide your miniatures, usually about every two to four years, you'll want to consider a couple of things. If you grow pumila-derived MDBs, you know about their summer dormancy. In the past, I've rushed to get them dug and divided early in the summer, around late June or July, just to get them replanted and back in the ground before they go completely dormant. This strategy works great if you live where early summer weather isn't super hot or humid. However, in areas of the South, you'd be wise to hold off dividing until maybe early September, when you have a better chance of reestablishing them in milder weather, even though they'll be dormant. If you grow any other MDBs, you can divide them in early summer, at least six weeks after they've finished blooming. Though you may have to divide them a little more frequently than some of your taller irises, the reward of having more and more little plants should more than balance out the minimal effort required to dig these sprites. And their hardiness, vigor, and lovable nature in full bloom make MDBs the best iris gifts to gardening friends who need a little iris love.

Cultivars You Should Grow

It's no secret that some of the earliest MDB cultivars proved a bit challenging in the open garden, struggling to disown their alpine genetic ancestry in favor of more garden-friendly characteristics. Gone are those days. With continued improvement of the cultivars from *Iris pumila*, the subsequent generations of breeding work between those outstanding cultivars, and crosses with the standard dwarfs (SDBs), the MDBs are vastly improved. Here are my favorites, the ones that I absolutely couldn't live without — dependable perennials that have thrived in my garden and in those of my friends around the country.

'AFRICAN WINE' (KASPEREK 1999)

From my friends Brad and Kathie Kasperek of Zebra Gardens in Utah comes this sweet-looking miniature with a zany name. Though I'm ever in pursuit of red irises for my garden, I came across this iris by accident — the result of Brad and Kathie's generosity in an order box. Another great companion for bulbs like dwarf daffodils or species tulips, this miniature is on my watch list every spring and on the lists of my clients as well! For many years, this has been one of our top-selling miniatures. Looking for a groundcover to plant underfoot that won't completely run this iris out of garden and home? Try *Sedum rupestre* 'Angelina'. The fresh chartreuse color of this stonecrop's foliage against the juicy red flowers looks smart and superb. Caparne-Welch Medal 2006.

ABOVE: 'African Wine' (Kasperek 1999)

'BETE NOIRE' (MARKY SMITH 2009)

Translated from French as "black beast," the phrase is usually intended to refer to someone disliked or avoided. However, you'll do right to associate with this dwarf as much as possible while it's in bloom. I can't help it — I love black flowers. When this miniature dwarf with black flowers came along, it didn't take me long to send away an order. Irresistibly velvety and shiny, this iris rose to the top of my favorites list in no time.

'BRANDED' (PAUL BLACK 2002)

I've always known 'Branded' as a little changeling — as the flowers age, the greenish butter color hazes whiter, and the overall effect is quite pretty if subtle. 'Branded' grows very well, no doubt taking a cue from its larger SDB-sized progenitors. Plant a few, and you'll have plenty to share with your friends in just a few seasons. Plant it where you can kneel down, and you'll probably pick up a slight spicy fragrance. Think herbally and underplant it with various thymes, for an amplified scent-sation. Honorable Mention 2004.

TOP TO BOTTOM: 'Bete Noire' (Smith 2009) 'Branded' (Black 2002)

'BUDDHA SONG'
(BONNIE DUNBAR 1970)

Here's a historical treasure worth growing. 'Buddha Song' resulted from a cross of a TB, the purple pepper plicata 'Rhages' (Mead-Riedel 1934), and the dwarf iris *Iris suaveolens* var. *mellita* (as *I. mellita*). The result — a purple bitone shaped in the most bizarre way, but wonderful all the same. It grows with phenomenal vigor and blooms for weeks in the spring, carpeting the rock garden with its flowers. If you can track a piece down, you're in for an unusual treat. Honorable Mention 1971.

ABOVE: 'Buddha Song' (Dunbar 1970)

'CREVASSE' (H. COLLINS 1975)

Very few people grow this lost gem, likely because it was never widely distributed, or even very popular in its day. 'Crevasse' has some of the most unusual flowers of any of the miniatures I grow, catching my attention with a sea green halo around white beards on the falls. I've got a clump situated near bluish gray stones, the strangest accidental combination of stone and plant: each seems to play off the plusses of the other.

ABOVE: 'Crevasse' (Collins 1975)

'CROUCHING TIGER' and 'HIDDEN DRAGON' (ERIC AND BOB TANKESLEY-CLARKE 2003)

This rather Zen pair of dwarfs are officially registered as species crosses (SPEC-X) in the AIS registry of irises. They resulted from a cross of a selection of *Iris pumila* (possibly *I. alexeenkoi*, another dwarf iris species of merit) with 'Commencement', a pumila-derived dwarf. Like all good couplets, you can't grow one without the other. They often herald the bearded iris season in my garden, at least in "normal" years (whatever those are), blooming sometimes as early as the last day or two in March though more often in early April. Perhaps better than other forms of *I. pumila*, they're superb rock garden plants, glowing for a brief week in the earliest days of spring in bouquets seemingly stuck right in the ground. A wise garden sage once told me that the cure for an alpine's ailment was more rock, more rock, and more rock. In this case, pea gravel mulch can help disguise these two when they enter dormancy. Like their wild-growing relatives, these dwarfs often enter dormancy in early July, passing out just in time to miss the first days of blistering heat. Nestle them up with a light layer of pea pebbles and forget them. 'Crouching Tiger', Award of Merit 2008.

'DOOZEY' (BEN HAGER 1994)

Ben Hager was the king of 20th-century iris breeding. Masterful at whatever class he turned his hand to, he left quite a mark on the MDBs, favoring sharp, eye-catching dwarfs with loud, articulate fall spots. 'Doozey' is no exception. I plant some of my most cherished plants near the front door — they're the first things I want to see on my morning forays into the yard. 'Doozey' grows just off my patio there, at the foot of a gray boulder, where its clump is multiplying at an athletic pace. Crisp white flowers look ink-blotted on the falls with a medium violet spot edged in the same icy white as the standards. A very special iris.

ABOVE: 'Doozey' (Hager 1994)

6

ABOVE, LEFT TO RIGHT: 'Crouching Tiger' (Tankesley-Clarke 2003)

'Hidden Dragon' (Tankesley-Clarke 2003)

'DOTTIE'S DOLL' (A. AND D. WILLOTT 2006)

From the moment I first saw a photograph of this plant during a program at an AIS national convention, I was struck with plant lust. I had to have it. Perky flowers. Sharp colors. Good growth habits. What more could any iris lover ask? So cute and adorable, it was hard to resist planting more than just a few, but they grew into fine, charming clumps. I enjoy them in the company of miniature daffodils, crocus, and various grape hyacinths. A newer cultivar that I highly recommend!

'EARLY SUNSHINE' (V. GRAPES 1955)

During the time I edited the newsletter of the Dwarf Iris Society of America, I had the pleasure of publishing a story about Vivian and Hazel Grapes, two sisters from Nebraska who bred hostas and dwarf irises from the 1930s into the 1960s. Of the 25 irises they registered and introduced, and that I read about with interest, only 'Early Sunshine' remains (barely) available. I'm happy to say that a clump has thrived in my saxatile garden for many years, blooming through well-mannered tussocks of Appalachian sedge *(Carex appalachica)* with near religious conviction. It blooms quite early and, though by aesthetic standards it isn't anything more than just a dwarf yellow iris, it is a fine memorial to two plant-loving women who thought it special enough to share with the gardening world.

ABOVE, LEFT TO RIGHT: 'Dottie's Doll' (Willott 2006)

'Early Sunshine' (Grapes 1955)

'FISSION CHIPS' (KEITH KEPPEL 2004)

All nuclear engineers (or fans of battered cod, French fries, and vinegar) who happen to be gardeners deserve to grow this plant. Bright orange flowers with paprika-colored beards shout out loud, proving that mighty garden plants come in all sizes. I was at Butchart Gardens once and saw them using this sharp-looking mini in containers with succulents and silver-colored plants. Delightful idea! Always one of the most asked-about miniature dwarfs in my garden. Caparne-Welch Medal 2011.

ABOVE: 'Fission Chips' (Keppel 2004)

'FLASHING NEON'
(A. AND D. WILLOTT 2005)

I joke that I keep a desert island list of plants — the essential gardenworthy plants that I couldn't possibly part with were I stranded on some obviously temperate, desert island. This mini makes the cut, embodying the concept of distinctiveness — you'll never confuse this with any other iris, ever. Tony and Dorothy Willott have bred and introduced over 360 irises, a good many of which were MDBs. Without question, 'Flashing Neon' is one of the best. If you've never taken a moment to lie flat on the ground staring at a miniature dwarf iris, I can honestly say you're missing out on another world. If, when the mood strikes, you can't decide where to start, get down in front of this one. Honorable Mention 2007.

ABOVE:
'Flashing Neon'
(Willott 2005)

'GNUZ SPREAD' (KASPEREK 1996)

Here's something special — a reblooming MDB that glows in yellow. Most all of Brad and Kathie Kasperek's iris introductions sport names with a safari theme, adding an often ignored but tremendously fun element to the garden — the lexicon of plant names. After all, who shows friends around the garden in silence? The way we talk about, and subsequently name plants says a lot about our passion for gardening. The word "spread" isn't carelessly placed in the name either. This little puppy can grow — a delicate euphemism for saying that it will eat other plants in its sunshiny, rebloom-prone path. It hails from the high plains of Utah, and if it will rebloom there, it should about anywhere. We enjoy a series of late stalks on it in Iowa in autumn, always glad to see another spot of springtime yellow against the falling leaves. Award of Merit 2000.

'IVORY FASHION' (A. AND D. WILLOTT 1996)

I practically trip over this variety every spring. It grows so well that it's managed to roam its way out into the gravel path through the rock garden, poking up creamy white flowers with red-brown feathering spots right in the walkway. Though fragrance is not my forte, my mother tells me it has a slight sweet smell — all the more reason to kneel down to its lowly, 5-inches-above-the-ground flowers and take a sniff. This little thing barely hits me on my shoes, but oh how adorable!

ABOVE, LEFT TO RIGHT: 'Gnuz Spread' (Kasperek 1996) 'Ivory Fashion' (Willott 1996)

'LITTLE BIRD' (LOWELL BAUMUNK 2010)

New to the market, this yellow- and chocolate-colored sparrow of a flower already has a spot in my garden. As an avid amateur ornithologist, birds hold a special place in my heart. Combining a passion for plants and birds isn't hard, but when something this cute comes along it's irresistibly easy. 'Little Bird' is the daintiest thing, sporting flowers with the best, perkiest form. While I love the wispier forms of MDBs more closely allied to *I. pumila*, I appreciate MDBs from SDB breeding that buck up and show a sunny face to the sky. 'Little Bird' does just that, though I would recommend planting it near strong colors for the best show — fluttering around at ground level on 5½-inch stems, it can easily hide away.

'RED AT LAST' (LEONA MAHOOD 1970)

The first time I sent a photo of this late-blooming mini to friends in a "happy spring" email, I think the servers at my ISP nearly crashed. Everyone couldn't get over how darn cute this little tyke was, shooting back replies to my message at lightning speed. Yet for all its chic and charm, this oldie remains a prize in the hands of MDB collectors. If I could stick one iris inside the back cover of this book to share with you, it might be this one (you don't think I could really choose just one do you?). And as far as red in bearded irises goes, it's pretty red by my standards. A three-year-old clump will fit in a tomato soup bowl! Honorable Mention 1974.

ABOVE, LEFT TO RIGHT: 'Little Bird' (Baumunk 2010)

'Red At Last' (Mahood 1970)

6

'SUN DABS' (TERRY AITKEN 2002)

In the early days of spring in the Midwest, little dabs of sunshine are often all we get in a 24-hour cycle; the other hours are occupied by blobs of wet and cold. Never down or out, 'Sun Dabs' easily forms a mass of bright, sunny yellow flowers that will reward for many seasons. I've given away more 'Sun Dabs' than I can keep track of on account of its rampant growth habits — a notable quality among smaller bearded irises. Plant it in the closest company of your hens and chicks (*Sempervivum*) and you're guaranteed an enviable spring show.

ABOVE: 'Sun Dabs' (Aitken 2002)

'TINGLE' (PAUL BLACK 2000)

My dear friend Paul Black named this seedling 'Tingle' because it reportedly gave him spine-tingling chills the first time he saw it. The first time it bloomed I got them too. It's just cute as a bug in a rug, as that old granny-ism goes. Imagine shrinking the form, fatness, and appeal of a tall bearded into a flower just a fraction of its size. The color certainly doesn't scream at you, but the personality of a clump of 'Tingle' definitely brings jazz to the scene. It's vigorous, blooms well through most any conditions (including a terribly vicious freeze once), and flowers without end in the spring. Mine are underplanted with various hens and chicks (*Sempervivum*). Award of Merit 2004.

'TINY TITAN' (TERRY AITKEN 2002)

From Terry Aitken's garden in Vancouver, Washington, comes this *orange* MDB, a significant color addition to a class long bereft of carotenoids. A notable award winner it will, I imagine, soon grow (if it doesn't already) in an esteemed spot in the gardens of many iris lovers. It grows excellently and blooms for several weeks in spring, glowing on wet days rather than sullying in the rain. Grow a carpet of this at the front of the border, and your neighbors will think you're up to some kind of garden magic. Caparne-Welch Medal 2009.

ABOVE, LEFT TO RIGHT: 'Tingle' (Black 2000)

'Tiny Titan' (Aitken 2002)

6

'TRIFLE' (BEN HAGER 1997)

My sense of smell isn't very keen; I don't remember the nuances of complex fragrances very well, if at all, nor do I detect odorous subtleties. So when, tall as I am, I don't even have to bend over to catch a whiff of 'Trifle', you know something's brewing in those nectaries. For whatever genetic reasons, 'Trifle' consistently ranks as one of the smelliest irises in the garden. At a meager 5 inches tall, this wee sprite fills the air with the scents of juice and fruit, quite a feat for something so small. A few plants quickly spread out into a lovely clump, guaranteeing a regular show of blooms and fragrance, and enough to share with all your garden friends.

ABOVE: 'Trifle' (Hager 1997)

'TRIMMED VELVET'
(DON SPOON 2006)

I'm not a fan of purple in irises. There, I said it! I guess it's just too typical (thanks a lot, van Gogh). But as with every garden rule, there's an exception. 'Trimmed Velvet' reblooms reliably for me in zone 5 in Iowa, and reportedly well for others south and east. The name couldn't be more apt. The velvety hue of the flowers is unbeatable, in spring or fall for that matter. In spring it joins a chorus of other miniatures in my rock garden, but in fall it often sings in the presence of autumn crocus (*Colchicum speciosum*) — a more than juicy combination of pink and velvet in the waning days of September. Like many rebloomers, it grows steadily, putting up consistent increase as it paces itself through two rounds of flowering in any given season. Even though it's purple, it's earned a spot on my desert island list. Award of Merit 2011.

ABOVE: 'Trimmed Velvet' (Spoon 2006)

'WATERMARK' (A. AND D. WILLOTT 2001)

No list of my favorite MDBs would be complete without this doll-face clumper. Aptly named, the otherwise white flowers have the finest turquoise rays extending from the beard. They're cute, whether singular or massed, and a plurality of flowers is never hard to come by given this variety's penchant for forming vigorous clumps within a few seasons of planting. This distinctive variety merits a home in your finest trough or nook nearest the path. Remember, MDBs are an intimate subject — plant for close inspection! Award of Merit 2007.

'WESTERN CIRCLES' (A. AND D. WILLOTT 1993)

This flower sports a classic pattern for miniatures, to my eye at least — yellow with a brown spot. Even though a hundred before it and after it have sported variations of the same, its personality as a plant is hard to deny. Plus, it's among the most popular MDBs with members of the Dwarf Iris Society. It's hard to argue with the votes of real iris lovers!

ABOVE, LEFT TO RIGHT: 'Watermark' (Willott 2001)

'Western Circles' (Willott 1993)

'WISE' (TOM JOHNSON 2001)

No less a breeder than Ben Hager once said that short irises should have short names, and so it goes with 'Wise'. This rather wise- and smart-looking miniature reblooms occasionally in my southern Iowa garden, though not reliably. Despite this, it blooms for up to three weeks in May, making it one of the longest-blooming miniature dwarfs in the garden. Single-budded stalks with velvety, imperial purple flowers and starkly white beards look smashing in the company of miniature daffodils, or the overlooked dandelion. Caparne-Welch Medal 2007.

ABOVE: 'Wise' (Johnson 2001)

6

ABOVE:
'Atroviolacea'
(Todaro 1856)

Gallery

6

OPPOSITE: 'Cinnamon Apples' (Black 1990)

ABOVE: 'Bugsy' (Hager 1993)

6

OPPOSITE: 'Blue Ash' (Willott 2001)

ABOVE: 'Self Evident' (Hager 1997)

ABOVE: 'Moi'
(Baumunk 2004)

7 Standard Dwarf Bearded Irises

> "Standard dwarf irises are one of the best garden perennial series developed in this country."
>
> **Bee Warburton, *The World of Irises* (1978)**

If the MDBs herald spring with marquee clumps of color and cute, the standard dwarfs (SDBs) in the weeks thereafter round out Act I with much the same and more. Boasting the very same bijou charm as their smaller cousins, the SDBs step it up a notch, literally, thanks to taller flower stalks. SDBs range in height from 8 to 16 inches tall, a fairly particular range for a less-than-fussy group of bearded irises. They're the perfect compromise for gardeners who love dwarf and dainty, but just can't handle things too small.

During chilly early spring days, the MDBs bloom at an easy pace, preserved by cool nights and mild days, long enough for me to enjoy every single one. But when the first SDB blooms in my garden, I feel as if the start gun to spring has fired. Clumps are off and blooming faster than I can get around to see each one, mostly due to the fact that I've got a hundred or so more SDBs than MDBs. The overlapping bloom season of MDBs and SDBs has fortuitously resulted in a great many hybrids between the two groups. As the popularity of SDBs grew in the last half of the 20th century, enterprising breeders rightly intercrossed the two groups, utilizing MDB parents for daintiness and earlier bloom and SDB parents for new color breaks, flower size, and form. The two groups work in perfect complement to each other.

Today, SDBs are a hot commodity on the iris scene, coming in second only to tall bearded irises in the number of new registrations each year. An explosion of breeding work has led this class to new frontiers, expanding the color palette to the point that it rivals the tall beardeds' in scope. No longer do standard dwarfs come in merely self colors and spots. Instead they show off plicatas, luminatas, and bicolors in nearly all shades, revamped spot patterns with remarkable clarity and contrast, and, not to be disdained, new self colors in tones and hues only fitting for smaller flowers. Despite a constant flood of new varieties, iris lovers keep planting them one after another, never seeming to get enough of the latest metamorphoses of pigments and panache. Loving small plants has its benefits, I suppose — you can always find room for "just one more."

In my opinion, the median irises — the SDBs, intermediate bearded (IBs), miniature tall bearded (MTBs), and border bearded (BBs) — blaze the path to an iris-filled future. Smaller gardens, whether they are so by choice or by default (the confines of modern living), necessitate a different scale of gardening, one more intimate and less panoramic. The plants in these gardens should fit the space, in more ways than one I suppose, but chiefly with regard to size. Gardens like this may have room for only a few irises, and a single, established clump of a tall bearded iris might just be too much, too big for the space at hand. Comparatively, a few clumps of standard dwarfs at establishment don't take up nearly as much space and make charming edgers, softening the rigidity of sidewalks and paver patios. Here begins a four-chapter-long case for median irises — smaller gardens deserve smaller irises with no sacrifice of beauty or sophistication.

Origins: A Product of Horticultural Intuition

Bearded irises have fascinated plant breeders since the introduction of the earliest wild-collected forms, for their diversity of shape, stature, and above all, color. As it relates to SDBs, that fascination grabbed the attention of Paul Cook and Geddes Douglas (for whom the SDB class's top medal is named), two men who lived just over 500 miles apart, in Indiana and Tennessee, respectively. The distance between these two men is worth noting because — quite possibly — it facilitated the magic that followed.

Regarded in his lifetime as an iris hybridizing genius, Cook's first notable contribution to the development of SDBs was his establishment of a stable race of *Iris pumila* from clones sent him by Bob Schreiner. His original intentions were not to completely transform the iris world, despite the ultimate result of his work; rather, Cook was after the bluest of the blue irises, wanting to sidestep lilac and lavender for azure and gentian.

The crosses that led to Cook's success weren't original to him. Earlier work by Schreiner and French cytologist Marc Simonet had yielded unworthy progeny that were reportedly discarded without further evaluation; these pioneers in ideas were most likely frustrated by a lack of quality tall bearded irises with good combining ability. Many TBs available at the turn of the century were diploids, making them difficult to cross with *Iris pumila* and other miniature dwarf species because of mismatches in chromosome numbers. Though crosses of this nature weren't completely impossible (the hybrids, if developed at all, were often infertile), the road to a dreamland of semi-dwarf irises must've seemed long and steep, from Schreiner's and Simonet's perspectives. I imagine the compost pile seemed a far easier alternative.

But Cook didn't let their experiences discourage his efforts — a reminder to all breeders that failure leaves as many opportunities as success. He placed pollen from two of his *Iris pumila* seedlings — a lemon yellow self numbered 343 and a blue bicolor — onto his TB seedling 10942, a light blue self. The results were a tide-turning surprise, though Cook didn't realize it at the time. Three SDBs were introduced from this cross in 1951 — 'Fairy Flax', a pale violet-blue self; 'Green Spot', the first iris with true green color on the falls; and 'Baria', a barium and citron-yellow bitone. 'Green Spot' became the type cultivar for standard dwarf beardeds, a class created by the newly formed Median Iris Society in the late 1950s. To this day, it remains a paragon of the class. 'Baria' was considered a color break of similar magnitude, delivering to the class a better, more vibrant yellow than previously available.

The next part of the story requires that 500-mile trip south to the garden of Geddes Douglas of Nashville. Given Tennessee's earlier bloom season, it was a simple matter for Douglas to mail TB pollen north to Cook, whose Indiana garden was two to three weeks behind in the flowering season, for crosses onto his stable line of *Iris pumila*. Similarly Cook could mail pollen from *I. pumila* south at the same time of year. Douglas applied the pollen to his TB seedlings in Tennessee, resulting in what he called "lilliputs," a moniker still encountered occasionally. The first of these came in 1953, the next generation of an iris family straddling the two states. Through the rest of the decade and into the 1960s, Douglas introduced two IBs and 17 more SDBs, earning his place in iris history as the co-founder of the SDB classification.

Since the days of Cook and Douglas, many notable irisarians have left their mark on SDBs. By virtue of their smaller size and durable multitude of flowers, SDBs stand up in adverse weather conditions about as well as any iris could. Making home just a foot or so off the ground, SDBs aren't visited with the troubles of loftier heights. Even through pelting spring rains and petal-shredding winds, SDBs weather the storm with grace and charm. If such a thing is possible, it would seem that this charm has been manufactured right into these flowers, courtesy of American breeders like Paul Black, Bennett Jones, Terry Aitken, Ben Hager, and Marky Smith. If you totaled up these fine folks' introductions, you'd have page after page of "must-have" lists. You'll see their names again in my favorites list ahead.

Worth Noting: Clump or Go Home

All this horticulturalizing resulted in a class of bearded irises worth boasting about. The first introductions grew well, multiplied in spades, remained healthy and overall disease-resistant, and maintained all the hardiness conferred upon them by their miniature dwarf parents. From the tall bearded side of the family came larger flowers with more substance, better and often flaring form, the tendency to branch and show off another bud or two, and a tent show of colors and patterns never before seen on irises so small.

The trends continue to this day: SDB flowers flare more, sport more buds, and are as colorfully entertaining as ever. Reblooming SDBs are more and more common as well.

These short and sassy perennials can take a sleepy May garden, still struggling to show off a few tulips and daffodils, to hip and happening with bold strokes of color. Their garden value stems from their performance en masse — a simple garden math equation where high bud count equates to more flowers in bloom over a longer stretch of time, which equals jaw-dropping floriferousness! Here's a bit of a gripe, though: from time to time, a few breeders have overlooked the balance between flowers and foliage. Nobody wants to have to dig through mounds of green leaves to find flowers to enjoy. You want to be able to stand on the patio, coffee cup in hand, and survey the garden, enjoying clouds of color hovering between bulbs and shrubs. Varieties with short, squatty stalks lower than the maximum height of the foliage deserve a home next to the compost and a stern scolding. Grow up and be seen!

Expert Pointers: SDBs in the Garden

Though I garden on a scale of acres in the country, I practice what I preach when it comes to median irises. I've boxed my yard up into little vignettes suitable for assembling intimate pairings of my favorite small plants. I'm also an unabashed lover of rocks and plants together (yes, I'm a rock gardener), and there's nothing smarter-looking than dwarf irises popping up between small, rounded boulders. If you're looking out the window at your garden and wondering where to put some standard dwarfs, let me give you some ideas.

Standard dwarf irises love an open sky and aren't quite as tolerant of shade as miniature dwarfs. Though a walk through my dry, shady backyard would reveal a few clumps of SDBs growing at shade's edge, I wouldn't recommend it if you've got other options.

The beauty of a standard dwarf iris is hardly singular — it's clump power or nothing — and in shade, that visual impact is lost when only a few stalks struggle up toward the light instead of many. Bottom line — give them light! Other than that, they're culturally a cinch. Treat them like any other bearded iris: plant in well-drained soil and shower them with love, though be patient if they don't overwhelm you the first year. That clump effect needs another growing season to really kick into high gear.

What else do you have planted in that frontyard border where SDBs belong? Daffodils and tulips? Check! Hyacinths and fritillaries? Check! All these spring-flowering bulbs time perfectly with the peak flush of color from standard dwarf irises. The combinations are endless, and at a time when so many gardens can look bleak and bare, why settle for just sprays of color here and there when you can have waves? One of my favorite spring vignettes in my own front garden is a mass of 'Spiderbaby' (Spoon 2005), a pinkish plicata that never disappoints, growing side by side with species tulip *Tulipa vvedenskyi* and a rambling, roving, run-you-over-when-you're-not-looking pink strawberry (*Fragaria vesca* 'Lipstick'). This swath of pink and red warms the garden and looks exceedingly romantic against tufts of sedges and just-emerging grasses nearby.

Like irises in general, standard dwarf irises let you pull colors into the garden palette that you might not find so commonly in other things. Take for instance another vignette in my own garden, put together this time by the cinnamon and chestnut blended SDB 'Flaming Embers' (Willott 2003) springing up around 'Apricot Jewel' tulips, variegated phlox (*P. glaberrima* 'Triple Play'), and the ever-present mountain bluet (*Centaurea montana*). What else at this stage of the gardening game could add such rich, potent cinnamon hues as this little standard dwarf? It's wild, catchy, and fun in one plant! You could probably guess that I don't like sleepy spring gardens. I'm ready to kick-start spring with color that shatters the memories of winter and rekindles those of summer. Spring is a time for gardens to come alive — a yearning that is always satisfied as I shuffle through the garden from clump to clump of standard dwarfs.

In contrast to their miniature cousins, SDBs throw up more than just one flower per stalk, usually at least two. With a little more room to throw off a branch, it's becoming more and more common to see SDBs with three to four or even more buds per stalk. Often you'll see two buds in the terminal position (the topmost flower on the stalk) and then another bud just below called a spur. But some SDBs that push the boundaries of the class have left iris lovers wondering whether the idea of a truly branched SDB is possible. Why not, right? More buds equals more flowers equals more show power. Some matters of taste enter in here I suppose, like whether the whole presentation becomes a sad bunch of half-seen flowers hidden among each other's petals, or whether the benefit of more flowers trumps any awkwardness of the flower placement. But maybe this is all a little esoteric. I'm all for more flowers. We can sort the rest out later.

Cultivars You Should Grow

With over 4,000 cultivars (like, holy cow!) listed by the AIS registry, where do I begin? Have no worries. I've managed to winnow the masses into my top most-beloved standard dwarfs, favored for their color, vigor, and reliability year in and year out.

'ABSOLUTE JOY' (TERRY AITKEN 2006)

What an absolute joy indeed to finally see a new twist on another of my listmakers, 'Pele': back in 1993, Terry Aitken really stirred up the SDB world with that introduction, and he's close to doing it again with this one. 'Absolute Joy' is a rising star for good reasons. Glistening pinkish orange with a purple fall spot, it blooms toward the end of the SDB run — a truly great closing act. Award of Merit 2010.

ABOVE: 'Absolute Joy' (Aitken 2006)

'BEING BUSY' (BEN HAGER 1993)

My great-grandmother often called me "Kelly doing, doing, doing" for my tendency as a child (and I suppose now) for always being busy. Imagine my elation when I found an SDB with busy colors to match my personality. A row of this in our production fields always looks photogenic, no matter the year. Like clockwork, it sounds off with yellow, maroon, and mauve patterned flowers at the peak of the SDB season. I'm always moving it around from spot to spot, tucking it in here and there among everything from shooting stars (*Primula*) and rock cress (*Arabis caucasica*) to creeping speedwell (*Veronica prostrata*) and Corbett columbine (*Aquilegia canadensis* 'Corbett'). Honorable Mention 1995.

ABOVE: 'Being Busy' (Hager 1993)

'BUTTONWOOD' (RICK TASCO 2005)

While I tend to get bored with plicata patterns, especially in taller cultivars, I adore them in the dwarf irises. 'Buttonwood' grows into a thick clump, sporting an annual flush of stems with three buds— in full bloom, it draws everything from smiles to (happy) tears. The dark garnet peppering on the flowers intensifies in cooler springs, making for a dizzying array of color against a strong cream-yellow ground. Like the best of the floriferous SDBs, clumps of 'Buttonwood' should be appreciated alongside paths or in the company of bright colored tulips, where their beauty shines to great advantage.

'CAT'S EYE' (PAUL BLACK 2002)

I used to joke that this was an 8:55 a.m. iris, which really had nothing to do with when or how it bloomed. Our nursery opens in the spring at 9:00 a.m., and the joke went that if you weren't there by 8:55, this thing would be sold out for sure! Few irises look as good in a clump as 'Cat's Eye', and few probably grow as rampantly and keep blooming just as reliably! Though not a true red, the heavily saturated red spot on the falls of 'Cat's Eye' is just plain seductive, no question about it. It's definitely on the desert island list, not only for its bold and raucous colors but because it grows into such a superior clump in the garden. Imagine it pairing it with red hens and chicks (*Sempervivum*) and a mat of *Sedum rupestre* 'Angelina' — a dynamic trio. Cook-Douglas Medal 2008.

7

TOP TO BOTTOM: 'Buttonwood' (Tasco 2005) 'Cat's Eye' (Black 2002)

'CHANTED' (BARRY BLYTH 1990–91)

I find that pink flowers either get gobbled up like a teddy bear special at Christmas or left to collect dust on the shelves like those pre-packaged sets of men's cologne. It's love-hate for most. I happen to love pink, so long as it's pink, mind you. Too often in the iris world, we settle for sullen pinks, with more hints of cocoa than rouge. When I say pink, I want pink. And fortunately, 'Chanted' gets pink right. It also sports blue beards, a combination long lusted for by breeders and unimaginatively dubbed "blue-bearded pinks." Prosaic monikers aside, I appreciate 'Chanted' not just for its good color but for its ability to thrive. Hybridizers and pollen daubers take note — this Aussie-bred iris has made a name for itself as a parent, as evidenced by over 150 registered descendants in the American Iris Society registry.

'CHOCOLATE SWIRL' (RICK TASCO 1999)

Ever in search of irises that look good enough to eat, I planted 'Chocolate Swirl' with the greedy ambitions of a confection-loving gardener. Swirled like the best fudges, a clump of this is reminiscent of a vat in a candy factory (a vivid memory of mine from a childhood tour through a chocolaterie). Chocolate brown flowers, though, come with a caveat — depending on the color of your soil, they can too easily get lost against the backdrop of their substrate (bark mulch, of course, doesn't help). To avoid this, plant them in striking companionship with other plants that offset their richly imbued colors — yellows, whites, oranges. Honorable Mention 2001.

TOP TO BOTTOM: 'Chanted' (Barry Blyth 1990–91)

'Chocolate Swirl' (Tasco 1999)

'CHUBBY CHEEKS' (PAUL BLACK 1985)

No list of "must-haves" in this class would be complete without mention of 'Chubby Cheeks', quite possibly the most influential SDB, legacy-wise, of all time. With over 200 registered descendants, 'Chubby Cheeks' gives rise to kickass SDBs, not to put too fine a point on it. Spelling out its virtues is like a vocab list for what makes a great iris — form, substance, vigor, and ruffling. As its apt name suggests, 'Chubby Cheeks' features some of the cutest, rounded flowers you could imagine, a trait that it passes on generously to its children. Though some purists may balk at fatter flowers across all the classes, I say go for it. To be purely analytical, more surface area on a flower equals more color and a better opportunity to experience color. In bearded irises, form begets function. Cook-Douglas Medal 1991.

ABOVE: 'Chubby Cheeks' (Black 1985)

'CONEY ISLAND' (KEITH KEPPEL 2005)

Though I'm no fan of mustard on my hot dog, I'll gladly recommend 'Coney Island'. The mustard of these flowers results from a chic blend of chrome, lime, and quince yellow, guilded into Art Deco bands around chubby, well-formed flowers. I love that brown beard too, which is an excellent example of monochromatic contrast. Despite our tendency to desire beards of opposite, alarming colors, sometimes all it takes is a little intensification of the pigment to make it special. Honorable Mention 2007.

'DEATH BY CHOCOLATE' (AUGUSTO BIANCO 2002)

Dieters have no fear, you're permitted to indulge yourselves with this little garden morsel. With flowers lacquered in rich milk chocolate, coffee, and chamois, it's probably no surprise that the flowers smell like chocolate mocha, too. Hailing from the garden of Italian iris breeder *straordinario* Augusto Bianco, this brown iris does anything but blend in to the ground below. Wouldn't it be fun to throw a chocolate-themed garden party and give everyone one of these as a gift?

ABOVE, LEFT TO RIGHT: 'Coney Island' (Keppel 2005)

'Death by Chocolate' (Bianco 2002)

'DEVIL BABY' (KEITH KEPPEL 2005)

'Devil Baby' features chubby flowers with excellent form (almost as if sized down from a tall bearded and plopped onto shorter stems) and dark wine black color that'll have every passerby stopping for a closer look. While I love black and chocolate flowers for their rock star colors (seriously, black and brown are not the norm), they often need a little contrast to make them pop. And really, what doesn't look good with black? I've experimented with bulbs, groundcovers, and early bedding plants like pansies and violas. But like every good gardener with iris fever, I went back to basics, so to speak, and put a clump of 'Devil Baby' in between clumps of the white SDB 'Invisible' (Black 2004). Tuxedo gardening, anyone? Award of Merit 2009.

7

ABOVE: 'Devil Baby' (Keppel 2005)

'ENCHANTED MOCHA'
(BARBARA AND DAVID SCHMIEDER 2002)

This unusual dwarf iris really set my head spinning when I first encountered it. Imagine lightly ruffled, perky petals draped in coffee pink with little whitish beards tipped tangerine. I suppose a list of combinations would run on endlessly — with such subtle but commanding colors, it would go well with yellows, pinks, and oranges, but also creams and whites. A deliciosity for the eyes and best enjoyed with a cup of morning brew. Honorable Mention 2004.

ABOVE: 'Enchanted Mocha' (Schmieder 2002)

'EYE OF SAURON' (PAUL BLACK 2009)

If you're a fan of *Lord of the Rings* and the fantastical world of the Shire, you'll need to grow this one just because. If you're a fan of ethereally striking flowers that call from across the garden, you'll have to grow this one because you need it. In a shameless reference to an old Mike Myers sketch on *Saturday Night Live*, it's all about the eye here. Pale violet-blue falls are emblazoned with a dark charcoal plum eye — in a word, bold! This variety is already earning rave reviews around the country for its distinctiveness and admirable growth habits. Breeders take note — the seedlings this thing throws are dazzling! Honorable Mention 2011.

'EYE OF THE TIGER' (PAUL BLACK 2008)

Purple prose warning: I could cloy on for hours about this one little iris. It's absolutely crazy! Nothing out there comes remotely close to glistening like 'Eye of the Tiger', and it's at the top of the dwarf iris section of my desert island list. Introduced in 2008, this new kid on the block is bound to make some waves. Why not grab it up and make sure it's shaking things up in your gardening neighborhood? Just in case you were wondering — of course it's a good grower. Honorable Mention 2010.

TOP TO BOTTOM: 'Eye of Sauron' (Black 2009) 'Eye of the Tiger' (Black 2008)

'GIGGLES AND GRINS' (CAROL COLEMAN 2006)

My friend Carol Coleman of Boise, Idaho, has introduced several great-growing, colorful irises. But my all-time favorite of her kids is 'Giggles and Grins' because it sparkles with distinction like few irises do. Pardon my micro-rant, but distinctive irises really are the crème de la crème for modern gardeners. With thousands of varieties on the market, who needs more of the same old colors and patterns, blah, blah, blah, ad nauseum? This one's different. The flowers defy description beyond saying bicolor with an artistic twist. A bright star in the world of fab dwarfs. Honorable Mention 2011.

'HELMSMAN' (MARKY SMITH 2002)

A plicata of Spanish orange and peach. Olé! If you need some orange to fill in and make a statement, 'Helmsman' is a great iris for the job. In my mind, I imagine a carpet of this under 'Fine Wine' or another of the many dark-leaved weigelas on the market. That veil of dramatic, blackcurrant foliage hovering over a swath of sparkling citrus makes my mouth water. Be daring in your combinations — it's your garden. Plant a statement that's quintessentially you! Honorable Mention 2004.

ABOVE, LEFT TO RIGHT: 'Giggles and Grins' (Coleman 2006)

'Helmsman' (Smith 2002)

'HONEYLOVE' (JIM AND VICKI CRAIG 2004)

I'm a sucker for brown (and black) flowers. Hunt me up some cinnamon and brown sugar, toss in some ruffling, and I'm there. 'Honeylove' grabs my attention and sets my taste buds a-watering every time I take a stroll around the garden. And it grows with a vengeance, ensuring you'll have plenty to share with your iris-loving friends. Lightly ruffled and flaring flowers show off brown stippling on yellow ground. Lean in for a sniff, and you'll catch a faint sweetness. Life should have more moments like this.

ABOVE: 'Honeylove' (Craig 2004)

'JIVE' (KEITH KEPPEL 2002)

I'm a sucker for orange. In the SDBs, it's easily come by, fortunately, and with irises like 'Jive' in the garden, gardeners can't help but want even more. As with many of Keith's SDBs, the clumps form fast and flower abundantly. Parades of orange flowers last for weeks — I'm always counting a stray bud or two opening long after the rest of the clump has finished, as if saying, "Just one more bloom, please!" Orange does something for me in spring that yellow doesn't. While I adore yellow, and yellow dwarf irises (and thermopsis and daffodils and . . .), orange adds a little extra zest to my life. For many years I grew a clump of 'Jive' in the vicinity of a crabapple tree, and there was nothing prettier for a day or two than falling fuchsia-blushed crabapple blossoms gracing the petals and nearby ground of this prize-worthy dwarf iris. Serendipity indeed. Honorable Mention 2004.

'IT AIN'T ME BABE' (LOWELL BAUMUNK 2007)

Another iris that I fell in love with instantly. A plicata hailing from such great irises as 'Rebus' (Gatty/Keppel 1996) and 'Chubby Cheeks' (Black 1985), lavender-flowered 'It Ain't Me Babe' does what all good SDBs should — forms vigorous, floriferous clumps in just a few seasons. I look forward to its thriving array of well-budded stems each spring in the company of *Veronica gentianoides* and a few reseeded sedges (*Carex*). Though the color itself isn't bold or distinctive, the overall effect, accentuated by bright orange beards, definitely is. A winner from the word go; and yes, it is the one you want.

ABOVE, LEFT TO RIGHT: 'It Ain't Me Babe' (Baumunk 2007)

'Jive' (Keppel 2002)

7

'PELE' (TERRY AITKEN 1993)

A must-have iris, no ifs, ands, or buts. Named for the Hawaiian goddess of volcanoes, this explosively colorful iris stops traffic — literally. A clump of this in front of my rock garden along the driveway at Rainbow Iris Farm frequently catches the eye of gardeners parking their cars, who of course see no harm in stopping in the middle of the road to step out for a peek. Avoid planting streetside unless you have good insurance. Cook-Douglas Medal 1999.

ABOVE: 'Pele' (Aitken 1993)

'RASPBERRY TIGER' (PAUL BLACK 2009)

Okay, here are your instructions. Stop reading, go buy one of these, resume reading, and then next spring rush out and stare intently at each flower. See the black veins? They're *awesome* and crazy cool. What could the future hold for SDBs with this parent in their blood? Black veins on white flowers? Black flowers with orange beards? I can't help but think of food-related names for all the possible results, so naturally I'm craving them. 'Raspberry Tiger' is a magnificent new dwarf iris that will surely earn a reputation as a top-award winner. The color, the clumps, the distinctiveness. It's almost too much for words, even for a hyperbolic iris lover. Honorable Mention 2011.

ABOVE: 'Raspberry Tiger' (Black 2009)

'ROSALIE LOVING' (DON SPOON 2003)

Don Spoon's excellent eye for color is apparent in this wonderfully fluorescent SDB, named for a prominent iris lover in the Mid-Atlantic region. 'Rosalie Loving' nearly glows, thanks to neon yellow haft marks that fade into a reddish fall spot. It's a slower grower for us in Iowa, but never fails to reward us each spring with several shimmering flowers. In milder climates, expect some rebloom. Honorable Mention 2006.

'RUBY ERUPTION' (CHUCK CHAPMAN 1997)

How can you not be curious about the wow factor of a plant called 'Ruby Eruption'? With a name like that, it's got to be red hot, and it is. The petals have a bright yellow ground heavily stained and marked in wild-and-crazy ruby lines. Holla! Truly, I've never even thought about what to plant this with. I just give it a corner to itself and let it do its thing. A fabulous vernal reminder of the power of the rainbow. Cook-Douglas Medal 2006.

TOP TO BOTTOM: 'Rosalie Loving' (Spoon 2003)
'Ruby Eruption' (Chapman 1997)

7

'SAWTOOTH SUNRISE'
(CAROL COLEMAN 2009)

My friend Carol Coleman from Idaho has bred some tremendously colorful SDBs, including this honey and gold plicata. Ruffled and perky, these flowers grace the tops of healthy clumps that increase well from year to year. As with many plicata-patterned irises, temperature affects the intensity of the pigmentation, so expect some variation in the stippling from year to year. Lightly ruffled and sweetly fragrant, there's much to love about this plant. While I've never seen a sunrise in the Sawtooths, I can only imagine this iris rivals it for beauty.

ABOVE: 'Sawtooth Sunrise' (Coleman 2009)

'SPIDERBABY' (DON SPOON 2005)

I just love this iris. I've grown it for many years and can't think of a single fault other than I never have enough of it (I'm greedy for color). My gushing emotions aside, it does have a tendency to flower a little close to the top of the foliage, but this is hardly a major demerit considering its excellent growth, delightful flowers, and reliable performance year after year. Some SDBs have generously colored flowers, but they show up only every few years. Rubbish. Plant something that thrives, and enjoy 'Spiderbaby' along a garden path for regular, daily viewing in the middle of spring. Honorable Mention 2007.

ABOVE: 'Spiderbaby' (Spoon 2005)

'TRUE NAVY' (BENNETT JONES 2001)

Remember Paul Cook and his quest for the bluest of the blue? He'd be mighty proud of Bennett Jones's 'True Navy', I suspect. Let this gentian beauty run rampant among white things, and you're in for a real visual treat. Or place a perfect specimen atop a pedestal and watch your neighbors weep. Award of Merit 2006.

'VAVOOM' (ALLAN ENSMINGER 1994)

Whoosh! The color explodes from this plant like nothing else. Aptly named and introduced by Allan Ensminger of Lincoln, Nebraska, who was known to fellow irisarians as the "Wizard of Odds" for his ability to concoct unthinkable and amazing irises, 'Vavoom' adds energy to the garden scene in the early days of spring. Those uranium green standards and neon canary falls look riveting surrounded by dark purple irises and grape hyacinths, or simply en masse, by themselves. Despite my innate tendency to pair wines with cheese or ties with dress shirts or plants with other plants, some beg to sing solo. 'Vavoom' may just be an iris in that mold — give it space to be the diva. Cook-Douglas Medal 2000.

ABOVE, LEFT TO RIGHT: 'True Navy' (Jones 2001)

'Vavoom' (Ensminger 1994)

CLOCKWISE FROM TOP LEFT: 'Amber Eyes' (Morris 2007)

'Cuore' (Bianco 2002)

'Clash' (Black 2003)

Gallery

ABOVE: 'Circus Dragon' (Jones 2002)

ABOVE: 'Flirting Again' (Aitken 2002)

ABOVE, LEFT TO RIGHT: 'Flower Child' (Byers 1989)

'Gaily Forward' (Dyer 1999)

ABOVE: 'Pugzilla'
(Kasperek 2010)

ABOVE: 'Grass Girl'
(Coleman 2008)

TOP TO BOTTOM: 'Tickety Boo' (Niswonger 2001)

'Shout' (Willott 2002)

ABOVE: 'What Again'
(Ensminger 1991)

8 Intermediate Bearded Irises

"The intermediates, easily grown, free-flowering and wind resistant, are gaining popularity all the time and rightly so."

Robert L. Jensen,
***Bulletin of the American Iris Society 285* (1992)**

I'll be frank — the thought of a well-grown, full-blossomed clump of intermediate bearded (IB) irises makes me swoon with iris love. Sure I've spoken glowingly and flatteringly of the two classes before this, but midway through the spring bloom season, I'm ready for the IBs to whisk me off my feet (just don't tell the dwarfs). For the plant lover who tracks spring by the calendar of the garden, the halfway mark of bearded iris season looks just as good as the beginning and the end but grows somewhere in the middle with regard to height.

Among the first bearded irises in my childhood garden was the IB 'Ask Alma' (Lankow 1987). This mid-size peach thing looked like a sized-down version of a taller peach thing I already grew. The sized-down part was cool. It wasn't miniature, because it hit me about hip high, but it certainly wasn't tall either. That just-so proportion earned it a proud spot in the border on the east side of our house, among orange double Oriental poppies (*Papaver orientale*) and other favorite irises like stormcloud blue 'Honky Tonk Blues' (Schreiner 1988) and prairie golden 'Ola Kala' (Sass 1942). It persisted for a few years before I neglected it (I ditched it for more amorous varieties, no doubt), and it eventually stopped flowering. A few years later when digging out the bed in late summer, I came across a cracked and faded tag alongside a withering rhizome — the Ask was gone but Alma was still there.

The IBs are the rising stars on the bearded iris stage — the proverbial "irises of the future" — because they look so fine and grow so well. We may yearn for estate gardens, but the fact is that most gardeners tend parcels smaller than an acre in size. In these urban and suburban gardens, the scale of the landscape is defined almost by default. Large plants, not including tress (of which there are often many), have a minimal role, while understory shrubs, perennials, and groundcovers fill out the rest of the yard. And choosing plants is challenging, with sunny exposures often limited by towering trees or the looming shade of houses or buildings. Even in the wide-open country where I make my garden, sunny exposures come with a caveat — if they're exposed to the sun, they're also open to rhizome-desiccating winter winds.

"Fenced in" or not, we manage to make beautiful gardens, so long as all the plants we choose to grow and tend in our landscapes, irises included, fit the context. An iris lover gardening on a tiny urban lot with one patch of sun probably can't grow dozens of blowsy tall beardeds, which tend to pounce impolitely on anything in their vicinity. They're big — duh. Fortunately for that iris lover, and anyone with limited gardening space, median irises make perfect choices for that sunny spot. Here at the crossroads of bearded iris genetics grow the IBs. Essentially, they're perfect. Boasting vibrant and varying color swatches, IBs look most often like smaller versions of their tall bearded ancestors. With pleasing proportions, often light ruffling, and rounded form, they're perfect for any gardener on a "tall bearded–lite" diet.

Origins: Covering the Middle Ground

The story of the intermediates is almost inseparable from that of the SDBs. In fact, the earliest IBs were sometimes registered as dwarfs, since the SDB designation wouldn't come along until later. Paul Cook's 'Baria', 'Fairy Flax', and 'Green Spot' were originally registered as IBs, not fitting particularly well into any category that existed at the time of their creation; they later became SDBs under the new classification system adopted by the Median Iris Society.

While the story of the modern IB starts with the love children of talls and smalls, the story of the class begins with the familiar *Iris germanica* (German flag). Pioneers of the American frontier are said to have toted them west as a reminder of eastern colonial gardens — the fairest of the fair in the gardens of an intimidating new land. Amble down a muddy road in mid-spring, and you're liable to come across naturalized patches of *I. germanica* waving purple and lavender flowers in such forlorn places as ditches and alongside dilapidated houses. Bright-eyed iris lovers interpret their persistence as resiliency. For anyone looking to dig out the ditch or tear down the house, they're probably just a weedy nuisance.

Most iris lovers with more than a few years' experience have cast *Iris germanica* as nongermane to the modern garden. So untrue! Though they may be far less dandy than the latest import from Australia, their simple presence reminds iris lovers just how far our favorite flower has come. Forms of *I. germanica* are still common throughout European gardens and are naturalized across North America (many of them, indeed, in the gardens of those of us who just can't bear to condemn them to compost). They have names like 'Nepalensis', 'Florentina', and 'Kharput'. Relations to *I. germanica* worth growing include *I. kochii* (which forms a stately clump and tolerates part shade) and *I. marsica*, an Italian endemic, first described from the Abruzzi National Park, east of Rome.

The story of *Iris germanica* is a little funny — despite Linnaeus's circumscription of the species in 1753, it's never been known to occur in the wild. Most taxonomists agree that what has long been referred to as the species *I. germanica* is in fact a loose collection of hybrids, which easily accounts for the diversity seen from one garden or wild clump to the next. Its sterility supports the hybrid hypothesis; its rampant vigor seconds the motion. Noted botanist Brian Mathew has written of apparent cultivars of this "species" naturalized in the wild in Turkey. How sterile hybrids come to vary and spread so widely has puzzled botanists for a long time. The flowers typically theme and vary around purple standards and falls with white or yellow beards. At any rate *I. germanica* bequeathed little to modern IBs, save its general appearance and size. By nature many forms are intermediate, with flowering stems never reaching more than 18 to 24 inches high, right smack in the middle of a crowded room of tall beardeds and dwarfs. It was that middle, median look that became the yardstick used to classify modern bearded irises.

Confusion over plant names and origins aside, if there's one human name to know when thinking about intermediate irises, it's Sass. Immigrants from Germany in the late 1880s, brothers Hans and Jacob Sass settled with their family on a farm in eastern Nebraska. Hans, the oldest at 16, had received some early training in botany and took a liking to irises, daylilies, and peonies, among other perennials. The humble Sass brothers, through their own individual efforts, would come to create some of the hardiest and most floriferous bearded iris varieties of the first half of the 1900s — each brother won two Dykes Medals; Hans in 1932 ('Rameses') and 1943 ('Prairie Sunset') and Jacob in 1941 ('The Red Douglas') and 1948 ('Ola Kala'). These varieties, built on the hardiness genes inherent to species like *Iris trojana* and *I. variegata*, proved supremely well adapted to the Midwest and are popular even today, thanks to the preservation efforts of devoted collectors. A nearly complete collection of their introductions grows at Mahoney State Park between Lincoln and Omaha.

The Sass brothers began their breeding work with IBs by crossing dwarf species from Europe with then-modern TBs. At the time these "dwarf species" circulated erroneously as *Iris pumila* (the true *I. pumila* wouldn't reach American shores until Bob Schreiner imported several clones in the late 1930s); most likely they were *I. lutescens* or other species in the chamaeiris complex. What with the difficulties of fertility and mediocre progeny, the Sasses had to grow a lot of seedlings to ensure their success — a game of odds. But through careful interbreeding and selection, they turned out some excellent dwarfs that founded their line of IBs to come.

Both brothers had an early intuition about the garden value of intermediates, particularly in the temperamental Midwest (their condensed proportions make them superbly windproof). But IBs aren't just intermediate in height. Blooming between the dwarfs and the tall beardeds, they fill an important gap in the spring flowering season, an absence hardly imaginable in today's iris-filled garden. The Sass brothers knew this, too. They introduced some of the first reliable rebloomers, which happened to be IBs, including the ever-popular 'Eleanor Roosevelt' (Sass-McDade 1933) and 'Autumn Queen'

(Sass 1926). The Sass brothers' early breeding work with intermediates, which yielded 18 introductions, earned them lasting fame — the highest award for IBs is the Hans and Jacob Sass Medal.

On the down side, the genetics of intermediates have caused a lot of grief. For decades IBs were considered mules — the resulting 44-chromosome arrangement just didn't want to pair up nicely with anything else during recombination. Many IBs were and continue to be derived from second-generation crosses and backcrosses of shorter plants with taller irises. In the last decade, thanks to the persistent efforts of breeders like Jim and Vicki Craig and Paul Black, fertility barriers have begun to fall as more *Iris aphylla* genes make their way into the median iris stock. Modern hybridizers should know the gamble before they begin, but with such a class — destined for greater appreciation and use — they would be wise to give IBs a serious, entrepreneurial look.

Worth Noting: At the Crossroads

If I drew a map of all the ways in which bearded irises have evolved at the hands of careful hybridizers armed with camel hair brushes, I probably would confuse us both. But the common station through which many of those trails have passed is the IB class. IBs have played an important role as a color conduit between the smalls and talls of the bearded iris spectrum. For decades, breeders longed for pinker SDBs; IBs came to the rescue, allowing hybridizers to move genes for pink flowers from TBs through the IBs and eventually to the dwarfs. The highway runs in the other direction, too. The eye-popping spot patterns known only in the dwarfs have climbed the scale of bearded irises to finally begin showing up in the BBs and TBs, thanks to crosses with IBs.

The IB class is home to a motley crew of bearded irises of mixed parentage, a horticultural melting pot that will likely boil over in the coming years as the iris world finds new ways to organize its rich diversity — good news for gardeners who always need more. Until then, its diversity of flower shape and size runs the gamut, from the classic look of Ben Hager's 'Cheers' (1975) to the round, flaring form of 'Tantrum' (Keppel 1997). Some shorter cultivars look like standards dwarfs; some in the middle look airier and freer, like MTBs; and some at the larger end of the scale are virtually indistinguishable from BBs (and these are increasingly common). The attitude of most iris lovers who love beautiful flowers — the more the merrier. Tolerance is a wonderful thing in the garden.

Expert Pointers: IBs in the Garden

If I run into a gardener frustrated with growing irises, chances are my magic solution involves an IB. My taste for these halflings grew about as quickly as many of them did in the garden. I began to realize that their size wasn't just contributing to their cute factor — it clearly allowed them to stand tall through violent spring thunderstorms, or warm blustery days in mid-May. I can only imagine how many irisarians, from the Sass brothers through to the present, have had a similar epiphany. The obvious durability of IBs has earned them major brownie points. They work hard in the garden view because at an average of only 20 inches tall, they don't take up a ton of space, still give off the same colorful ambience and floral glam of their taller cousins, and thrive with ease. I grow many IBs in the company of columbines (*Aquilegia*), whose jester-like flowers fluttering in air always look comedic and entertaining. Lady's mantles (*Alchemilla mollis* or *A. alpina*) also look suave, cloaking the spreading fans at ground level in soft or shiny foliage and yellow-green flowers.

When selecting IBs for your garden, give some attention to how the flowers look on the stalks. If you look at a clump of IBs straight on, do you see several flowers held in a pleasing arrangement or a mosh pit of color so busy that your eyes demand their union break? The flowers on IBs should sit high above the foliage with enough space to appreciate them all. This isn't just some detailed law of minutiae — if I had a dime for every time some gardener complained about an iris with bunchy stalks that got so heavy it broke or fell over, I'd be rich (and reveling in schadenfreude). Nobody has time for varieties that send up only a few stalks or even several weak stalks that end up falling onto each other in a grand mess. IBs should have sturdy stems, preserving the durability of their TB ancestry in concert with overall smallness from the SDB side of the family. They should be the best middle child you could ever hope for.

IBs look handsome in arrangements, but they're a second to the miniature tall beardeds, which bloom at approximately the same time. Though they lack the flexuous stalks of the MTBs, their stems work well as features in small to mid-size arrangements. Many old-fashioned IBs like 'Eleanor Roosevelt' boast a tremendous (verging on overpowering) sweet fragrance. *Iris germanica* has a similar reputation; most questions about a certain purple iris that smells like grape soda trace back to one of these old-fashioned purples.

Though not an absolute, IBs often boast a type of hybrid vigor, particularly if born of strong parents, that breeders have wielded to advantage. This trailblazing quality might require you to divide them more often, but it's a trade-off I hope you'll deal with. Their abundance ensures a steady supply for your garden club's plant sale or plenty to share with friends. Take care to site IBs in plenty of sun, though a little afternoon shade won't hinder their success if your landscape has large trees like mine. IBs, for whatever reason, don't seem as prone to rot diseases as their taller cousins — in overly wet years, this becomes a moot point of course.

Some varieties also send up a series of stalks over the course of a few weeks, overlapping the SDBs, border beardeds and tall beardeds with copious sprays of flowers. Profuse flowering habits are a definite plus in this section, which has something to do with their size. Think about going to a bakery and sampling your favorite chocolate chip cookies — when they're small, it's easy to eat a dozen. Roll them out into decadent patties of dough, and the stomach starts to whine after just one or two. The same principle applies to median irises, and particularly IBs. The same space might be easy to fill with a tall bearded variety that would send up fewer, larger flowers on larger stalks. But plant an IB and suddenly you crave more flowers. An established clump of IBs should boast many, showy flowers and dazzle the senses when in bloom. If I haven't made the point already — any garden, short on space or not, needs to grow a few IBs.

Cultivars You Should Grow

It wasn't quite as difficult to jot down a list of favorites for this class, maybe because I love IBs so much that I've developed extra-rigid criteria for picking winners. I don't know for sure. But I chose each member of this short list based on all the factors outlined earlier — a bumper crop of flowers, strong stalks, and superb growth habits, all inherent virtues of the very best IBs. I really do believe that more and more of these irises will hit the market in the years ahead, and that's great because our gardens need them!

'ABBEY CHANT' (GEORGE SUTTON 1998)

There are so many things to love about this IB — I'll try to keep it succinct. First off the flowers, namely the beard. That blue spot against a bright patch of yellow and white makes a smart complementary spark. It always boasts nice stalks for cutting, too, and the musky fragrance smells great from a vase (or so I'm told). Finally, its vigor. It grows and grows, even in less-than-ideal soils and never fails to shower on the flowers each spring. A well-rounded, top-performing IB should command attention on account of its karma — flowers en masse at just the right height and in balance with the whole plant. Done and done. Possible rebloomer, but likely only in milder climates (read: central and southern California, its homeland).

ABOVE: 'Abbey Chant' (Sutton 1998)

'BLUE EYED BLOND'
(ALLAN ENSMINGER 1989)

What's a garden without a blue-eyed blond? She's a showgirl too. Vixenish clumps of yellow flowers sporting blue beards awake the senses on cloudy days in spring — virtually a bouquet planted in the garden. I consider this a garden staple, easily moved around to fill in here or there, wherever some amount of strong color and good growth is needed to make a statement. Hans and Jacob Sass Medal 1995.

ABOVE: 'Blue Eyed Blond' (Ensminger 1989)

'CALLIGRAPHER' (MARKY SMITH 2007)

8

If you need to write a new storyline into your garden "novel," a diva plant is never a bad idea. Diva plants own the moment, just as Bernadette Peters does in a Broadway show. When the spotlight's on, they've got it. One of my favorite diva irises of recent vintage, 'Calligrapher' is grounded with cream tinted by chartreuse; bands of smoky red and violet encircle tightly proportioned flowers and offset orange beards. Hints of spice perfume the air, especially from a mass of flowers. Good-growing, smart-looking, and destined for fame. Honorable Mention 2009.

ABOVE: 'Calligrapher' (Smith 2007)

'CINNAMON FLASH' (TERRY AITKEN 1999)

I'm a fan of the overlooked and underappreciated, irises or otherwise. I'm a particular fan of this apparently forgotten IB of Terry Aitken's that sports one of my favorite colors — cinnamon — in both flower and name. Always multiplying and a reliable bloomer, garden visitors always stop for a second look at this remarkable bicolor. As I've said before, brown as a color is all too rare in flowers, and when it happens with such artistry, it makes a gardener smile. A rebloomer out of 'Champagne Elegance' (Niswonger 1987).

'DAZZLING' (PAUL BLACK 2008)

An IB of extraordinary pedigree, there's not much more to say than what the cultivar name says already. Reminiscent of British breeder Cy Bartlett's 'American Patriot' (1997), white-capped flowers float above a sea of lustrous blue, rimmed white and accented with an orange-tipped white beard. A clump in the garden looks like an armful spilled in mid-border, a colorful serendipity that happens reliably each spring. Here's one instance where I'd prefer monochromatic plant combinations — the sheer purity of colors warrants subtle companions, something simple and old-fashioned like money plant (*Lunaria*) or white columbines (*Aquilegia*). Honorable Mention 2010.

TOP TO BOTTOM: 'Cinnamon Flash' (Aitken 1999) 'Dazzling' (Black 2008)

'ELEANOR ROOSEVELT'
(SASS-MCDADE 1933)

Some of you may sneer at my inclusion of "just another old purple iris." But this iris holds a special place in my heart for its indefatigable performance year after year. Plus, if you have a nose for great iris scents, you'll love catching a whiff of this flower's rich, grapey odor. It carries on the air, too — our production beds fill the air with plumes of fragrance that waft the half-mile up the road to our neighbors, who seem to always know when iris season begins! Earlier flowering than other intermediates, 'Eleanor Roosevelt' would grow in concrete, and thus lends itself to cultivation by iris beginners who for whatever reason may struggle to get their first clumps going.

ABOVE: 'Eleanor Roosevelt' (Sass-McDade 1933) — and Sadie Jane

'FAST FORWARD' (TERRY AITKEN 2002)

I can't say enough good things about this reblooming intermediate. Though it possesses some colorfully thematic similarities to its pod parent 'What Again' (Ensminger 1991), it pulls off distinction like few other modern irises can, sending up a flurry of stalks each spring and usually like clockwork again in summer, often just after the Fourth of July holiday. I joke that the fireworks of these flowers usually last all of five minutes in my Iowa garden, melting out under oppressive humidity. But it gets points for trying! You'll never have to worry about running out of this one — its vigor is impressive. If you're feeling generous, it's a great passalong iris for neighbors, or donate the extras to your local iris club for their sale. Honorable Mention 2006.

ABOVE: 'Fast Forward' (Aitken 2002)

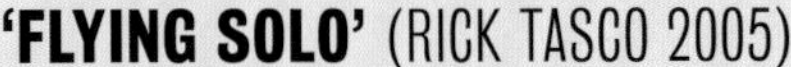

'FLYING SOLO' (RICK TASCO 2005)

I may be fond of this primarily because it's made such a huge clump right off the patio. I see it every day it's in bloom and watch over it the rest of the season, when the show has shifted to the heleniums, daylilies, and coneflowers in its vicinity. It gets a little extra attention in the fall and a little more sprucing up in spring. It's growing alongside the nerve center of the garden — it has to look its best. Annually, this space-ager does just that, sporting clean soft pink flowers with tiny little horns that take off from the ends of rusty tangerine beards. A great cut flower in a pinch, and plentiful enough after a few years to share with any neighbor who needs a congenial patio companion.

'GENE'S LORA LAVELLE' (KELLY NORRIS 2009)

Given my love affair with the class, it's no surprise that my very first introduction was this IB. Sure I'm a little biased, but nature pulled a rabbit out of the genetic hat when I made a cross, back in 2003, between 'Tantrum' (Keppel 1997), a red and mustard plicata IB, and 'Blatant' (Byers 1990), a reblooming TB of similar colors. Of the eight seeds I collected (crosses involving intermediates are notorious for low seed counts due to fertility and chromosome arrangement issues), three germinated. Two of those seedlings survived to transplant, and this, the one that survived to flowering, was eventually named 'Gene's Lora Lavelle', after devoted patron Louis Garr's parents. Glowing dramatically from 30 feet away, this iris puts the "stun" back in "stunning." I only wish it had a few more buds, but a nice healthy clump more than compensates with extra stalks.

ABOVE, LEFT TO RIGHT: 'Flying Solo' (Tasco 2005) 'Gene's Lora Lavelle' (Norris 2009)

'GNU RAYZ' (KASPEREK 1997)

Flaunting a dizzying array of lines and dots, 'Gnu Rayz' knows how to entertain the senses. It's also one of the most vigorous IBs I've ever grown, forming a hulking clump in just a season or two. Because it produces so many plants each with so many flower stalks, you are guaranteed a full-on spring show that lasts for over two weeks. If I had to recommend just one modern IB that knows how to grow, this would be it. Hans and Jacob Sass Medal 2004.

'GOLDEN MUFFIN' (O. DAVID NISWONGER 1986)

An aptly named, comfort food sort of bearded iris. You know when you're feeling blue and just crave a bakery fresh treat (or a giant bowl of mashed potatoes)? 'Golden Muffin' answers that call, when you urgently need a plant to make a new border or garden seem like home. I've grown this honey bicolored IB since I was a kid, and while I admit I don't pay it enough attention every spring, I'd definitely notice its absence. It's at home wherever I grow it, always flowers, and goes well with just about any other iris or perennial I put next to it. Award of Merit 1990.

ABOVE, LEFT TO RIGHT: 'Gnu Rayz' (Kasperek 1997)

'Golden Muffin' (Niswonger 1986)

'JOHN' (ALLAN ENSMINGER 1990)

I don't know who the "Wizard of Odds" was honoring with this name, but this iris is far from any old regular Joe that might live next door. It's decorated in the strangest of color combos: chocolate brown standards hover over straw yellow falls, a pairing that tantalizes the senses. Chocolate break, anyone? Plus it flowers and flowers, growing into handsome clumps (a compliment to its namesake, no doubt) that repeat their performance spring after spring. If you're looking for different, be sure to pick some up. Award of Merit 1994.

ABOVE: 'John' (Ensminger 1990)

'MAN'S BEST FRIEND'
(PAUL BLACK 2008)

Here's an iris you'll either love or hate. If you don't dig brown, just skip over. In the Midwest, I enjoy rich, saturated flower color, a dapper duo of chestnut and violet-gray, much like breeder Paul Black does in the Pacific Northwest; in the South, the flowers come off mellower, some say to the point of washing out. But whatever the climate, the floriferousness of a clump of this IB is admirable to say the least. I love a gorgeous flower just as much as the next iris lover, but if it's *that* gorgeous, I want lots and lots of them. Maybe I'm just impatient or have high expectations, but you can never have too much of a beautiful thing. Honorable Mention 2010.

ABOVE: 'Man's Best Friend' (Black 2008)

'MANY MAHALOS' (TERRY AITKEN 2003)

The IB class was long bereft of good oranges it seems, until 'Many Mahalos' came along — for which we give it many thanks! Offering the possibility of rebloom in milder climates, this well-branched, heavily budded IB is vaguely reminiscent of an outsized MTB in form, but that shouldn't be perceived as a negative. An excellent show stalk if you're planning to make a run at the top prize at the flower show this year. Award of Merit 2010.

'MARIPOSA WIZARD' (RICK TASCO 2004)

IBs fit the bill for smaller spaces where TBs just outsize everything. 'Mariposa Wizard' is a perfect case in point — it's a sized-down, proportionately lovely version of 'Mariposa Skies' (Tasco 1996), its TB pod parent. Good-growing and fine-flowering, this bitone will rebloom in milder climates. If you're a northern gardener, don't count on it, but relish the surprise if and when it does. Award of Merit 2008.

ABOVE, LEFT TO RIGHT: 'Many Mahalos' (Aitken 2003)

'Mariposa Wizard' (Tasco 2004)

'MIDSUMMER NIGHT'S DREAM' (LOWELL BAUMUNK 1999)

Though I'm an unrelenting critic of blue and violet in iris flowers, even I can't pass up the silken image of a mass of 'Midsummer Night's Dream'. Seemingly plucked from the pages of Shakespeare, this romantic iris has a luscious quality to it that makes me melt. Add on its tendency to rebloom in early summer and late fall, and I'm sold. The clump increases well, and I always admire its clean foliage, even in years when everything shows dots of leaf spot and rust. Hans and Jacob Sass Medal 2006.

'ON GOLDEN POND' (PERRY DYER 2000)

Why this perky and pretty yellow IB has been ignored by the AIS awards system baffles me. Though perhaps just another yellow, what iris garden can really have too many clumps of golden yellow beaming from all heights throughout the bloom season? It's a staple garden color. With 'On Golden Pond', you'll get a reliable show of flowers year after year without much effort, even in lackluster soil (as mine unfortunately happens to be growing in). Fine foliage, good overall plant health, bushy beards. and just darn pretty. Plant at the feet of some bluestars (*Amsonia*) for instant complementary kaboom.

ABOVE, LEFT TO RIGHT: 'Midsummer Night's Dream' (Baumunk 1999)

'On Golden Pond' (Dyer 2000)

'PAN FOR GOLD' (CHUCK CHAPMAN 2007)

A yellow-stitched plicata, this novel flower boldly presents itself atop handsome stalks with ample buds and branches. I've only recently added it to my own garden but have enjoyed its healthy growth and sparkling garden persona around the country. Hailing from Canada, it's no doubt going to be hardy. Genetically speaking, it's a typical IB cross of an SDB (Chuck's award-winning 'Ruby Eruption', a personal favorite) and a TB, the splattered 'Hyenasicle' (Kasperek 1998).

ABOVE: 'Pan for Gold' (Chapman 2007)

'STAR IN THE NIGHT' (PAUL BLACK 2009)

I'm in love. Breathtaking to behold, 'Star in the Night' glows like a Saturday night date all ready to go by Thursday morning. Like any fine woman's best pearls, the polished white beards atop satiny black falls are the perfect accessories to an otherwise sleek piece of formalwear. Expect handsome growth in a variety of climates, six or seven buds, and well-placed branches, which allow you to enjoy every last flower as it unfurls. Careful, you're drooling. Walther Cup 2011.

ABOVE: 'Star in the Night' (Black 2009)

'STARWOMAN' (MARKY SMITH 1998)

This IB is the reigning queen among all four classes of medians these days for managing to capture enough votes to win a Dykes Medal. A plicata with blackish blue-purple banding on a white ground, 'Starwoman' grows phenomenally well (a characteristic that repeats throughout this list of my favorite intermediates, you'll note). Ain't no room for wimps in my garden! And yes, despite its rather "ordinary" colors, by iris standards, this one stands a chance of making my desert island list. A clump of it planted alongside golden banner (*Thermopsis*) will capture hearts and minds. Dykes Medal 2008.

'TANTRUM' (KEITH KEPPEL 1997)

I always say this one throws an absolute fit in the garden. In all honesty, brick red and golden mustard — a challenging color combination for pastel lovers — may not quite fit your garden scheme in spring. But if you're a fearless painter of colors in the landscape, you'll feel right at home with this one raging forth in front of a stand of Oriental poppies (*Papaver orientale*). Perky, flaring flowers with rounded form show off wild plicata markings, just like a modern IB should. Go loud or go home. Honorable Mention 1999.

TOP TO BOTTOM:
'Starwoman'
(Smith 1998)

'Tantrum'
(Keppel 1997)

Gallery

ABOVE: 'Exotic Artistry' (Willott 2005)

ABOVE: 'Rimaround'
(Aitken 2007)

ABOVE: 'Intoxicating'
(Black 2009)

ABOVE: 'Jump Start'
(Keppel 2002)

8

ABOVE, LEFT TO RIGHT: 'Fortune Hunter' (Black 2004)

'Bottled Sunshine' (Nichols 1995)

9 Miniature Tall Bearded Irises

"By crossing and selecting smaller things, I believe we can have the color patterns in our MTBs that are found, for the most part, in the tall beardeds."

W. Terry Varner, *Bulletin of the American Iris Society 268* (1988)

Miniature tall bearded irises possess an almost wooing charm. Among the first to win me were two classic varieties — 'Bumblebee Deelite' (Norrick 1986) and 'Dotted Doll' (Fry 1987). I acquired them, planted them, and tripped out when they bloomed the next spring, since I hadn't really expected much in the way of a show until the second year. But this vigorous duo was stunning, forming miniature clumps, three stalks each, from pencil-skinny rhizomes the fall before. That did it, I was hooked. But it wasn't until several years later, when I inherited about 250 more cultivars (just a few) from an iris friend, that I really let my passion explode. Now I think of the class as if it were my family; I'm all too eager to talk about my pride-and-joy offspring to strangers on the bus or in line at the grocery store. Of all the bearded iris family, these dapper mid-spring doers, nestled right in the middle of the spectrum, are a truly carefree group, easy to grow and thriving rambunctiously, their delicate stalks of would-be-airborne flowers fluttering in place on well-branched stalks.

Like a flock of migrating birds, a clump in full bloom is a spectacle to witness — at least, a clump of an exceptional variety is. As with any group of irises, duds lurk under cute names and flattering descriptions. But the real test of a miniature tall bearded iris' merits comes down to two words: clump effect. Same as with the dwarfs — smaller flowers simply show off better in droves. Each one is like a piece of hand-painted china to behold, but a full place setting sells the eye a lot faster. If you come across MTBs that can't do their thing dozens of minikin flowers at a time, consider a more floriferous choice. But just because they're delightful en masse doesn't mean that the individual qualities of the flowers take a backseat. The more colors and patterns there are within each of the bearded irises classes, the greater the possibilities for collecting and designing with them. Smaller yards, which more than welcome daintier irises like MTBs, deserve just as much color and glam as gardens measured in acres.

Origins: For It Was Mary

With any luck and without even knowing it, you've probably seen a miniature tall bearded iris. Most are descended from the diploids *Iris pallida* and the familiar *I. variegata*, the queen mother of this classification, whose brown and yellow flowers enliven cemeteries and old homesteads in mid-spring. Visitors to my nursery often bring them to me to identify, cosseting their vase-full with heirloom pride, along with a story about how they came to own and grow them. From those cherished stems blossomed a class of bearded irises — small in stature, few in number, but mighty in their ability to produce bevies of flowers.

The MTB class owes its existence to the discerning eye of Mary Williamson, daughter of iris breeder Bruce Williamson, who fondly referred to them as table irises when her father simply saw them as runts. Mary was the first woman to receive the Dykes Medal, winning it in 1940 for her 1936 introduction 'Wabash'. It was her record-keeping and watchful eye that plucked these table-sized flowers from the rows of her father's tall bearded seedlings of dubious parentage; these likely involved popular diploids of the time like 'Juniata' (Farr 1909) and 'Shekinah' (Sturtevant 1918), as well as significant influences of *Iris variegata*. Together with her friend Ethel Anson Peckham, Williamson took stock of these runts and saw their potential as cut flowers, appreciating their finer stems in comparison to the somewhat inelastic stems of their row mates.

Williamson introduced her most notable miniature tall bearded varieties (registered as intermediates, since the MTB class didn't yet exist) after her father's death. One of them, 'Pewee' (1934), a grayish white with yellow beards, won the first Williamson-White Award in 1968. But despite her best efforts, miniature tall bearded irises lagged in popularity until the 1950s and '60s, when California iris lover Alice White, the other half of the now Williamson-White Medal, rekindled interest in the group. The group was formally recognized by the Median Iris Society and the American Iris Society as an official class, one with refined ornamental features of graceful proportions, not simply a crowd of stunted tall beardeds.

As Mary Louise Dunderman, Ben Hager, and other hybridizers began to explore the class, the pace of advancement quickened. Smallish, strappy flowers perked up with flaring, wider form, grew vigorously, and shone in shades of pastels. Dunderman made some 50,000 crosses in her Ohio garden across her lifetime, focusing all the while on the pixie personalities of her favorite plants. She raised nearly 20,000 seedlings from these crosses, but — truly discriminating — she introduced only 44 irises, 41 of which were MTBs. Displaying the shrewd precision of her efforts, her introductions won a wall of honors, including six Williamson-White Awards and one Williamson-White Medal. Some of these — the shimmering white 'Crystal Ruffles' (1986), the rose-cream plicatas 'Rosemary's Dream' (1982) and 'Carolyn Rose' (1971) — remain tremendous cultivars for modern gardens.

Hager's foray into MTBs proved one of the more challenging ventures of his long reign. His game plan was to miniaturize tall bearded irises onto stems and plants akin to *Iris aphylla*, the well-branched MTB-sized tetraploid that was beginning to have an almost lusty influence on the minds of iris lovers. His first attempts with the class were in 1956. Over the next two decades he crossed, inbred, and crossed again to work through fertility issues and shape the iris of his daydream into a garden plant worth growing. His classic 'Abridged Version' (1983) is a curious smoky pink with tangerine beards — a digest edition of some smoky pink TB that could never look as hot. Hager's most enduring legacy to the median classes remains his tetraploid MTB introductions, which show up in the studbooks of Jim and Vicki Craig, Charlie Nearpass, Kenneth Fisher, and other tetraploid pioneers who continue to pursue truly miniaturized tall bearded irises.

The continuing MTB challenge has been an expansion of the color palette, which some hybridizers gave up on, citing the limitations of diploidy. Colorful diversity doesn't lack in MTBs, even if it doesn't abound. Orchid pinks like 'Rave Review' (Craig 1992) look stunning accented by fire-hot beards. Blues like the modern king 'Sailor's Dream' (Fisher 2004) and blue bicolors like 'Ozark Dream' (Fisher 1992) are unrivalled in color saturation. Yellows like 'Chickee' (Dunderman 1980) sparkle in the spring sun. Romantic blends of roses, iron browns, and reds like 'Maggie Me Darlin'' (Guild 1985) and 'Fiesta Flirt' (Fisher 2001) reward close inspection. The rainbow isn't short on possibilities or lacking in taste in the miniature tall bearded class.

Worth Noting: Tetraploid Frontiers?

The steady stream of new tetraploid MTBs coming onto the market could facilitate a conversion of the class from diploids to tetraploids, as seen in the tall beardeds in the early 20th century. But I hesitate to think that the diploid charm of the class, timeless and nostalgic as it is, wanes in modern days. In fact, I think the class will evolve to appreciate both and encourage hybridizers to give gardeners more and more choices for their gardens. Ben Hager, Jim and Vicki Craig, and others sought to miniaturize tall bearded iris flowers onto daintier stems while not sacrificing any of the colors of their taller progenitors; others like Mary Louise Dunderman and Dorothy Guild delighted in the miniatures because they were already miniature, harkening back to a historical look lost in the evolution of the voluptuous tall beardeds.

Regardless of the direction of horticultural evolution, miniature tall bearded irises will always be expected to have clear, richly colored flowers atop flexuous, thin stems. Their small size demands clean, healthy foliage in proportion to the flower stalks. Some varieties have leaves that tend to brown and curl at the ends, and while not a fatal flaw, it's certainly not the best look when a troupe of irises is trying to tap out its flowering routine in mid-spring. More so in this class than others, purple spathes show up and attractively so, giving the buds a Technicolor look as the petals arise from an enclosure of purple. *Iris purpureobractea*, a naturally MTB-sized species, was originally described for this very feature. While not used extensively yet in hybridizing, *I. purpureobractea* has yellow flowers that startle as they unfurl against the purple tissues of their spathes, and a few keen iris lovers have already taken note of that ornamentation. If their work pans out, expect a line of miniature tall bearded irises with not only showy flowers but stems and buds, too. This purple coloration also shows up as a flush of red-violet at the base of the fans in some varieties, even those not of *I. purpureobractea* descent — yet another attractive feature that survives ephemeral flowers.

The underlying trait of interest is bud count. By now you can probably speak this as a mantra — more buds, more buds, more buds. Miniature tall beardeds don't lack for buds, fortunately; they, like their small cousins the miniature dwarf beardeds, compensate for their smaller flowers by offering up more of them. Flowering, after all, has everything to do with reproductive biology, and the more a plant can maximize its opportunities for discovery and subsequent pollination, the better. Happily, many buds on many stems delight humans, too — and would-be pollinators just happen to come along for the ride. The end game is that MTBs of the highest caliber should have eight to nine buds, though many varieties gladly offer more. Even one with less than seven shouldn't be discounted; fewer buds might make a case for beauty when stems are on the longer side of the class (21 inches or more), or when flowers have descended from larger parent plants. But in my garden, I prefer fewer buds to be offset by more stems.

Miniature tall beardeds are a valuable specialty cut crop, though the market hasn't really exploited them for that use beyond the kitchen table or church altar. While many irises have appeal in the vase, stems of MTBs look professional when others look amateur. Rocketing from a centerpiece along a rigid line, they have few rivals. Breeding lines of MTBs with perhaps fewer buds and flowers that sequenced in unison would amount to a smart project for an enterprising hybridizer, not to mention florists would go gaga over the creations. I've nearly tied stems in a knot without breaking them apart — that's versatile!

Finally, notwithstanding the ever-ravenous appetite for rebloom, there remain only a handful of available rebloomers in this class, including 'Lady Emma' (Jones 1986), 'Merit' (Fisher 1996); 'Maidenhood' (Craig 2008); and the Doodle series from Charlie Nearpass — 'Emma Doodle' (Nearpass/Chesapeake and Potomac Iris Society 2003), 'Lucy Doodle' (Nearpass/Chesapeake and Potomac Iris Society 2003), and 'Claire Doodle' (Nearpass/Spoon 2000). Reblooming irises with as many buds as miniature tall beardeds can boast would be extremely valuable additions to the herbaceous garden. Somebody should "get on that."

Expert Pointers: MTBs in the Garden

If I were limited to one sentence to summarize my thoughts about growing MTBs in the garden, I'd say that they should be planted liberally and in swaths across the herbaceous border. Their flowers, often near 3 inches in diameter, look adorable with a whole host of spring-flowering perennials, or simply underplanted with a colorful groundcover for showy contrast. Whether flaring to semi-flaring, dangling to slightly ruffled — they always maintain a poise and dignity all their own. With flowers so delicate, even for those that are tetraploids, how could anyone with a heart deny them a place among the poppies (*Papaver*) and pincushions (*Knautia*)?

Miniature tall bearded irises are such essential garden plants in my mind that chalking up a list of ideal companion plants seems almost silly. I've recommended for many years that gardeners try them alongside the just-awakening flushes of ornamental grasses — the combination of sword-shaped foliage and grassy blades later in the season looks just like you designed it for that particular eyeful of fun. Take note of the logistics though, since a volcanic clump of maidenhair grass (*Miscanthus*) will engulf dainty MTBs; smaller native grasses like sideoats grama (*Bouteloua curtipendula*) and little bluestem (*Schizachyrium scoparium*) more aptly fit the bill.

I've always marveled at the durability of the flowers of miniature tall bearded irises — paradoxically, they weather wretched rainstorms and wind with relative ease, as if something so small goes unnoticed by the spring furies of Mother Nature. However, substance is still important, simply because smaller flowers lack the tissue mass of larger flowers. But even if the first round of flowers flies to smithereens on a windy day, the buds to follow will compensate for their loss. That endless flow of flowers makes a humble, even half-dozen assortment of MTBs last for weeks in spring. I'm amazed each year at how long they stay with me in the garden, overlapping the latest standard dwarf beardeds and intermediate beardeds, and holding fast well into and occasionally through tall bearded season.

Cultivars You Should Grow

MTBs go beyond graceful — their simple practicality, bearing petite flowers on downsized stems, makes them a superb choice for windy gardens. They're artful too, the perfect cut flower for a Mother's Day bouquet. With less than 625 cultivars of MTBs listed in the American Iris Society registry, I've long harbored the ambition to collect them all. Despite the 300 or so in my garden at present, I'm unabashed in my critiques of most of them. Here are 25 of my favorites, though if you asked me on another day I might easily list off as many more.

'ACE' (LYNDA MILLER 1999)

Lynda followed Ben Hager's advice about short irises having short names. My indifference to purple and white plicatas aside, I really am fond of this perky MTB, mostly because it grows exceptionally well. The plants always look healthy, and I have a habit of throwing an extra one in as many iris shipments as I can each season. A clump or a small row of white dotted deep violet flowers perfumes the air with a light musky scent. If purple flowers in spring are on the menu, I'll ask for this one! Williamson-White Medal 2005.

9

ABOVE: 'Ace' (Miller 1999)

'AGLOW AGAIN' (KENNETH FISHER 2004)

As far as tetraploid MTBs go, this is one I rush out to see just as soon as I know it's in bloom. It's so soft, subtle, yet rich with pink and peach overtones in a romantic way. I imagine a bouquet of these might grace a candlelit table some night, fluttering in the air along with the flickering flames. I hope I've made it clear that MTBs make great cuts, and this variety blends well with any buxom array of spring flowers suitable for the vase. As a garden plant, it makes a fine specimen too, growing amply and often remaining in bloom for two weeks; it has also rebloomed occasionally in a variety of climates across the United States. An excellent companion for both softer pastels and stronger, juicier colors.

ABOVE: 'Aglow Again' (Fisher 2004)

'APRICOT DROPS' (TERRY AITKEN 1994)

A remarkable cross between 'Abridged Version' (Hager 1983), an MTB, and Terry's own SDB 'Pele' (1993). Genetics worked in his favor to produce a hybrid that maintains the MTB charm of its pod parent while bringing on board color genetics from its pollen parent. Deservedly award-winning, 'Apricot Drops' was a major advancement in carotenoid colors in the MTB class. Softly blended apricot flowers hover on wiry, well-branched stems in vigorous clumps. A smart color for blending with bright lavender and magenta pinks, like that of peonies and primroses (*Primula*). Williamson-White Medal 2003.

'BUMBLEBEE DEELITE' (J. AND G. NORRICK 1986)

This has to be one of the most familiar and recognizable bearded irises of the 20th century. Narrowly missing the Dykes Medal on two different occasions, 'Bumblebee Deelite' was a rallying cry for MTBs and a testament to the popularity of median irises in the United States. Handsome and dramatic en masse, this MTB grows superbly, guaranteeing a supply of flowers for years after planting. A showstopper that no garden should be without! Williamson-White Medal 1993.

ABOVE, LEFT TO RIGHT: 'Apricot Drops' (Aitken 1994) 'Bumblebee Deelite' (Norrick 1986)

'CARLA BETH' (WYSS/NORRIS 2012)

This iris sort of discovered me, instead of the usual vice versa. Several years ago I began an inventory of the 250-some MTBs I'd inherited, taking note of any mismarked accessions before adding them to our sales collection. I came across a tag with a name I didn't recognize, did a little research, but couldn't find anything about this "Carla Beth." So I emailed the friends who were the source of the collection and mystery solved: the name had been reserved by breeder Betty Wyss, but she passed away before completing the paperwork to fully register it. We decided to complete the process for her and plan to introduce this juicy-colored MTB in 2012. Excellent stalks and bud count, and a color pattern that ages to a milder version of its former self — all make this an iris worth growing.

ABOVE: 'Carla Beth' (Wyss/Norris 2012)

'CEDAR WAXWING' (EARL ROBERTS 1974)

I enjoy ornithology and birding, and while I'm not a collector per se of things with bird names, I have to admit I'm fond of both this iris and its avian namesake. A small yellow beard adds a point of contrast to an otherwise earth-tone flower with light tan standards and mulberry falls faintly edged with tan. For any interested hybridizers, its pedigree involves pink amoena seedlings, 'Kaleidoscope' (Katkamier 1929), and *Iris variegata* var. *reginae*. I've often remarked to visitors that due to its vigor and floriferousness, a clump of 'Cedar Waxwing' should really be called a flock. Williamson-White Award 1977.

'CLAIRE DOODLE' (NEARPASS/SPOON 2000)

It took me a few years to realize how in love I was with this iris — sort of a Harry and Sally kind of situation. At first, I could take it or leave it. Its cool lavender-blue flowers with darker venation are nice but didn't send me screaming across the yard to find someone to share them with. But it's what it does with those flowers that eventually brought me around to the "Claire" campaign. With the tetraploid *Iris aphylla* in its genes, this iris branches very well, displaying the flowers in an attractive, unobstructed way. Better yet, it reblooms, at least in milder climates (zone 6 and above). I've yet to see rebloom stalks in my zone 5 garden, but I keep hoping for a surprise. 'Claire Doodle' is also proving to be a valuable parent in breeding, particularly when combined with tall beardeds.

TOP TO BOTTOM: 'Cedar Waxwing' (Roberts 1974)

'Claire Doodle' (Nearpass/Spoon 2000)

'CLOWN PANTS' (TOM SILVERS 2006)

Technically speaking, 'Clown Pants' is actually a species cross (SPEC-X, in iris registration lingo) — a clone of *Iris variegata* crossed with *I. suaveolens* var. *mellita*. But from a horticultural standpoint, the plant is handily an MTB, and any value it has as a parent will be exercised in the improvement of this class. The flowers are charming — pale yellow overlaid with purple striping that blends into a burgundy wash at the edge of the fall. I start to smile just thinking about it, jesterly as it is. It flowers well, too; buds upon buds upon buds grace the garden for weeks each spring. A superb weed worth sharing for prettiness and charm. Plant a hedge of it and enjoy.

'CRYSTAL RUFFLES' (MARY LOUISE DUNDERMAN 1986)

Ruffling in MTBs is fairly uncommon since diploids rarely produce flowers with enough bounce and bob to produce the illusion of wavy petals. 'Crystal Ruffles' is an adamant exception to the rule, waving in the purest white on well-branched stalks at the peak of spring. It's been a difficult parent for breeders to wrangle into submission, so the ruffling hasn't shown up in much more than just a few registered and introduced progeny. Breeder's worries aside, 'Crystal Ruffles' forms bountiful clumps that unfurl into swarms of doves in the early phase of the MTB flowering season. Definitely a looker worth having around. Williamson-White Award 1991.

TOP TO BOTTOM: 'Clown Pants' (Silvers 2006)

'Crystal Ruffles' (Dunderman 1986)

'DIVIDING LINE'
(CHUCK BUNNELL 2005)

This is one of the most popular MTBs in the country, with a slew of awards and honors (all entirely warranted) to boot. It grows terrifically well all over the United States, forming (as a top-notch MTB should) a massive clump that puts on a weeks-long floral display in spring. The flowers garner the most attention though, aptly showing off a namesake lavender dividing line that slices through a violet spot on pale purple falls. It definitely gets points for distinctiveness and will easily be one of the standard MTBs for decades to come. Williamson-White Medal 2011.

ABOVE: 'Dividing Line' (Bunnell 2005)

'DOLLIE AND ME'
(LYNDA MILLER 2011)

This is a rare recommendation of a plant that I've not yet grown in my own garden but that I've very recently fallen in love with in my travels. The pairing of typical colors — yellow and light violet — gets a dose of distinctiveness from rosy haft marks, sort of like a plain face touched up by a little blush. Boy, ain't she purdy! With another favorite MTB of mine, 'Ben A Factor' (2000), bred by Lynda's husband, Roger, in her background, this tetraploid showgirl will romp across your garden stage, demand the spotlight, and perform admirably for a two-week engagement without pause or fail. A hands-down endorsement of a very lovely new iris!

ABOVE: 'Dollie and Me' (Miller 2011)

'FAIR HALDIS' (JEAN WITT 1975)

I had no idea what Haldis meant when I first grew this iris. I've since learned it's a girl's name of Norse origins, with various meanings of "stone spirit" and "weapon of the goddess." Amazing the lore that is woven into humble garden plants. Indeed the flowers of 'Fair Haldis' are quite humble, slightly tailored, tannish striped white. Their beauty comes en masse, when a generous quantity of them hovers above rampantly increasing plants. A staple garden plant of merit. Honorable Mention 1979.

'HONORABILE' (LÉMON 1840)

You may recognize this rough and ready stalwart from a visit to the cemetery or a stroll by that decrepit old house in the neighborhood. Across the country, this oldie but goodie crops up in bygone places, a remnant of a long-ago garden. These haphazard growing conditions are testament to its garden performance — it's tough as nails and grows like a weed, always putting up a shiny show of cadmium yellow flowers with falls flushed mahogany over bronze. Also a notable progenitor of many sports, including 'Sans Souci' (Van Houtte 1854), 'Sherwin-Wright' (Kohankie 1915), 'Kaleidoscope' (Katkamier 1929), 'Joseph's Coat Katkamier' (Katkamier/Tankesley-Clarke 1930/1989), and 'Brown's Mutant' (Mahan 1993).

TOP TO BOTTOM: 'Fair Haldis' (Witt 1975) 'Honorabile' (Lémon 1840)

'HOT NEWS' (STEPHANIE MARKHAM 2009)

And what hot news it is! In a class of irises dominated by simple yellows and purples, 'Hot News' turns heads with its rich, jewel-tone red flowers. Born and raised in the Northeast, this spicy-looking MTB fills out into a suave clump with plenty of vigor to go around. As modern-day "queen of the MTBs," breeder Stephanie Markham has other tricks up her sleeve for keeping these diploid cutesters flashy and fun for modern gardens. Call it poor taste in color combos if you like, but I'm dying to plant this next to something bright pink like dianthus or sea thrift (*Armeria maritima*). Honorable Mention 2011.

ABOVE: 'Hot News' (Markham 2009)

'JACK'S PICK' (CHUCK BUNNELL 2006)

I'm a big fan of Chuck Bunnell's irises. Chuck was a protégé of Jack Norrick and picked up the latter's eye for color and glam in the MTB class. 'Jack's Pick', reminiscent in flower of some expensive, bejeweled amulet, no doubt earned its name for being the pick of the litter. It grows well across the country, even in Texas, where I first saw it — a part of the country not known for growing the finest clumps of MTBs on account of the heat of late spring and early summer. 'Jack's Pick' might as well be your next MTB pick for the garden. It is handsome in every respect. Honorable Mention 2010.

ABOVE: 'Jack's Pick' (Bunnell 2006)

'LADY EMMA' (FRANK JONES 1986)

Some of my more astute iris friends chuckle at my inclusion of this rather plain yellow iris in my list of favorite MTBs. But life isn't all about colorful characters swooning over you at every moment. Sometimes the best companions are the reliable friends who show up — even in the garden — just when you need them most. 'Lady Emma', while lacking rouged flowers of head-turning color, is a rebloomer, and does so with a certain conviction in climates cool to mild. It's a bloody weed too, so you'll never be without it once you've had it around a year or so. Honorable Mention 1988.

ABOVE: 'Lady Emma' (Jones 1986)

'LUCY DOODLE' (NEARPASS/SPOON 2003)

Here's one of a handful of tetraploid MTBs on my list of favorites. It's not that I have anything against them; rather, there just aren't tons from which to choose — yet. An involved parentage including TBs and other tetraploid MTBs gave rise to this ruffled flower. I marvel at its superb branching; it packs loads of buds all over the place in a perfect arrangement that looks just as complete in the garden as on the show bench. One 19-inch stalk can have nine to 12 buds, which means you can expect flowers for well over two weeks on an established clump. Plus tendencies to rebloom (especially in milder climates)! What more could you want?

'PEEBEE AND JAY' (BARBARA AND DAVID SCHMIEDER 2006)

Plant lovers know what it's like to fall in love with a plant over and over again, and that happens to me every spring when this iris comes into bloom. Though I was never a dutiful eater of this iris's namesake sandwich, I more than enjoy its elementary school colors on the petals of irises, in this case orangey brown standards over jelly purple falls. Reminiscent of the slightly older 'Siren' (Fisher 2000), but with better and more intense coloration. Award of Merit 2011.

TOP TO BOTTOM: 'Lucy Doodle' (Nearpass/Spoon 2003) 'Peebee and Jay' (Schmieder 2006)

9

'PLUM QUIRKY' (RILEY PROBST 2005)

The ideal MTB flower dances in my mind, lilting with grace and strength in the wind, flashing color, and blooming tenaciously for weeks and weeks until I demand it stop because I just can't stand it anymore. Few irises come close to that standard. But one that really knows how to kick its skirt up is 'Plum Quirky', a devilishly cute creation of Riley Probst's that turns heads and wins awards. The purple patterning on its delicate little falls washes down the length of the petals to a flared end. In a word — flirty. Award of Merit 2009.

'PUG' (EUGENE KALKWARF 2001)

It took a few years before I got around to ordering this iris, and I'm still grumpy that I waited so long! Never put off growing a great plant, at any cost. This dapper MTB, bred in Lincoln, Nebraska, sports a cloud of white-stitched cinnamon and gold flowers that make me think of the colors of hard butterscotch candy. It grows madly, romping about its garden spot to form a sizable, showy mass of flowers that nobody can walk past without stopping to coo. Now if I could only find a little pug (of the canine sort) to set next to a clump for a play-on-words photo op! Honorable Mention 2004.

TOP TO BOTTOM: 'Plum Quirky' (Probst 2005)

'Pug' (Kalkwarf 2001)

'RAYOS ADENTRO' (CAROL MORGAN 2007)

Here's a showstopper iris with an arresting visual aesthetic. Bold, blackish red-purple standards give way to falls of the same color with erratic white hafting that leads inward to a golden beard. Definitely a diva iris with more than enough stage presence to hold its own or shine bright with a cast of supporting flowers. Consider planting in the vicinity of white for contrast, or merlot and burgundy for complementation. Incidentally, the name is Spanish for "rays within." Honorable Mention 2010.

ABOVE: 'Rayos Adentro' (Morgan 2007)

'REDROCK PRINCESS' (JEAN WITT 2006)

Another great addition to the color range in the MTB class. Blended rose-red, tan-orange, and medium brown, this lightly ruffled little flower makes quite a statement en masse — a photo-worthy clump that I'm always sorry to see finish. 'Redrock Princess' deserves a royal court of companions — don't be afraid to try juicy, dynamo colors like melons and pinks. Its award-winning distinctiveness coupled with its fine growth habits make this MTB "one to watch" and most certainly one to grow. Award of Merit 2010.

ABOVE: 'Redrock Princess' (Witt 2006)

'SPRING BLUSH' (KENNETH FISHER 2002)

This wonderful tetraploid MTB became one of my favorites within just a few seasons of planting it. I love the tetraploid MTBs for their slightly larger flowers, glowing colors, and robust plants. 'Spring Blush' reminds me of tropical fruit hanging from a vine waiting to be picked, succulent and tender in color and appearance. The flower stalks boast excellent numbers of buds and branches, ensuring a handsome floral display for the two weeks this clump graces the garden setting.

ABOVE: 'Spring Blush' (Fisher 2002)

'SUN SPIRIT' (JIM AND VICKI CRAIG 2007)

If your gardening diet needs a dose of citrus, what better iris to grow than this one? 'Sun Spirit' is the first tetraploid orange MTB, a major breakthrough stemming from years of work in the Craigs' garden in Oregon. It has what iris lovers like to call "triple terminals," or three buds in the terminal position, a bonus for those of us sticklers who demand blooms, blooms, blooms for as long as possible. The flowers are just exceptional in all respects — substance, form, and color. A dynamo clump that opens up a palette of opportunities for combinations with yellow columbines (*Aquilegia*), Chinese pagoda primrose (*Primula vialii*), or mountain bluet (*Centaurea montana*). This iris is going places — grow it now so you can say you knew it when! Honorable Mention 2010.

'VIBRANT ROSE' (WITT 1990)

I love irises (plants, really) with names that actually evoke an image or describe the plant in question, a name so vivid that it is easily discerned by even the most undiscerning consumer. The name and the iris — 'Vibrant Rose' — does just that, catcalling from across the garden so that I might walk past for a closer look. Its flowers drip with painted rose colors, blended into a shiny alloy that looks smart against all sorts of other colors, irises and perennials alike. Like most MTBs (except the worst, which shall not be named), it increases abundantly, ensuring a steady supply of flowers for many years after planting. 'Vibrant Rose' has more than once run me out of house and home in the garden, so feel free to give it a harsh division every few years and share the wealth with your gardening friends. A striking look with pink weigelas or yellow columbines. Honorable Mention 1992

TOP TO BOTTOM: 'Sun Spirit' (Craig 2007) 'Vibrant Rose' (Witt 1990)

9

ABOVE: 'Ben A Factor' (Miller 2000)

Gallery

ABOVE: 'Baubles and Beads' (Miller 1997)

TOP TO BOTTOM:
'Chian Wine'
(Guild 1977)

'Petit Louvois'
(Mahan 2006)

ABOVE, LEFT TO RIGHT: 'She's A Doll' (Miller 2010)

'Blue Chip Stock' (Black 1998)

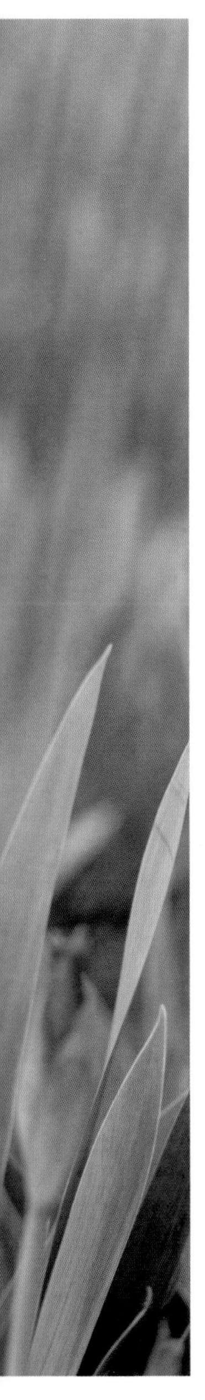

ABOVE: 'Enriched'
(Craig 2000)

OPPOSITE: 'Orange Starlet' (Fisher 2008)

ABOVE: 'Maggie Me Darlin'' (Guild 1985)

OPPOSITE: 'Merit' (Fisher 1996)

ABOVE: 'Dodger' (Miller 2007)

OVERLEAF: 'Abridged Version' (Hager 1983)

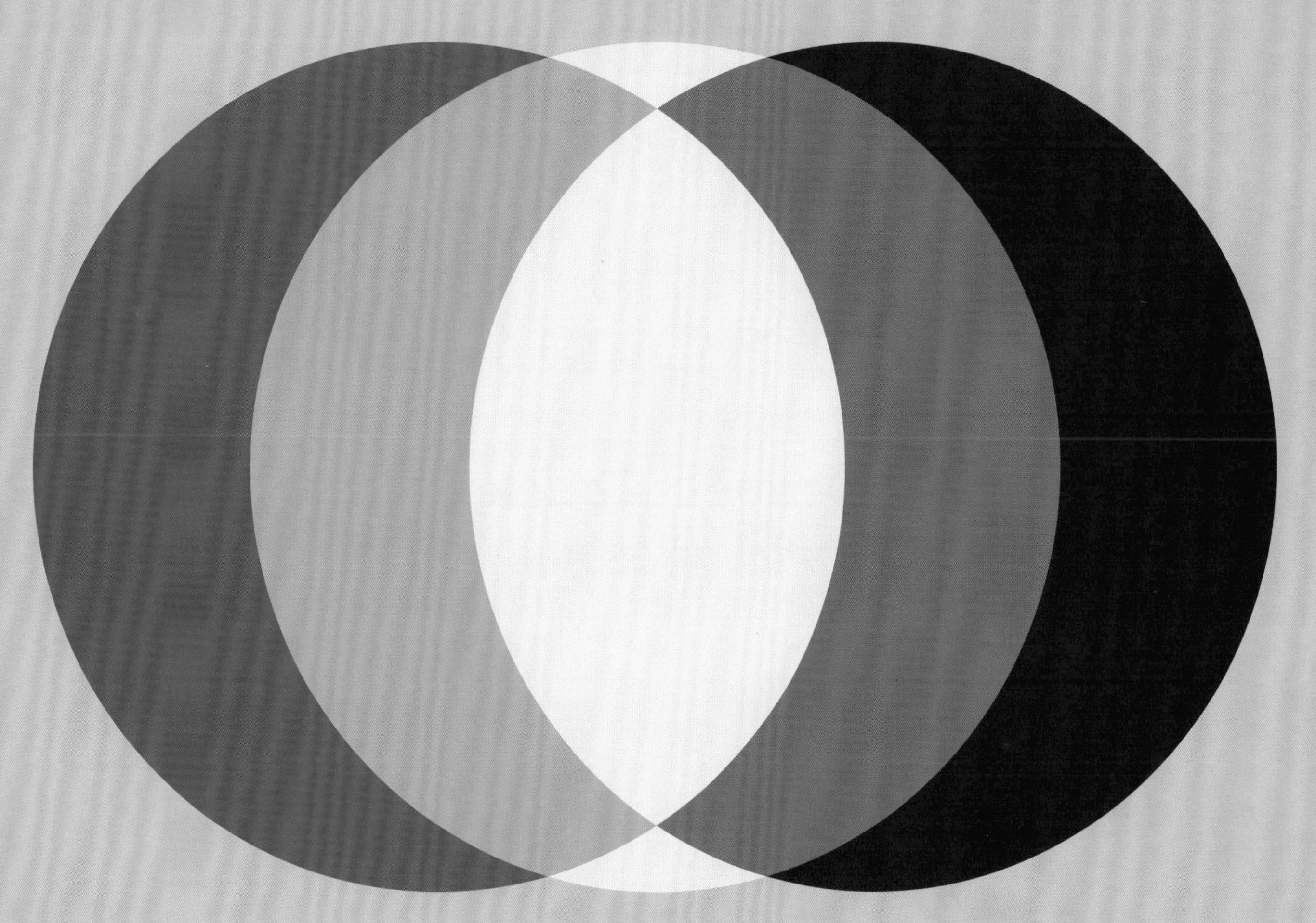

10 Border Bearded Irises

"The uses of border irises in the garden are as varied as the imagination."

Bennett Jones, *The World of Irises* (1978)

The first time I heard of "the rose formula," a near mathematical device used by rose fanatics to precisely size up flowers the rest of us would simply call "lovely," my mind reeled. I accept the fact that I'm an obsessed plant lover, minding the condition of my garden far more than that of my living room or kitchen on a daily basis. But the thought that fellow plant lovers, with a strain of the same virus that afflicts me, had let their passion evolve into something formulaic seemed borderline absurd. It turns out I hadn't heard it all. In truth, iris lovers have their own formula for precision, though perhaps not as neatly ordered as that of rosarians. Specifically, it applies to border bearded irises, exactingly wrought from the short segregants of tall bearded crosses and consummated into the finest attempt at human-mediated perfection the iris world has known.

Gushing prose aside — describing exactly what perfection means in reference to a border bearded iris is a little challenging. Perhaps because they're identical to IBs and MTBs in height, by definition between 16 and 27½ inches tall, I overlooked the charm of border bearded irises for many years. Maybe "overlooked" isn't the right word — I always grew some, but their individuality never struck me. But then one spring, I just got it — the kind of in-the-garden epiphany that makes you realize that an iris isn't just an iris anymore. It's a look, like a wink or a nod, that happens at the right moment and makes the heart flutter. And that moment, silly and nerdy as it may sound, had a practical side, too. It was a cold, wet spring that year. Most TBs sulked in the aftermath of a late freeze, as did a good many other things. Left standing? A rigorous band of survivors whose beauty in any other year might have gone unnoticed. Many of these were border beardeds.

Origins: Paradigmatic Proportions

The idea of the border bearded iris began with soft-hearted, bright-eyed breeders in the 1940s who just couldn't bring themselves to compost the shorter members of their iris patch. One of these early characters was Harold Knowlton, who would become the godfather of the class, in part because of his deliberate efforts to breed and promote these refined, smaller plants. His namesake medal is now the highest honor a border bearded iris can attain, save the Dykes Medal.

In Knowlton's day, BBs were not the goal but rather the sideline, if you will, of other taller breeding work. You can imagine what a collection of sidelines looks like — variation (often of the unflattering sort) abounded. Many of these TB-derived runts bloomed sparsely, grew poorly, and had no justifiable garden value beyond their pint-sized novelty. Early BBs were registered as IBs, since the BB class didn't exist until the late 1950s; but many carried the colloquial name "border irises," coined by Geddes Douglas to describe the shorter irises that sometimes dropped out of his TB breeding. Early varieties like 'Black Forest' (Schreiner 1944) were the first poster children for this new type of bearded iris, but they really were larger than desired and ultimately advanced what soon became an un-hip look: larger flowers on stunted stalks. Knowlton saw potential, though, in a redeeming race of small-statured seedlings descended from tall beardeds, emphasizing that by selecting for proportion and balance, a suitable cultivar could result. Two of his 1950 introductions, both from TB parents, would become the standard bearers of the class — 'Pearl Cup' (a white and pale blue bicolor) and 'Crickett' (an orange and red variegata).

Despite Knowlton's early guidance and a further clarification of the standards for the new class in the 1960s, many hybridizers routinely introduced varieties that simply didn't have a proportionate look, sporting flowers that looked too big to belong on stems and plants just a little bit smaller than their TB parents. Knowlton, along with other BB pioneers like Bee Warburton, Lynn Markham, and May Belle Wright, had a precise goal in mind as they refined the look of the class: vigorous, broadly adaptable bearded irises with precise floral dimensions. These visionaries saw an array of carefully balanced flowers, 5 inches or less in width and no more than 8½ inches tall in combined height and width, atop sturdy stems inherited from their taller cousins. A little esoteric, perhaps, but these rigid standards came to define a class of irises like no other, a telling example of the passion for growing plants and the lengths to which bright-eyed iris lovers will go in pursuit of idyllic, rainbow beauty.

In the early 1990s, most BBs could still be traced solely to tall bearded forebears. Only a few breeders carried on breeding programs involving crosses of border beardeds to each other ("border beardeds on purpose," as Lynn Markham put it), and fewer still had pulled *Iris aphylla* into the mix, though its influences were beginning to show, thanks to the pioneering work of Jim and Vicki Craig. *Iris aphylla* adds a host of desirable traits to the BB pot, not least of which is its outstanding winter hardiness. Its narrow, generously produced foliage gives clumps a dense, clustered look with a certain grassy appeal. If you're searching for that look, varieties like 'Slick' (Markham 2003), a pure *I. aphylla* selection, and 'Understated' (Markham 2001) are some irises to play with. 'Slick', with its intensely saturated purple flowers, stops traffic in spring.

Experiences of gardeners in southern climates suggest that *Iris aphylla* isn't always the most successful iris during long hot and humid spells. This anecdotal evidence may link back to provenance, since some interior or high-altitude collections of *I. aphylla* may not possess a great adaptation to wet summers. Overall though, the improvements in vigor, generous branching, and bud count — all necessary virtues of iris love — offered by *I. aphylla* promise that a heyday for border beardeds can't be far away. New varieties, with advances in color patterns that parallel that of other classes, enter the market each year, particularly from well-regarded hybridizers like Terry Aitken, Paul Black, Lynn Markham, and even broken-colored specialist Brad Kasperek. Cultivars from these breeders build on strong genetics across a wide color range and ever tantalize iris lovers as their mug shots arrive, glittering and glamorous, on the pages of catalogs in the depths of winter.

Worth Noting: The Flux of Flowering

But let's forget, for a moment, the niceties of size and balance and proportion. The real controversy (verging on horticultural crisis) is what to do about BB bloom time. As breeders have crossed BBs with themselves and virtually all other classes of bearded irises, particularly the ever-expanding selection of fertile IBs, the span of flowering has widened immensely. Border beardeds, by class definition, bloom with the TBs, but some varieties join the garden scene as the MTBs unfurl. I don't have a preference, frankly, so long as they make the scene with fervor and spirit.

A roller coaster lies ahead, and that's a good thing only if you like carnivals and amusement parks. As breeders continue to push the boundaries of crossability between various classes of bearded irises, the flowering seasons and all other characters that we use to horticulturally define not just BBs but all our flowers will continue to scatter in every direction. Fortunately, in horticultural nomenclature, we can make, break, and change the rules as the game runs away from us. The changes in store will be liberal ones, if they are to accommodate the diversity produced by amateur hybridizers.

Expert Pointers: BBs in the Garden

The border bearded class offers only subtle diversity in comparison to the other classes, but its members are well worth growing and loving just the same. Green-thumbed theorists posit that color trumps all features of smaller and smaller-flowered bearded irises, a statement I wholly endorse; but no matter what the color — sunset orange or chamois pink — it should never bleach or burn either. Nor should the opportunity to sparkle be squandered on flowers with poor form and finish, the botanical equivalent of runny makeup and mussed hair. And if I haven't already been picky enough: a BB's fleeting moment on the garden stage shouldn't be wasted on too much ruffling or excessive ornamentation; smaller flowers just can't afford it, because there's less surface area available for such decoration. But if you like lace and ruffling on flowers, as I tend too, my picky prescriptions may not matter much. Ultimately, go with what looks good to you.

Border beardeds function as garden plants in much the same way as IBs. They tolerate the wind with grace, fill the voids where taller irises would overwhelm, and should grow well if given a sunny spot and well-drained soil. If you have a large island bed or garden border, you'd do well to plant them closer to the edges, like you would IBs or MTBs. Like many irises, they're tough on their own feet, but crowd them out with the sky-raising herbaceous perennials of mid- and late summer and you're asking for trouble. Other than that caveat, I can't think of any perennial that would look out of place alongside a handsome clump of border bearded irises. Their versatility only accents their desirability as specimens of the finest efforts in iris breeding.

But a warning about less stellar efforts. Despite an abundance of handbooks, and rulers, and stern scoldings from sage irisarians with decades of wisdom, border beardeds that don't quite measure up to standard still make their way into commerce. I won't name names, but some are simply ungainly, short TBs that "grow out of class" in plush climates or (in the Midwest) wet springs. Growing out of class is strictly frowned upon. Who wants to plant a 16- to 27½-inch-tall-at-maturity iris that instead takes a Herculean leap to 3 feet? It's happened — no joke! Such poor efforts by hybridizers end up frustrating and disappointing even the most tolerant iris lover. It's okay to practice tough love in the garden — shape up or ship out.

Cultivars You Should Grow

Border beardeds often get knocked as being "just stunted talls," a derogatory phrase that even I, with the best of intentions, have spouted offhand in an effort to concisely describe their place in the classes of bearded irises. My descriptive failings aside, border beardeds deserve a special place in gardens. It's easy to love the charm and proportion of the truest-of-the-true border beardeds, those cultivars that really measure up. Here's a list of some easily cultivated BBs that no iris aficionado should be without. It's no surprise that many of my choices have won the Knowlton Medal and, in one notable instance, even the Dykes.

'ANACONDA LOVE' (KASPEREK 1999)

Grab your Panama Jack hat and let's venture deep into the jungles of — your garden. I love plants that take me places, draw me in for a closer look, and captivate my attention, just like 'Anaconda Love'. This iris sports solo-spotlight regalia — soft pink and beetroot purple streaked silvery white — so plant it where it will shine. Call it a focal point, traffic obstruction, or obscene, this good-growing iris delivers a knockout performance in the garden and deserves all the attention it gets. Knowlton Medal 2006.

ABOVE: 'Anaconda Love' (Kasperek 1999)

'BATIK' (ALLAN ENSMINGER 1986)

One of the most talked about irises of its day, 'Batik' goes where no iris before it did, at least in terms of class and style. Allan Ensminger wandered into the world of broken-colored irises in the 1970s, seeking to stabilize these frenzied flowers into an aesthetically justified chaos. 'Batik' has notoriously inconsistent growth habits in my garden (and, apparently, all rural southwest Iowa gardens visited by people named Kelly), despite being within a few hours of its Lincoln, Nebraska, "home" — but I digress and forgive. Across the rest of the world, it does well, and seeing it in a full-on mass is visually arresting. If you're something of a purist, you probably just can't quite deal with the unstable array of white and silver smattering underlying blue-purple. But if you're a little irreverent, carefree, and open to splashes of drama in your garden, you couldn't have found a better iris. Makes a great cut stem, if only for the conversations you'll have about it. Knowlton Medal 1992.

ABOVE: 'Batik' (Ensminger 1986)

'BOOM BOOM BLONDE'
(GORDON AND LORRAINE NICHOLSON 2002)

I like to think of myself as a champion of underused plants, whether irises or not. This attractive BB, an unusual reverse amoena, remains very much overlooked in the iris world, largely because of a lack of availability. Stunning blonde-bombshell standards contrast near-white falls for a clump effect that's charming at only 26 inches tall. Anyone who walks by it in my garden stops for a second look, peering down into a salon of tight chignons and updos. Though it could grow a little faster to meet demand, there's nothing wrong with a plant testing my patience every now and then.

'BROWN LASSO'
(BUCKLES-NISWONGER 1975)

No list of outstanding BBs would be complete without the famous 'Brown Lasso', one of only three non-tall bearded varieties ever to win the Dykes Medal. Yellow and purple bicolored flowers get just a little sexier with a chocolate-kissed rim around the edge of the falls. Dependable and reliable, chic and consummately beautiful, 'Brown Lasso' has for many years, and will for many more, be the standard against which all BBs are measured. In few words — a lesson in proportion. Dykes Medal 1981.

TOP TO BOTTOM: 'Boom Boom Blonde' (Nicholson 2002) 'Brown Lasso' (Buckles-Niswonger 1975)

'BUNDLE OF LOVE' (PAUL BLACK 2007)

Out of the powerhouse parent 'Dolce' (Black 2003) comes this perfectly proportioned BB blend, swaddled in baby pink and cream. I swear, each flower looks soft, and there are many of them for sure, festooned on well-placed branches along 26-inch-tall stalks in vigorous, full-bodied clumps. An excellent garden plant with great showmanship potential; cut stalks look great in a vase. Award of Merit 2011.

'CHICKASAW SUE' (JAMES GIBSON 1983)

This was one of the first named bearded irises I remember growing as a kid. Ever since it hit the market, it's garnered the attention of many fawning iris lovers for its ruffled cinnamon brown plicata flowers, so much so that you can find it (or at least a plant labeled as it) at big box stores! It has a reputation for reliability, always growing and flowering well year after year — and surprising me anew each spring, since I've long passed it by for newer things. But here's my homage to an old garden friend, worthy of cultivation even today. Award of Merit 1989.

ABOVE, LEFT TO RIGHT: 'Bundle of Love' (Black 2007) 'Chickasaw Sue' (Gibson 1983)

'CHRISTIANA BAKER' (FRED KERR 1999)

The forebearer of Fred's Dykes Medal–winning champ 'Queen's Circle' (2000), 'Christiana Baker' tops my list of the purest colored irises. With flowers of pristine white edged in a sharp rim of deep sea blue, the sheer cleanliness of the presentation will cause you to break stride and step in for a closer look. The potential companions for this flower in the full garden are limitless, but my mind tends to think a little more monochromatic in this case, opting for a clump planted under a fringetree (*Chionanthus virginicus*) with lupines (*Lupinus*) and any white allium like *A. cowanii*. Sounds spring dreamy! Knowlton Medal 2005.

ABOVE: 'Christiana Baker' (Kerr 1999)

'CLASSIC NAVY'
(LANKOW-AITKEN 1999)

Though I'd be lying if I said I excluded them entirely, I tend to eschew irises that flower in traditional purples and blues. I'm certainly in the minority here — purple and blue color the memories of irises for many, from their earliest childhood days. If you're looking for that spot of blue reminiscent of your grandma's garden, a clump of 'Classic Navy' would look smart. Self-colored, gently ruffled, and blooming late with a seemingly endless supply of buds and stalks, an established clump makes a stunning centerpiece to a garden bed or border. Consider throwing in some chartreuse sedges (*Carex*) and a clump or two of golden garlic (*Allium moly*) for a zinging combination. Award of Merit 2004.

ABOVE: 'Classic Navy' (Lankow-Aitken 1999)

'CROW'S FEET' (PAUL BLACK 2006)

Here's one instance where the idea of crow's feet shouldn't send you running shrieking from the mirror, or the garden. Rather, this alarmingly different bicolor features dramatic purple stripes down falls accented by bright orange beards and white standards. I think this is one of those irises that you'll either embrace with open arms or pass over with a simple "no thanks." It's a definite diva if you're trying to pair it with other plants, but if you're just collecting and want to add the latest, flashiest BB, it'll fit in while standing out. An award winner with a bright future as a must-have garden plant — help prove me right! Award of Merit 2010.

ABOVE: 'Crow's Feet' (Black 2006)

'CUT ABOVE' (TERRY AITKEN 2005)

Talk about an iris that defies description and sends me looking for a thesaurus. In an intense twist on metallic tones in flowers, 'Cut Above' boasts juicy bronze standards that seem to shimmer above coppery yellow falls that fade to white in the center (in the end, the color of a bearded iris's fall often resolves itself to the color of the beard: it's a make or break element of the floral anatomy). All together, it's one jiving ensemble. Honorable Mention 2007.

'EYE CANDY' (KEITH KEPPEL 2004)

My garden won't ever be without this charming pip of a safrano pink BB, sized down from TB relatives like 'Happenstance' (Keppel 2000). The flowers are ruffled, with fat form and plastic substance. The well-budded stalks of 'Eye Candy' usually close out the bearded iris season for me, blooming very, very late. I think you'll agree, pink never looked so good. Knowlton Medal 2010.

ABOVE, LEFT TO RIGHT: 'Cut Above' (Aitken 2005) 'Eye Candy' (Keppel 2004)

'FLEECE AS WHITE'
(PAUL BLACK 2005)

What a great name for a white flower, right? 'Fleece As White' is destined for greatness as a well-formed, excellently branched, and superbly budded iris. Coming from the genetics of Paul's 'Dolce' (2003), 'Fleece As White' carries on a new look that's catching on in the iris world — sturdy stalks with well-placed branches and buds that yield a weeks-long floral show while sporting a classic clump effect courtesy of its ancestor *Iris aphylla*. If you think irises don't last long enough, you either need to buy more or plant cultivars with exceptional qualities that guarantee their spotlight shines for weeks instead of days. Start here. Knowlton Medal 2011.

ABOVE: 'Fleece As White' (Black 2005)

'JUNGLE SHADOWS'
(SASS-GRAHAM 1960)

Famously described by a visitor to my garden as "the ugliest most beautiful iris I've ever seen," this paradoxically pretty flower will either leave you giddy with geeky excitement or nauseated. I grow it just for the unusualness, since nothing else on the face of the horticultural planet looks anything like it. I have no idea what you would pair it with in the mixed border. I grow it in a bed full of nothing but irises, sort of like a museum gallery for the absurd and bizarre. An oldie but a goodie. Knowlton Medal 1967.

ABOVE: 'Jungle Shadows' (Sass-Graham 1960)

'NICHE' (JOE GHIO 2007)

Though of unknown parentage, it's likely that 'Niche' is a dropout BB from a TB family; in other words, it drew the short end of the evolutionary stick. Its boldly patterned flowers can't be missed in the garden. In a Texas garden, I saw it planted near red yucca (*Hesperaloe parviflora*) to lavish effect, the red beards accenting the red tubular flowers of its succulent companion. This variety is reminiscent of the lovely TB 'Gypsy Lord' (Keppel 2006), though of a slightly different rendition of blue-violet. Award of Merit 2011.

'ORANGE POP' (LARRY LAUER 1998)

Despite lots of cultivars on the market in orange tones, the list of good-growing oranges that look sharp and sparkly numbers far fewer. I'm fond of 'Orange Pop' because of its clean colors and standout growth habits, though I wouldn't characterize them as rampant. If fragrance tracks on your radar, you'll certainly notice a profoundly sweet aroma from each of these flowers, which makes for an excellent reason to cut them and bring them indoors to enjoy if rain or wind threatens. Knowlton Medal 2004.

TOP TO BOTTOM: 'Niche' (Ghio 2007) 'Orange Pop' (Lauer 1998)

'PUT UPON' (MITCH JAMESON 2012)

A Rainbow Iris Farm introduction from our friend Mitch Jameson of St. Joseph, Missouri, 'Put Upon' is another dropout from TB breeding but measures up in swell fashion to all the particulars of the BB classification. Finely formed flowers of nearly perfect dimension open atop 26-inch stems later in the bloom season. When this first bloomed in our trial beds, I was beyond impressed by its burgundy brushstrokes "put upon" its strong apricot ground. Mitch has a playful knack for naming irises, which in this instance results in a clear image of the patterning of the flower. Definitely a BB worth having in the garden, if only for its unusual pattern and coloration.

ABOVE: 'Put Upon' (Jameson 2012)

'RASPBERRY SILK' (DON SPOON 2000)

As evidenced by their high incidence on this short list of BBs, I enjoy the flauntingly ostentatious patterns of broken-colored irises. I gripe and gripe about distinctiveness, so why not live my words? Irises like 'Raspberry Silk' won't go unnoticed, with flames of fruity colors smattering pink-infused white ground. This Virginia-bred BB grows well and enhances its flirtation with ruffled curls and a slight, sweet fragrance. A runner-up to the 2003 Honorable Mention, and a definite winner in my book.

ABOVE: 'Raspberry Silk' (Spoon 2000)

'RUFFLED RASCAL'
(FRANCIS ROGERS 2009)

I need to clear the air here. I *love* darktop irises and probably always will, enchanted as I am with rainy blue and purple standards floating like storm clouds above pristine white falls. But like any fad, the charm is beginning to wear thin: breeders just can't help but introduce one or 20 new ones every year. How many do we need? Well, as an avowed iris nerd, I've bought most of the 20 or so I come across every year. You never know when you might find another winner. Sure enough, this darktop BB is a lovely incarnation of the pattern and adds to it lots of heavy ruffling, an unusual trait for BBs. The smaller flowers, ruffles, and slight fall flare endear it to me — I'm a sucker for pretty on a good plant.

ABOVE: 'Ruffled Rascal' (Rogers 2009)

'SILGREY'S BEAUTY'
(W. TERRY VARNER 2007)

I've grown enough irises in my life to trust my blink instinct as to whether or not I like a variety. It's a quick mental calculation, from one who's observed, loved, and composted more than a fair share of plants. But I either ignored my blink the first time I saw this one, or I was just dead wrong. It's taken several years for me to warm up to it, but I've come to really, *really* like it. The color truthfully doesn't do much for me, but it's soft and subdued in a way that ultimately adds to the garden tapestry. The real heartthrob for me is staring at its perfectly sculpted flowers on excellently branched stalks, every flower positioned for viewing — a truly drool-inducing experience. For companion plants, again I go to my standard mental image of yellow columbines, especially the dwarf *Aquilegia canadensis* 'Corbett' (though the bloom seasons might not line up exactly right). Other possible combinations include plants with golden foliage, like *Brunnera macrophylla* 'Diane's Gold' or *Tanacetum vulgare* 'Isla Gold'.

'TEAPOT TEMPEST'
(LYNN MARKHAM 1999)

Lynn Markham has dedicated her breeding career to producing border beardeds that measure up, one inch at a time. 'Teapot Tempest' takes the cake for superbness, a love child of Lynn's BB 'Angel Feathers' (1973) and the purple TB 'Pops Concert' (Waite 1981). Neon purple flowers glow from across the garden on well-branched, nicely budded stalks that power their way through the final weeks of the bloom season. An iris with lessons to teach us all about the fineries of perfection. Knowlton Medal 2008.

TOP TO BOTTOM: 'Silgrey's Beauty' (Varner 2007)

'Teapot Tempest' (Markham 1999)

'WOOING' (MITCH JAMESON 1993).

My friend Mitch Jameson of St. Joseph, Missouri, has a knack for breeding nifty bearded irises. One that takes my senses for a spin is 'Wooing', a delicate pink with staying power during vicious Midwestern springs. Substance, form, and spirit accompany the well-budded stalks of this pink delight. Excellent, healthy growth guarantees a clump at all times in your garden. A child of the famous and award-winning BB 'Pink Bubbles' (Hager 1980).

ABOVE: 'Wooing' (Jameson 1993)

'ZINGERADO' (LOWELL BAUMUNK 2004).

Talk about a clump queen. This thing will own the garden when it's in bloom. A captivating creation by Colorado-based iris breeder Lowell Baumunk, 'Zingerado' inherited a brilliant fall spot pattern from its IB pod parent 'Zing Me' (Blyth 1990–91), put to good aesthetic use on silver ground inherited from the Dykes Medal–winning TB 'Silverado' (Schreiner 1987). I find the effect most flattering from a distance, and dream of some day planting a row of these throughout a long border to watch them erupt into rhythmic interplay late in spring. Loads of charm and garden potential. Award of Merit 2010.

ABOVE: 'Zingerado' (Baumunk 2004)

Gallery

OPPOSITE:
'Monsignor'
(Vilmorin 1907)

TOP TO BOTTOM:
'Bermuda Triangle'
(Cadds 2000)

'Magic Quest'
(Tasco 2007)

PAGE 288: 'Minnesota Mixed-Up Kid' (Worel, reg. 2003, ca. 1970)

PAGE 289: 'Border Guard' (Ghio 2003)

ABOVE: 'Banana Royale' (Aitken 2009)

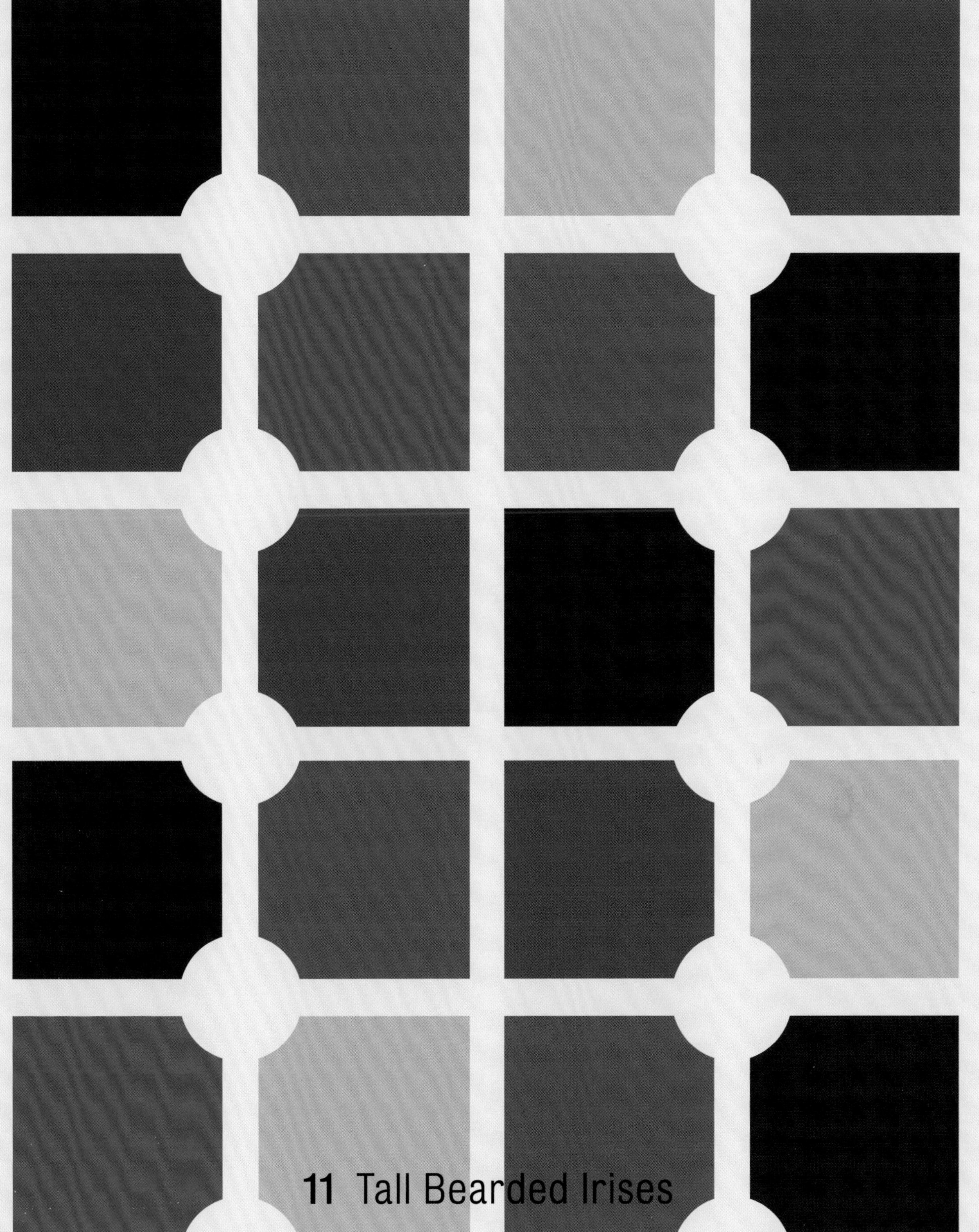

11 Tall Bearded Irises

11

"IRIS: mention the word to the average person and he will think of tall bearded irises… truly the extroverts of the iris world."

Melba Hamblen and Keith Keppel, *The World of Irises* (1978)

My earliest memory of anything called an iris was in fact a tall bearded iris, though I'm fuzzy on the specifics. Both my grandmothers had irises in their yards when I was a kid. A few forlorn clumps of something grew near the house I grew up in before I had my own garden, though I can barely remember what color they were. I saw them in cemeteries, around my elementary school, and in gardens around my hometown. My first vivid memory of tall bearded irises, though, is from the first spring in my first garden — I nearly hated them! They were all droopy and blue, and they were everywhere, bound to consume the house if I didn't stop them. Later that summer I grabbed a spade and tore into the mangled, overgrown clumps of whatever weedy clone of *Iris pallida* grew around our home, hell-bent to see bare dirt by the time I finished. Any incipient romance I had for irises prior to that day was lost. I spaded hundreds over the fence into the pasture, content at my efforts as a 10-year-old to landscape a new yard.

But in those brash, juvenile actions grew the seeds of iris love. Those tall bearded irises, liberated by division, bloomed madly along the fence the next few springs.

My intolerance faded, and a few autumns later a more seasoned 12-year-old brought rhizomes of those formerly forlorn tall bearded irises back to their garden home. As it turned out, they weren't all just droopy blues — amid those wildlings were a whole cast of other historic cultivars, some that I later identified as faithful standards like 'Aladdin's Wish' (Murawska 1943) and 'Fascination' (Cayeux 1927). In those old standbys, I finally got it. There they were, blooming in a pasture without care or fuss as if sending some polite, subliminal request to cross over the fence and take their place alongside the Oriental poppies. Like kings and queens returned from exile, they were restored to their rightful garden thrones.

Tall bearded irises are emblematic of the American garden, rooted since the 19th century in a rich horticultural tradition. True, a full cast of divas beg for attention in the verdant spring garden. But seriously, what other genus of hardy herbaceous perennials easily cultivated in temperate gardens boasts the array of colors, patterns, and forms offered by bearded irises, and tall bearded irises specifically? Nothing! For gardeners planning an outdoor space that looks grand in as many seasons as possible, the way forward comes with embracing the emblems of each season, and the flamboyant tall beardeds are the royalty of spring flowers.

Many gardeners I know remember tall bearded irises wavering in May winds in dooryard gardens. Inevitably they were blue, the sweetly perfumed cultivars of *Iris pallida* still found in old cemeteries and alongside dilapidated houses. Despite their age, they remain important in the garden. Cultivars that have been around for 30 years or more (called "historics" in the iris world) deserve their spots in the modern garden along with the latest, greatest introductions. Thirty years may not seem like a long time, but with so many varieties of bearded irises entering the market each year, the attrition rate over time is quite high. Those old flags of memory that have survived, perhaps while neglected, start to seem fairly potent and valuable.

Horticulturally speaking, tall bearded irises grow over 27½ inches tall and typically bloom the latest of all bearded irises, usually rounding out the second full month of the spring bearded iris season. Many boast stems with three to four branches, which support anywhere from seven to 12 buds. Though there are some varieties with fewer buds, seven has become the norm in order to ensure two to three weeks of bloom from an established clump. Breeding work continues to push the number of buds per plant higher, and this would seem to be an improvement — more buds equals more flowers equals a happy gardener, after all. But the biological pendulum starts to swing here when the plant itself is weakened by its own exuberance. Too many flowers, while enchanting to behold, come at a great cost to the plant's resources. There is no hard and fast rule about this — varieties with 12 buds can be just as vigorous as those with seven. It's just a matter of good selection, something that iris lovers trust breeders to do.

For anyone less interested in fancy scientific binomials and more interested in the classiness of good-looking flowers, tall bearded irises never disappoint. In full force they're a spectacle, valued for consistent performance year after year (varieties unable to remain consistent and consecutive deserve a place in the compost pile). There's nothing high-brow about growing an enviable collection of tall bearded irises. Nothing could be easier.

Origins: The 20th Century and Beyond

The early origins of tall bearded irises are recounted elsewhere in this book, so let's pick up the story, already in progress, with the passionate amateurs and pivotal events that marked the 1990s. These people and their developments paved the way forward and continue to motivate a new generation of iris lovers.

The 1990s were full of color, at least in the iris world. One explosive new combination was black bitones with orange beards, as seen in the highly successful varieties 'Local Color' (Keppel 1996), 'Tom Johnson' (Black 1996), and 'Romantic Evening' (Ghio 1996). Keith Keppel and others had pursued this ideal of a dark, near-black iris with tangerine beards for years, employing progressive varieties like 'Gallant Rogue' (Blyth/Keppel 1990) and 'Cabaret Royale' (Blyth 1975) along the way. While iris lovers swooned over the latest dark and dreamy irises, the gardening public's fascination seemed to grow in step with the release of each new variety. Along the road to better blacks came luscious, ruffled dark violet irises like 'Hail the Chief' (Gartman/Ghio 1995) and 'Diabolique' (Schreiner 1997), both with excellent garden-appropriate branching and astounding vigor. Black irises won the Dykes Medal twice in the 1990s — in 1996 with 'Before the Storm' (Innerst 1989), representing the black patent leather category, and in 1999 with 'Hello Darkness' (Schreiner 1992), representing the sooty blacks.

Orange, a color nearly impossible to find in other spring-flowering perennials, continued to improve as well. Citrus juices flowed from the flowers of 'Cordoba' (Ghio 1998), 'Fringe Benefits' (Hager 1988), and 'Viva Mexico' (Maryott 1996). Dessert was served up in a clump of 'Pumpkin Cheesecake' (Niswonger 1995). What's more, they weren't just pretty faces — varieties like 'Avalon Sunset' (Schreiner 1994) retained an incredible amount of vigor, forming fast clumps in just a few seasons. For too long, orange varieties had weak stalks, poor substance, and insipid growth — but no longer. The breeding sensation of sunny blends continues — with caution: vibrant colors can easily burn in hot sun.

The search for a true red bearded iris, of any class, reached a fever pitch in the 1990s. Some breeders suggested employing high-cost molecular techniques like the "gene gun" to blast genes for lycopene pigment production into clusters of iris cells growing on sterile, agarose media in a laboratory. Some suggested crossing with reddish and brown irises, carefully selecting redder and redder shades in each succeeding generation. Whatever the effort, few earth-shattering advances were made in the class, but many of the side-products were high-quality irises, like a duo of Oregon-born reds — 'Dynamite' (Schreiner 1997) and 'Mallory Kay' (Johnson 1998). The conversation about red TB irises continued into the new millennium with Rick Ernst and Cooley's Gardens of Salem, Oregon, famously undertaking an over $1 million project to bioengineer a true red iris.

All this work and interest aside, the red grail iris remained just that, and in the first decade of the 21st century, eight of ten Dykes Medals were awarded to traditionally colored blue or purple irises. However, a quick glance at Dykes Medal winners since the late 1990s reveals a growing appreciation for space-agers and other novelty flowers. Others to break onto the scene were Brad and Kathie Kasperek's now famous broken-colored irises, several new flatties, and more and more horned or spooned iris varieties — there's definitely an increased focus on the beauty of the appended iris blossom! And in 1998, for the first time (and henceforth), Wister Medals were awarded to the top three tall bearded irises; this rule change followed the medal's creation by only five years, suggesting that tall bearded irises, in view of their enormous and expanding number of annual introductions, needed higher proportional awards recognition from the AIS.

Throughout the 1990s, many proclaimed that the era of the reblooming iris was upon us; and this objective has trumped all aspects of tall bearded iris development ever since. But even with their laser focus on this one trait, to the near exclusion of all others, rebloom remains a frustration for many iris breeders. Precient irisarian Anne Lowe took to task the sidelining of the landscape value of bearded irises in a tersely eloquent essay in the April 1991 *Bulletin of the American Iris Society*:

> I'm getting tired of excusing inherent faults in an iris on grounds of the weather or the climate in which we live. I am busy and life is too short to bother with irises which bloom every other year (maybe). I do not subscribe to the theory that a good iris is one which increases faster than it rots. I am not willing to subject myself to the tending of certain frail and rotting plants year after year, nor do I feel that I must prove myself by coaxing a noted "difficult-to-grow" variety to bloom. What is the alternative other than switching back to growing vegetables?

And Lowe's parting words are as true now as they were then, emphasizing the challenges ahead for gardeners who make flowers for the masses:

> It appears to me that the challenge to hybridizers of the '90s (and even into the 21st century) will be to develop irises that are hardy garden perennials; irises that can be grown by the average gardener anywhere — and still retain the glorious colors and full, ruffled form which we now have . . . this is a tall order indeed.

Disappointingly, Lowe's fervent interest in the landscape hardiness of tall bearded irises, and really all bearded irises, remains lost even now on many iris breeders, who remain much more enchanted by floral development than plant development. But iris lovers know the difference. As lovely as irises are, none of it matters if the plants below the flowers aren't strong and dependable.

Worth Noting: TBs as Tough Perennials

As one of the easiest herbaceous perennials to hybridize, tall bearded irises have largely come from the efforts of amateur breeders. But at a rate of hundreds of new varieties a year, the market burgeons with varieties that should've stayed home instead of coming to the party. This is smart advice from one gardener to another: find out what varieties do best in your area before investing in new additions to the garden. Ask your local iris club, if you have one, or call a local garden center or nursery that carries irises and get their advice. Otherwise, be brave and experiment! Overall, with such an amazing heritage to build from, tall bearded irises are one of the most versatile, easy to please groups of perennials you can grow. They're forgiving plants for beginning gardeners and coveted treasures for seasoned collectors.

Though planted for their mind-blowing flowers, a tall bearded iris must be a good perennial first. No mass display will happen year after year if a plant lacks the fortitude to increase appropriately and develop high-quality flowering stalks. Gardeners should expect nothing less — we don't let the refrigerator get by on only keeping the food cool some of the time, and by the same token we shouldn't let on-again, off-again bearded irises grow on. The foliage of a tall bearded iris should look crisp, stand erect, and look lush and full. Strappy, floppy foliage looks hellish on the best of days, and morbid on the worst.

Though iris fanciers (iris lovers who dote on their irises like children) don't mind, pampering should never be a requirement for growing tall bearded irises. Staking a prize-worthy stalk the night before a thunderstorm on the other hand is just good manners, but even then that's nearing the limit — what fun are flowers if stalks can't support them? Tall bearded stalks should always remain sturdy and have branching that supports all the flowers for the gardener to see and enjoy. If the branching is too sparse or too full, the floral presentation goes from glamorous to ugly. Where am I going with all this foot-stamping and finger-pointing? Just here: hardy perennials like tall bearded irises should never be capricious or fickle.

Expert Pointers: TBs in the Garden

The tall bearded class boasts an ever-expanding range of bloom times that stretch the stereotypical two-week window into four weeks or more of unquestionably lovely flowers — provided you're growing varieties across the available spectrum. One of the most unheeded pieces of advice for growing irises: take note of the flowering season when buying new bearded irises. Virtually all reputable iris growers list this information, provided by the breeder at the time of registration, in their catalogs. There are caveats, of course. Keep in mind that a California breeder's early to mid-season flowering variety might be totally different from a New Jersey breeder's: in California an early flowering variety might bloom in late March whereas in New Jersey not until early May. Not only would the window of flowering times differ, but the inherent biases of each breeder can, too. There's no good way to standardize phenology (the study of the sequence of flowering), but an early-mid-late system at least attempts to provide gardeners with some framework for how TBs bred elsewhere might perform in their own garden.

You don't have to love geography to appreciate the consequences of flowering time as it relates to weather and climate. Early blooming tall bearded irises can overlap the border bearded, intermediate, and miniature tall classes, providing the hybridizer with an opportunity to mix up the iris genome a little bit more and the gardener with the necessary overlap to keep a constant stream of color flowing through the garden. But in northern climates, where late freezes loom well into iris season, early tall bearded varieties may not have much to offer if their much anticipated flowers turn to mush after a night or two of below-freezing temperatures. Late freezes can also stunt and mangle flower stalks. Trust me, there's nothing more heart-wrenching than watching a tall bearded iris flower unfurl 6 inches above the ground in a sadly contorted blob that barely resembles the iris you thought you knew. After raising irises through many persnickety Midwestern springs and watching my favorite early flowering cultivars do everything from rot in the fans to twist in curvilinear loops, I would advise planting later flowering varieties if erratic spring temperatures show up routinely in your local forecast.

By contrast, I can't think of a single reason for not having an abundance of midseason varieties in your garden, other than that you'll likely have so many of them you won't know which way to look. The more bearded irises that last into early summer, the better; giving up the last of tall bearded iris flowers for the other perennials of summer is always hard.

While an excellent choice for northern gardeners, later flowering varieties tend to flirt with the boundaries of early summer in the South. Basically they melt or scald in the intense sun. Flower color plays a role in how badly they look after "a day at the beach." Dark, intensely saturated flowers seem to suffer the most from basking. But throw in high humidity, a baking wind, and heaven forbid poor floral substance, and you'll have the most fetching collection of late-flowering crepe paper the neighborhood ever did see. Early blooming TBs are better for these mild spring (or toasty summer) gardens, in southerly or coastal venues.

Once you've made an appropriate bloom-time choice of cultivars, loving tall bearded irises in the open garden couldn't be easier. Growing tall bearded irises with other plants is the most fashionable advice I can give you; alone, while elegant and regal in their own right, they lack pizzazz. Looking lonely just isn't in the cards for a clump of tall bearded irises, so matching them up with other late spring perennials and shrubs will guarantee the most value and enjoyment. But while I obviously recommend overlapping your various plant loves into one garden to grand effect, the power a bulked-up row of bearded irises has during spring flowering is undeniable. Along the driveway, a row of handsome tall bearded irises in full flower will instantly delay your guests, coming or going. Don't expect the same in the off-season, however; though tall bearded irises hold their foliage semi-deciduously through late summer, the absence of their formerly show-stopping colors is keenly felt. Planting in drifts of color brings a two-fold result — sensational displays at peak performance and underwhelming blankets of nothingness in their lowest hours.

While tall bearded irises hold up better in competition with other taller garden plants, they ultimately like a halo of space in the herbaceous border. The overhead canopy of plants can shade out clumps, drip water around the rhizomes, and basically choke them out, colloquially speaking. Reduced air circulation and more water lead to rotten rhizomes, leaf spot, and, if mulch is present, the perfect breeding grounds for iris borers. You can easily avoid all these pitfalls simply by giving your irises a little space — breathing room to own the spring stage. Whether marking garden paths, billowing from mid-border, or planted along a fence, tall bearded irises look at home in virtually any sunny space with good-draining soil. Fragrant varieties earn their keep as potent aromas meet inquiring noses leaning in for a closer sniff. Position these varieties and any with intricate patterns close to the audience — an intimate engagement suits them. The best, most vigorous varieties will spill color into view, leaving the landscape awash in their most salient virtue. Many historic TBs can tolerate a little shade if the overreaching limbs of taller trees grow overhead, particularly alongside that back fence that every garden seems to have; for whatever reason, these rugged old-timers can persist in these drier, shadier zones of the garden — the perfect solutions for a commonplace challenge.

If you obsess over just the right color combinations in your garden, you won't have any trouble finding a tall bearded iris to fit the bill. Not only is their color range vast, from bold to subtle, but with so many eccentric and eclectic patterns showing up on various degrees of wavy petals, it's easy to feel a little overwhelmed. Patterned irises ratchet up the aesthetic complexity in a fun way, but even for a pattern-crazy iris lover like me, a little goes a long way. Don't forget to let these garden divas shine — sometimes they make the perfect focal point or centerpiece in the garden border; however, patterns and strong selfs, like sultry blacks and reds, look quite good with lighter, mellower companions. Contrast is the goal. It's easy to chock a garden full of very loud TBs, but if you long for a little more harmony between your favorite plants, consider a balancing act between dominant colors and more subdued understudies. Likewise, if bold just isn't your style, softer-colored tall bearded irises look remarkably showy en masse, alone or with other shades, hues, and tones of the same color. Whatever your taste or preference, the perfect choice awaits in the tall bearded category. Other perennials wish they had it so good.

Cultivars You Should Grow

I cowered at the thought of trying to settle on a short list of my favorite TBs. Seriously, there are tens of thousands of varieties in existence. But then I stopped, took a deep breath, and gave it some thought — if I were to have only a few, which would mean the most to me and my garden? Without further ado, here's a toe-dip into the deep waters of the tall bearded realm.

'ALAN M. TURING' (MITCH JAMESON 2001)

Named after the British mathematician credited as the founding father of computer science and artificial intelligence, this is a lovely epitaph to a brilliant man and a standout tall bearded iris, for two reasons. First and foremost — the flowers. In a word, arresting. The dark metallic purple-blue that coats the falls is bordered by the finest rim of glistening red-purple. Second, it blooms late in the season, a welcome thing in the TB market, which is dominated by early flowering varieties. If you're a cold-climate grower with turbulent springs, you're guaranteed that this and other reliably late varieties will bloom unhindered by the perils of weather.

ABOVE: 'Alan M. Turing' (Jameson 2001)

'ALDO RATTI' (AUGUSTO BIANCO 1998)

Italian breeder Augusto Bianco breeds amazing irises, most of which don't get nearly enough traction in the U.S. market. Of all the darktops floating around these days, I'm hard pressed to find one that rivals the style and panache of 'Aldo Ratti'. Possessing exceptional vigor too, this bleeding blue TB quickly clumps up into a stellar patch of prima donna. A blue color that goes perfectly with false indigos (*Baptisia*) and Shasta daisies (*Leucanthemum* × *superbum*). If you're thinking on a larger scale, try planting clumps around existing fringetrees (*Chionanthus*) or snowbells (*Styrax*) for a cool monochromatic vignette. Enjoy light wafts of sweet perfume after cutting the stems for a bouquet.

ABOVE: 'Aldo Ratti' (Bianco 1998)

'ATTRAZIONE FATALE'
(AUGUSTO BIANCO, REG. 2006)

I'm absolutely nuts over this flower. It looks like two completely different irises have been glued together to form this one awesome, colorfully august flower. A total standout in the garden, 'Attrazione Fatale' (Italian for "fatal attraction") definitely woos you with its feminine standards ruffling around in mallow rose with a seductive beige flash and masculine rust-red falls. The flowers are a little smaller than modern tall beardeds and have a more classic architecture — not huge or overly ruffled, just tastefully put together. 'Attrazione Fatale' grows well and will have the neighbors lining up for a piece come dividing time.

'BEFORE THE STORM'
(STERLING INNERST 1989)

This now classic tall bearded iris has ridden a wave of popularity since its introduction. Critics debate whether it or its offspring, 'Anvil of Darkness' (Innerst 1998), takes the cake for the blackest iris on the market. You'll just have to grow both and decide for yourself! Throw in a pleasantly sweet fragrance and penchant for strong growth, and it's no wonder this TB roared through the AIS awards system to its top honor. Dykes Medal 1996.

TOP TO BOTTOM:
'Attrazione Fatale' (Bianco, reg. 2006)
'Before the Storm' (Innerst 1989)

'BE ORIGINAL' (JOE GHIO 2009)

For an iris raised just blocks from Monterey Bay, this astoundingly lovely TB has really earned my respect for performing so admirably in Iowa. And Wisconsin, and Missouri, and British Columbia. To look good in all these climates, season after season, earns it high marks. It's going to be a pleasure to watch this thing work its way through the AIS awards system, through which it will surely fare well. For gardeners, it's a very classic array of colors that will look like an old garden friend perked up with a facelift and a few more ruffles. Dreamy stalks of flowers always seem to find me first. I love it when I catch a plant's attention! Honorable Mention 2011.

'CHARIOTS OF FIRE' (TERRY AITKEN 2000)

I made it clear I love orange in my commentary on SDBs. But strong-growing, vigorous oranges in the TB class have seemed an unmet goal, at least from my Midwestern perspective. I've enjoyed 'Avalon Sunset' (Schreiner 1994) for years but have wanted something more modern to satisfy my need for ruffles and full, rounded form. Former AIS President Terry Aitken has a series of oranges worth growing, and this one is a favorite. Orange meets yellow, amber, and a white flash to paint the luscious, rounded petals of this stands-tall tall bearded iris. Strong stalks refuse to give in to windy days, and the clumps grow and grow, unconcerned by frigid winters and humid summers. A winner. Award of Merit 2005.

ABOVE, LEFT TO RIGHT: 'Be Original' (Ghio 2009) 'Chariots of Fire' (Aitken 2000)

'CONJURATION' (MONTY BYERS 1989)

This skyscraping space-ager TB always marks the final strains of the spring season, blooming well into the early days of June in Iowa. 'Conjuration' is known for many fineries — vigor that just won't quit, nicely formed flowers with white-orange horns that jut out from the beard's tip, as if on some garden-scale lunar quest, and some of the finest candelabra branching you'll ever witness in all of irisdom. While many take those last words to be indicators of an iris's worth on the show bench, I think it's even more admirable when that wide branching actually looks good in the garden. In this case, 36- to 40-inch-tall stems elevate those branches well above the foliage and into the company of perennial companions nearby. Imagine a flock of flowers rising up toward the boughs of weigela or beautybush (*Kolkwitzia amabilis*). Dykes Medal 1998.

ABOVE: 'Conjuration' (Byers 1989)

'DECADENCE' (BARRY BLYTH 2004–05)

One of the most popular irises in the world, among iris connoisseurs. Breeders revel in the groundbreaking potential of its never-before-seen color pattern: creamy apricot standards flushed rose over plum burgundy falls with an apricot rim. Its flowers have wide, ruffled form but can at times get a little "soft," particularly when stressed by rough-and-tumble spring weather. Growth habits vary across the country (it sure doesn't love my garden in the Midwest), but growers in the West shouldn't have any problems at all. These shortcomings aside, its sheer novelty value makes it worthy of a top spot. The planting combinations are endless too, and you may just end up giving it a little space of its own to shine. Loud? Maybe, but every garden needs a little commotion, right? Wister Medal 2010.

ABOVE: 'Decadence' (Blyth 2004–05)

'FLORENCE DAYTON'
(RON DE LA MOTTE 2003)

With a penchant for promoting the unsung, I couldn't help hum a few bars of tuneful praise for this newer addition to my garden. This space-ager forms a classy clump, with exceptional vigor and branching, and boasts ruffled bicolored flowers of cream and burgundy edged with cream. An easy-on-the-eyes concoction of fluttering petals, she has caught the eyes of at least a few judges. Honorable Mention 2006.

ABOVE: 'Florence Dayton' (de la Motte 2003)

'IMMORTALITY' (LLOYD ZURBRIGG 1982)

I notice this list contains only one rebloomer. I suppose that says less about my opinion of rebloomers and more about my head-over-heels sickness with iris love in May — I guess you could say I got a little sidetracked. But if I'm only going to name one, 'Immortality' is a surefire bet, probably one of the most reliable rebloomers across the entire country. Though its substance can get a little tissuey, particularly when soaked with spring rains, I wouldn't be without a clump, even if only to remind me in August of the spring that was. Fast-growing and with plenty of buds, this iris keeps me happy in whatever season it blooms, something I can't believe I'm saying about a white flower at all! Award of Merit 1990.

ABOVE: 'Immortality' (Zurbrigg 1982)

'JESSE'S SONG'
(BRYCE WILLIAMSON 1983)

Any disparaging remarks I've made about the appearance and appeal of purple and white plicatas stand suspended for just one iris. I'll confess to a closet obsession — I love 'Jesse's Song'. It grows and grows without care, blooms and blooms without fuss. What more could a plant-crazed, time-limited gardener ask? The flowers, though not sporting my favorite colors, have "just pretty" ruffling that still gives the petals a chance in the fierce winds of spring. Every stalk approaches perfection, and many Queen of Show honors have gone to absolutely flawless stalks of 'Jesse's Song'. At Rainbow Iris Farm, we have a field bed of almost 250,000, and it's a sight to see. Dykes Medal 1990.

'JOYCE TERRY'
(TELL MUHLESTEIN 1974)

What a glamorous old gal. A bold stroke of color in its day and now, this iris is timeless — virtually unrivalled, even yet, for the cleanliness of its color and pattern. 'Joyce Terry' doesn't increase as much as I would like, but it's reliable, flowering every year without fail. It earns a special spot on my list because of its distinctiveness, classic charm, and clean-cut good looks. Just because it doesn't sport fat, ruffled flowers, gaudy colors, and cloying fragrance doesn't mean it deserves any less of a spot in the garden. Here's one to plant for the sake of our horticultural heritage. Award of Merit 1978.

ABOVE, LEFT TO RIGHT: 'Jesse's Song' (Williamson 1983)

'Joyce Terry' (Muhlestein 1974)

'KING OF LIGHT' (LOWELL BAUMUNK 2007)

This yellow has been ignored by the AIS awards system, which should earn some blind judges a smart kick in the shins. Seriously, what's not to love about a strong-growing, well-formed, eye-blistering yellow iris with Colorado hardiness? It glows . . . glows. My gushing appraisal stems from a frustration similar to the one I have with orange TBs — too few modern, well-formed varieties actually have the stamina to grow beyond the West Coast in less-than-plush climates. I hope 'King of Light' represents a turn toward breeding tough varieties in glamorous colors for the whole of modern gardens, not just a few.

'LEADING LIGHT' (SHOOP/KEPPEL 1999)

Another great example of a superb modern orange, though much more tropical in coloration than others, that knows both how to beat the heat of Texas and skate through the bitter winters of Iowa without missing a beat. Easily one of our most popular irises at the nursery, we've grown this stud for a number of years and have never been let down by its performance. In the garden, it sings, gloriously at that. Plant liberally. Honorable Mention 2001.

ABOVE, LEFT TO RIGHT: 'King of Light' (Baumunk 2007) 'Leading Light' (Shoop/Keppel 1999)

'MAY DEBUT' (PAUL BLACK 2008)

My friend and mentor Paul Black has been pursuing a line of small-flowered tall bearded irises for the last several years. His logic: tall bearded irises should be clumping powerhouses, so why not add more, smaller flowers to those towering stems to increase the mass impact? The strategy is certainly resulting in some interesting irises. I'm rather smitten with one of them, namely 'May Debut'. Though the flower color is nothing to write home about, the unique effect of the clump does inspire double and even triple takes in a garden setting. I think these small-flowered TBs will do famously in herbaceous borders, particularly when massed with other taller perennials that help shuffle the eye upward toward the proverbial cloud of flowers hovering overhead. Some stalk space seems wasted in some varieties, with all the array of smaller flowers concentrated toward the top, but that's all a matter of breeding and selection. This new look might catch on, or it might not. What do you think?

ABOVE: 'May Debut' (Black 2008)

'OLA KALA' (JACOB SASS 1942)

Another historic iris I couldn't live without, it was among the rhizomes I tossed over the fence that time in my haste to thin a dim patch of "just blue" irises. The next spring, much to my surprise, flags of many colors — including this renowned yellow — called forth from their pastured exile. So back across the fence they came, this time with greater care, and there they've stayed. The Nebraska-bred 'Ola Kala' has grown on me as a favorite for its consistent vigor and dependable floriferousness. *Ola kala* is, loosely, Greek for "okay," and it's strictly okay by me. Dykes Medal 1948.

ABOVE: 'Ola Kala'
(Sass 1942)

'PARISIAN DAWN' (KEITH KEPPEL 2006)

If any of the newer irises on this list are destined for fame, this surely is *the* one. Bicolored peaches with colorful beards and contrasting, rimmed falls have been coming along for years, but reigning supreme over this comely color class is 'Parisian Dawn'. Indescribably classy, bounteously ruffled, and replete with enough buds to enjoy it for weeks. Is it warm in here? Award of Merit 2010.

ABOVE: 'Parisian Dawn' (Keppel 2006)

'QUAKER LADY' (BERTRAND FARR 1909)

You read right — 1909! This historic cultivar, despite having smaller flowers that don't exactly gleam, has a soft-spoken princess charm that stops me in my tracks each spring. It looks more like an MTB on skyward stalks than a TB, and its pedigree ('Squalens' × *Iris pallida*) tells us why: the cross marked an early combination of diploid selections of species irises, which paved the highway of bearded iris development. If your garden needs a vintage touch in lovely pastel hues of bronze and lilac, look no further.

ABOVE: 'Quaker Lady' (Farr 1909)

'RING AROUND ROSIE' (RICK ERNST 2000)

This Oregon-born TB was another phenomenal color break in bearded iris breeding. It's given birth to a whole line of bicolored cultivars with sandblasted falls bordered by yellow and brownish rims, traits owed to the influence of 'Wild Jasmine' (Hamner 1983). 'Ring Around Rosie' blooms in middle to late TB season, closing out the annual iris show with a stellar performance. Excellent stalks formed from well-budded branches guarantee the finale will last for two to three weeks on an established clump. If you're an iris breeder, or considering daubing some pollen, be sure to buzz by this one next spring. Wister Medal 2007.

'STARRING' (JOE GHIO 2000)

I've grown thousands of bearded irises, so it really takes something exceptional to make me look twice, let alone stare. This is an iris that makes me stare, and usually long enough that someone comes looking for me. I suppose it's because it comes closer than any other iris to being black and white. Buxom "tuxedo" flowers with a brick red beard couldn't look better. The falls, while not completely black, are uncommonly saturated with color. Yummy! Solid performer across the country and worthy of every honor it's received. Wister Medal 2007.

TOP TO BOTTOM: 'Ring Around Rosie' (Ernst 2000) 'Starring' (Ghio 2000)

'TEN CARAT DIAMOND' (GARY SLAGLE 2013)

Rainbow Iris Farm will introduce this ground-breaking, head-turning white after evaluating it — and loving every spring of it — for the last several years. Yes, in general I've got a beef with white bearded irises; too often they lack substance, something I talk about at length in Chapter 4. But 'Ten Carat Diamond' throws up flowers that could easily be mistaken for plastic. Rugged, beautiful, and altogether hot, this white iris deserves a place in modern gardens. Gary's got a superb eye for show-quality stalks but doesn't forget to breed into his irises tough stems so those flower-laden branches don't collapse on themselves. In a word — exceptional.

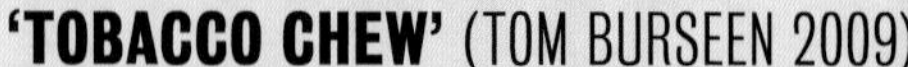

'TOBACCO CHEW' (TOM BURSEEN 2009)

My Texas friend Tom Burseen knows how to bestow loud, raucous names on equally loud, raucous irises. I once remarked after seeing what seemed like a dump truck load of this cultivar's flowers in a garden that it was so offensively ostentatious it was pretty. It's true! This space-ager is yet another great example of an iris that "works" almost entirely because of its beard, in this case a long tobacco-colored horn that slides off the crest of the fall into a little, sometimes lavender-tipped hook. Your eye immediately locks in on that beard, displayed against a pale pink background; and (at least for me), this leads you on a mind-shuffling path to check out every single one you can find in a clump. Honorable Mention 2011.

TOP TO BOTTOM: 'Ten Carat Diamond' (Slagle 2012) 'Tobacco Chew' (Burseen 2009)

'WINTRY SKY' (KEITH KEPPEL 2002)

I can't profess to having a favorite plant of any kind, and it's just lunacy to think that I could distill my passion for a genus so broadly diverse as irises into one favorite, let alone a couple dozen of each section. But just between you and me, when I hear the phrase "favorite iris," my mind quickly jumps, if only for a moment, to this startling reverse amoena from Oregon iris king Keith Keppel. Since the first day I saw it in the catalog, I had to have it, needed to have it. So ruffled, so profound in its coloration, I can't imagine a garden without it. While bold and dramatic, the colors aren't brassy, making it especially well suited for gardens with a cooler palette of colors that still need a little touch of glam. Admirable growth, buds, branches, and all that stuff. It's just darn gorgeous. Wister Medal 2010.

ABOVE: 'Wintry Sky' (Keppel 2002)

'WON'T' (MITCH JAMESON, REG. 2007)

As of yet unintroduced, this up-and-coming hunk will knock your socks off once it hits the market. With standards burnished in red-glowing bronze and lavender falls bordered by bronze, the color combination alone will make you do a double take. The story behind the name is pretty funny, too. Mitch had two seedlings that he hoped would bloom in time for his local club's spring show. One did (it was named 'Will') and the other didn't ('Won't'). Colors like these make the combo game fun to play — just imagine this iris paired with the reds of lupines and Oriental poppies (*Papaver orientale*), or the blues of mountain bluets (*Centaurea montana*) and bluestars (*Amsonia*). A clump of this should have no problem settling in and looking fabulous.

ABOVE: 'Won't' (Jameson, reg. 2007)

OPPOSITE: 'Cordoba' (Ghio 1998)

Gallery

ABOVE: 'Kona Waves'
(Annand 2005)

ABOVE: 'Spring Madness' (Johnson 2009)

11

OPPOSITE: 'Dreamsicle' (Schreiner 1995)

ABOVE, LEFT TO RIGHT: 'Chief John Jolly' (Parkhill 2003)

'Decker' (Jameson 2001)

ABOVE: 'Thornbird'
(Byers 1989)

ABOVE, LEFT TO RIGHT: 'Trumped' (Burseen 2008)

'Edith Wolford' (Hager 1986)

ABOVE: 'Stile Libero' (Bianco, reg. 2007)

OPPOSITE: 'Montmartre' (Keppel 2008)

ABOVE: 'Labor'
(Cayeux 1926)

ABOVE: 'Private Eye'
(Johnson 2010)

ABOVE: 'Belle De Provence' (Baumunk 2006)

OPPOSITE: 'Santa' (Shoop/Keppel 1998)

OVERLEAF: 'Exposé' (Ghio 2004)

PAGE 333, CLOCKWISE FROM TOP LEFT: 'Stairway to Heaven' (Lauer 1993)

'Gypsy Lord' (Keppel 2006)

'Pursuit of Happiness' (Johnson 2007)

ABOVE: 'Reckless Abandon' (Keppel 2010)

ABOVE: 'Whipped Honey' (Jameson 1996)

OPPOSITE: 'Burst of Glory' (Jedlicka 2008)

ABOVE: 'Fantasy Ride' (Duncan 2009)

ABOVE: 'Frosted Pumpkin' (Maryott 2002)

Sources of Bearded Irises

Aitken's Salmon Creek Gardens
Terry and Barbara Aitken
608 NW 119th St.
Vancouver, WA 98685
(360) 573-4472
flowerfantasy.net

Chuck Chapman Iris
8790 Wellington Rd. 124
Guelph, ON N1H 6H7
Canada
(519) 856-0956
chapmaniris.com

Comanche Acres Iris Gardens
12421 SE SR 116
Gower, MO 64454
(816) 424-6436
comancheacresiris.com

Fred Kerr's Rainbow Acres
P.O. Box 2191
North Highlands, CA 95660
(916) 331-3732
rainbowacres2.homestead.com/iris1.html

Iris Colorado
Lowell Baumunk
10918 N. Sunshine Dr.
Littleton, CO 80125
(303) 908-2450
iriscolorado.com

The Iris Garden
Yard House, Pilsdon
Dorset DT6 5PA
United Kingdom
01308 868797
theirisgarden.co.uk

Keith Keppel Iris
P.O. Box 18154
Salem, OR 97305
(503) 391-9241
keithkeppeliris.com

Mid-America Gardens
Paul Black and Thomas Johnson
P.O. Box 9008
Salem, OR 97305
mid-americagarden.com

Rainbow Iris Farm
Kenny, Krystal, Kelly, and Kody Norris
3149 Kentucky Ave.
Bedford, IA 50833
(712) 523-2807
rainbowfarms.net

Rockytop Gardens
Phil Williams
P.O. Box 41
Eagleville, TN 37060
(615) 274-6426
rockytopgardens.com

Schreiner's Iris Gardens
3625 Quinaby Rd. NE
Salem, OR 97303
(800) 525-2367
schreinersgardens.com

Snowpeak Iris and Daylilies
38956 Lacomb Dr.
Lebanon, OR 97355
(541) 259-2343
snowpeakiris.com

Stout Gardens at Dancingtree
Hugh and Jennifer Stout
432 NE 70th St.
Oklahoma City, OK 73105
(405) 642-4190
stoutgardens.com

Superstition Iris Gardens
Rick Tasco and Roger Duncan
2536 Old Highway
Cathey's Valley, CA 95306
community.webshots.com/user/rickt103

Sutton's Iris Gardens
16592 Road 208
Porterville, CA 93257
(888) 558-5107
suttoniris.com

Winterberry Gardens
Don and Ginny Spoon
1225 Reynolds Rd.
Cross Junction, VA 22625
winterberryirises.com

Horticultural Classification of Bearded Irises

1 **Miniature Dwarf Bearded (MDB)**
Up to 8 inches / 20 cm.
Earliest to bloom.

2 **Standard Dwarf Bearded (SDB)**
8 to 16 inches / 21 to 40 cm.
Begin bloom as MDBs are ending. Median.

3 **Intermediate Bearded (IB)**
16 to 27½ inches / 41 to 70 cm.
Bloom season overlaps the SDBs through TBs. Median.

4 **Miniature Tall Bearded (MTB)**
16 to 27½ inches / 41 to 70 cm. Bloom with the BBs and TBs, but blooms are smaller than those of a BB. Median.

5 **Border Bearded (BB)**
16 to 27½ inches / 41 to 70 cm.
Bloom with the TBs. Median.

6 **Tall Bearded (TB)**
27½ inches / 70 cm and above.
Last to bloom.

Photo Credits

Terry Aitken
pages 217 (left), 249, 275

Lowell Baumunk
pages 115 (bottom), 116 (left), 118, 120 (top), 124 (left), 125, 152 (left), 159–164, 310 (left), 330

Paul Black
pages 34, 110 (bottom), 306

Barry Blyth
page 110 (top right)

Tom Gormley
page 177

Thomas Johnson
pages 106 (bottom), 107

Doug Kanarowski
page 108

Keith Keppel
page 109

Fred Kerr
page 105 (top; bottom left)

Becky and Elizabeth Rankin
page 47 (top right)

Schreiner's Iris Gardens
pages 47 (bottom right), 105 (bottom right), 303 (bottom)

Marky Smith
page 143 (top)

Hugh Stout
page 41 (right)

Mike Sutton
page 110 (top left)

Rick Tasco
page 213 (left)

Mike Unser
pages 29 (bottom right), 35, 36, 38 (right), 41 (left), 120 (bottom left), 129, 130

All other photographs are by the author.

Index

Published in 2012 by Timber Press, Inc.

The Haseltine Building
133 S.W. Second Avenue, Suite 450
Portland, Oregon 97204-3527
timberpress.com

2 The Quadrant
135 Salusbury Road
London NW6 6RJ
timberpress.co.uk

Design by Holly Gressley
Printed in China

Library of Congress Cataloging-in-Publication Data

Norris, Kelly D.
Cultivating the rainbow : a guide to bearded irises for beginners and enthusiasts / Kelly D. Norris. -- 1st ed.
p. cm.
Includes bibliographical references and index.
ISBN 978-1-60469-208-2
1. Irises (Plants) 2. Irises (Plants)--Varieties. I. Title.
SB413.I8N67 2012
635.93438--dc23
2011038466

A catalog record for this book is also available from the British Library.